The

Coat

"Motley's the only wear"
(As You Like It: 11.7)

L'abbé Bérenger Saunière (1852-1917)

The Fool's Coat

The Tarot Fool is the Holy Innocent,
whose function is always to ask "Why?"

Vi Marriott

THOTH PUBLICATIONS
Loughborough, Leicestershire

First Edition 2005

A CIP catalogue record for this book is available from the
British Library.
Cover design by Bob Eames

ISBN 1 870450 99 X

Printed and bound in Great Britain

Published by Thoth Publications
64, Leopold Street, Loughborough, LE11 5DN
web address: www.thoth.co.uk
email: enquiries@thoth.co.uk

Contents

Quotations under Chapter headings are from *The Collected
Works of William Shakespeare*

Illustrations

* Photographs by courtesy of Neil Hudson Newman

The Fool

Introduction

The Fool's Coat

"God give them wisdom that have it.
And for those that are fools, let them use their talents"
(Twelfth Night II.5)

The Fool's Coat is made up of scraps and patches of many colours, stitched together to hide his nakedness. So is Truth made up of bits and pieces of imagination, deduction, assumption and downright lies, cobbled to cover the bare facts. Ask any three witnesses to describe an event, and you will get six different accounts, though each imagines his version to be the right one.

Historical mysteries are always popular. Did Richard III or Henry VII kill the little Princes in the Tower? Was Amy Robsart's death suicide or murder? What happened to Marie Antoinette's diamond necklace? Who was the man in the iron mask? Gallons of ink, acres of paper, and enough energy to power an intergalactic rocket have been spent on such questions. The biggest problem is that researchers always want to include every hypothetical fact or shred of evidence. The main issue disappears under a cloud of conjecture, and what does it matter if one statement contradicts another? The answer can always be put down to someone's misinterpretation of history, which of itself is essentially relative, depending upon who is the narrator.

The important precept which should be engraved in gold before the eyes of every researcher is "Remember Occam's Razor". Doctor Occam was a 14th century intellectual, and his rule was paramount: "The simplest solution is most likely to be the true one". Researchers must be selective, even at the risk of being accused of ignoring what does not fit their theses. Most likely it is not applicable, and therefore irrelevant.

The "mystery of Rennes-le-Château" is now too well known to want retelling, but solutions and theories have spread over such an enormously wide area that by now the origin of the story is almost forgotten, ranging from the discovery of untold gold or the holy grail to invasion from outer space, the coming of the apocalypse, discovery of the remnants of Atlantis, sacred sex, prehistoric temples, and the quest for the body of Christ or Mary Magdalen. When Henry Lincoln bought the paperback of "Le Trésor Maudit" as holiday reading, he little realised he was initiating a whole new industry. Rennes-le-Château literature is now so prolific that it requires a book to itself to list the bibliography. New books regularly appear, theories escalating into fantasy. Even the BBC is not immune.

What follows, therefore, does not aim to take into account every scrap of information, possibility or hypothesis that surrounds the Rennes-le-Château mystery. It does not claim to be the whole truth, or even part of the truth. It is, like most of the books written about Saunière's mythical treasure, a personal interpretation. A probability based on possible facts.

Chapter One

Cucullus non facit monachum"

(Twelfth Night 1: 1.5)

The Saunière Saga

How it all Started

If Henry Lincoln is not the "only begetter" of the Rennes-le-Château mystery, he can legitimately claim to be the accoucheur. In *Key to the Sacred Pattern*, he gives a lively account of how in 1969 he first came across Gérard de Sède's book *Le Trésor Maudit*, and thought it would make a good item for the BBC TV "Chronicle" programme. This ultimately grew into three full length TV documentaries, and with Michael Baigent and Richard Leigh he produced the blockbuster best seller *The Holy Blood and the Holy Grail*, published in 1982 and still in print.

Le Trésor Maudit was a judicious mix of fact and fiction. It was "Georgette Heyer" history, fiction based on an authentic period background. De Sède was a reputable author with several semi-historical books to his credit, and had originally been approached by Pierre Plantard and Philippe de Chérisey to rewrite a book about Saunière and Rennes-le-Château for which they had failed to find a publisher. It had all the ingredients guaranteed to appeal to the romantic imagination - an occult society of ancient lineage, hidden treasure, glamorous or notorious celebrities, documents in secret code, a lost heir, midnight graveyard excursions, and illicit liaisons. Also, although having more holes in it than a colander, there was enough basic, and even provable fact to make it sound feasible. How could it fail? De Sède's rewrite was published by René Julliard in 1967 and met with sufficient success to warrant a paperback edition still being sold on bookstalls two years later.

The original contact between Lincoln and the Plantard cabal was the journalist Jean-Luc Chaumeil, their spin-doctor, and it was at the gallery in Paris owned by Chaumeil's mother that Lincoln first met them. Plantard told Lincoln that he was of royal blood, descendant of the Merovingians, the true kings of France. He stated categorically that the Prieuré de Sion was the *eminence gris* behind the Rennes-le-Château mystery, and that "Jean Cocteau was the last Grand Master, everybody knows that". The current Grand Master was, of course, Plantard himself.

Plantard, the main protagonist and consistent upholder of the truth of his own assertions, was either unfortunate or untactful in dealing with his colleagues. Some of those involved in the original project later came forward to debunk the story as invention, and the supporting evidence as forgery. Gérard de Sède, Jean-Luc Chaumeil, and Philippe de Chérisey, parted company with him on uneasy terms, and later gave interviews in which they stated that the whole Rennes-le-Château mystery was a hoax.

As Lincoln says, if this were true why go to such incredible lengths to create something of extraordinary complexity, not only in resurrecting the original story, but in manufacturing supporting evidence by way of considerable documentation over a long period of time. What purpose did it serve?

The originators seem to have gained very little, in either prestige or money. De Sède went on to write other books. De Chérisey died suddenly in July 1985. Jean-Luc Chaumeil was involved in an acrimonious dispute during the early 1980's when Plantard was threatening him with a legal action for libel. This however seems not to have come to anything, and apart from Chaumeil's assertions on the BBC TV "Timewatch" programme on 17 September 1996 that he had indisputable evidence of forgery, he has remained silent.

Inevitably there are many writers and researchers who refuse to believe that it is all a hoax, maintaining that such heresy was the result of pique, mischief making or malice on the part of the mystery's detractors. Tourists continue to invade Rennes- le-

Château, to the embarrassment and profit of the locals, and books still pour from the press. The attraction of historical mysteries is that they are open to endless interpretation - if facts cannot be proved, neither can they be disproved.

Lincoln spent an enormous amount of time checking background and facts. His sharply diagnostic journalist's mind would accept nothing without proof, and he employed local researchers in France to investigate more fully. He himself says the deeper he delved, the more complex the story became. There were endless dead ends, and everything was shrouded in a dense mist of misinformation. People whose names were quoted did exist, but either claimed to be ignorant of any connection with Rennes-le-Château or Plantard, or were dead. But Lincoln never quite disclaims that there is, or was, some truth in the basic account.

After his extensive research that resulted in *The Messianic Legacy* (1986), the sequel to *The Holy Blood and the Holy Grail*, Lincoln presumably decided the subject was exhausted, and switched his investigations to sacred geometry, writing two new solo books, *The Holy Place* and *Key to the Sacred Pattern*, thus initiating a new spate of speculation about ancient temples, sex magic and visiting magi from outer space.

At a meeting of the Saunière Society on 6 December 1992 he said that his theories were "based on hearsay and made no claim to be statements of final truth", but that the geometry was "not subjective". As always, he remained coolly aloof, provoking but not participating in the heated arguments that ensued.

The Saunière Romance, as if...
The gospel according to
Gérard de Sède and Henry Lincoln

One summer day in the mid 1890's a shabby young priest climbed up the long steep road to the village of Rennes-le-Château. Father Bérenger Saunière was about to install himself in his new parish of St Mary Magdalene, and if he was not very excited by the prospect, at least he knew just what to expect. He was familiar with the area, having been born only 5 km away at Montazels, near the little market town of Couiza, and as a child had enjoyed exploring the countryside.

Languedoc scenery is awesome rather than beautiful. It has none of the terracotta and lavender prettiness of adjacent Provence, and the climate is temperate rather than Mediterranean. Bare jagged mountains, crowned with the ruins of Cathar castles, plunge to steep river valleys where winter vegetables, sunflowers and fruit orchards line the banks; and the high upland pastures support flocks of small hardy sheep that grow excellent woolly fleeces. The ancient villages were built in the most strategic places for defence, which means the most inaccessible. They are closed and secret, cherishing still their Cathar or Templar heritage.

The cretaceous limestone of the eastern Pyrenees has little surface water, but is honeycombed with caves, and underground streams that burst out in unexpected places. Rennes-le-Château has a spring that it is said has never failed. The foothills are clothed in maquis - rough scrub and herbs - and on every available fertile scrap of land flourish the vineyards, for this is wine country, and the delicious sparkling white Blanquette of Limoux has been made here since the 17th century.

Rennes-le-Château owes its origin to the garrison town of Rhedae, founded in the 5th century by the Visigoths on the plateau at the foot of the hill where the village now stands.

Rhedae was the capital city of Razès, and was destroyed in 1170 by the army of the King of Aragon. In the 14th century Pierre II of Voisins, Seneschal of Carcassonne, fortified the hilltop and the town prospered until it was destroyed in 1362 by a Spanish invasion. All that was left standing was the old church of St. Mary Magdalene and a few houses. Rhedae ceased to exist, and declined into the rural village of Rennes-le-Château.

Fr Saunière found the church sad and mildewed, windows broken, the roof leaking. The presbytery was dark, damp and derelict. Nothing daunted, he arranged to lodge with one of the villagers, and with the aid of a small loan from the Town Hall, set about repairing the worst of the damage.

Shortly afterwards Saunière was visited by a young nobleman, Jean-Stéphane de Hapsburg, who arranged for adjacent bank accounts to be opened for himself and Saunière, in order to facilitate the transfer of considerable sums of money from his own to the priest's account. There has inevitably been speculation among Rennes-le-Château writers that this money was a down-payment from the Hapsburgs either for Saunière to search for an unidentified "treasure" or a bribe to keep quiet about anything he might find.

A little over a year after his arrival at the village, the church was weatherproof and serviceable, and Fr. Saunière was installed in his presbytery with Marie Denarnaud, his eighteen-year-old housekeeper, in attendance. For all her life Marie was devoted to him, becoming his intimate friend, and some say his lover.

One of the first renovations undertaken was the replacement of the old altar, and it was in one of the supporting columns, an ancient Visigothic pillar, that Saunière found some documents - two parchments on which were written excerpts from the New Testament in somewhat eccentric script, and two genealogies that detailed the survival of the Merovingian royal line after usurpation of the crown by the Carolingians.

Historians maintain that King Dagobert II and his son Sigisbert, then only three years old, were both assassinated in the Forest of Woevres near Stenay in 679, but according to the Rennes-le-Château genealogies Sigisbert was in fact saved by his sister, Irmine, Abbess of Oeren, and taken to his mother's house in Razès (the ancient name for Languedoc) in 681. She was a Visigothic princess, Giselle de Razès, Dagobert's second wife, and their son was born in 676. He succeeded his grandfather, Bera II, as Count of Razès, and it was then that he adopted the name of "Plant-ard", that is to say "living branch". He and his wife Magdala were buried in the church of St Mary Magdalene at Rennes-le-Château, and it was their grave that Saunière exhumed in 1891. According to the genealogies, they were the ancestors of the true Kings of France, whose descendants were living in Saunière's time, and are still living today. The contemporary pretender was Pierre Plantard, the Grand Master of the Prieuré de Sion, the custodians of the treasure of Rennes-le-Château. The true nature of the treasure is ambivalent.

However much Saunière and Marie studied the documents they could not understand them, so Saunière took them to his Bishop at Carcassonne, who sent him to St Sulpice in Paris, where he was put into contact with Emile Hoffet, an expert palaeographer, nephew of the Director of the St. Sulpice Seminary. During his stay Saunière visited the Louvre and acquired copies of three paintings - *The Shepherds of Arcady* by Nicholas Poussin, *The Temptation of St Antony* by Tenier the Younger, and an anonymous portrait of Pope Celestine V.

On his return to Rennes-le-Château, Saunière dug up and destroyed the two gravestones of Marie Négri d'Ablès, Dame d'Hautpoul, the inscriptions of which were reputed to have been carved by Fr. Bigou at the time of the French Revolution, and provided the key words needed to decipher the New Testament parchments. It is assumed that Saunière in fact had, by now, arrived at the decoded but ambiguous messages expressed by these documents.

He then began behaving in a very strange manner, wandering around the countryside collecting stones, ostensibly for the grotto he was building in the churchyard. He and Marie visited the cemetery at night, and dug up ancient graves, much to the annoyance of the local residents. He also travelled a good deal, and left pre-prepared letters with Marie which she sent out in reply to any correspondence received, so that no-one should know about his absence. He bought and sold stamps and postcards, and dealt in antiques which he said were given to him by wealthy patrons. He presumably discovered the "treasure", but whether this was material or spiritual is never disclosed. Possibilities range from vast sums of gold, to a fabulously important mythological object, or a dangerous and marketable secret, which he was paid either to reveal or to keep.

Meanwhile restoration of the church continued, and the interior was decorated in an extravagant style which was said to illustrate the secret hiding place of the treasure. This was described in *La Vraie Langue Celtique et le Cromleck de Rennes-les-Bains*, an extraordinary book written by Saunière's friend Fr. Henri Boudet, priest of the neighbouring church of St Célse and St. Nazaire at Rennes-les-Bains, which presupposes Boudet was also familiar with the "secret".

As soon as the refurbishment of his church was finished, Saunière started work on the domaine. He built the Villa Bethania, laid out gardens where he kept bizarre pets, and constructed a rampart around the hilltop, underneath which was an orangerie. At one end of this promenade was a conservatory for exotic plants, and at the other he built as his library the Tour Magdala, a neo-gothic fortress-like tower with a roof look-out. It was all very expensive.

Saunière did not live in Bethania, but continued to inhabit the presbytery. At Bethania he entertained rich and famous guests, among them the Marquise de Bourg de Bogas, and the glamorous diva, Emma Calvé, who was perhaps also his mistress. Both ladies were said to be interested in the occult. The entertainment at Bethania was lavish, with the best of wine and food provided.

When Mgr Billard the Bishop at Carcassonne retired, and a new man was appointed, Saunière was asked to account for his expenditure. Saunière refused. He produced some accounts, but said others had been lost, or that he had paid bills in cash and had no receipts. Asked about his income, he said it was earnings from his own small commercial ventures, gifts from grateful parishioners, and the proceeds of the alms-boxes in the church. The Bishop did not believe a word of this, and repeated his request in rather stronger terms. Saunière again refused. He said it was his money anyway, that he had personally paid for the restoration of St Mary Magdalene so that he did not have to account for the cost, and the Church dignitaries should be grateful to him. Ordered to make a Retreat of Penitence, Saunière pleaded ill-health. Summoned to appear before the ecclesiastical court, he said he was too unwell. The Bishop accused him of simony, that is selling masses, and placed him under an interdict which forbade him to practice as a priest and also suspended his stipend. Saunière referred the matter to Rome, which meant it fell into abeyance during lengthy investigations which were never resolved. The Bishop endeavoured to transfer him to another Parish, but Saunière promptly resigned, beating the Bishop's decree by one day. The new priest could not move in, because the Rennes-le-Château Mayor immediately leased the presbytery to Saunière for five years with renewal options. Saunière never did, in fact, reveal the source of his wealth or the amount of his expenditure. When his will was read, it was discovered that he owned nothing at all. The property was all in Marie Denarnaud's name.

When Saunière died at the age of 65, his body was seated in a chair of state, and villagers filing past each plucked from his robe one of the red tassels adorning it. According to tradition the tassels at the fringes of the robes worn by the Merovingian "priest kings" had miraculous curative powers. Did Saunière consider that he also was of royal descent? It has been hinted that there was something peculiar about his death, and that Marie had ordered the coffin some days before Saunière became terminally ill, but this was found to be a misreading of the Undertaker's invoice and unfamiliarity with the French way of writing dates. The account was actually paid six months later. His deathbed confession to Fr Rivière of Espéraza disturbed that divine so much that he never smiled again.

So says the story of Bérenger Saunière and the treasure of Rennes-le-Château according to the early authors... Amid the froth of rhetoric there are some small pebbles of truth.

Saunière - Entrepreneur of the Impossible.

Who was Saunière? The original story, de-mythed of the ensuing accretion of occult, geographical, geometric and sci-fi suppositions, is simple. Bérenger Saunière existed - his baptism as "François Bérenger" (he early dropped the François) by Father J. de Bussy, Parish priest, on 12 April 1852 is recorded in the church register of St. Cecilia, Montazels, where his parents, Joseph Saunière and Marguerite Hughues, were married on 20 January 1850. Bérenger was born the day before he was baptised, 11 April 1852, in the same year as the Second Empire, and died on 22 January 1917. His cause of death was reported as high blood pressure and cirrhosis of the liver. His body lies in the cemetery behind his church of St Mary Magdalene at Rennes-le-Château which he served for more than thirty years, the plot having been ceded to him by the Council in perpetuity for services rendered. Somewhere in between the "mystery" evolved.

The common practice was for graves to be leased for only a certain term. Saunière himself had cleared a number of old graves from the churchyard much to the annoyance of some of the locals who on 12 March 1895 complained to the Bishop. M. Cros, the Vicaire General, wrote to Saunière enquiring into the matter, and Saunière explained that he was removing old graves in order to make more room in the burial ground. The church Minute book of 1857 ruled that there were to be no burials less than 35 - 40 metres from the adjoining houses and that the cemetery could only be enlarged so long as it did not endanger public health. If the cemetery was to continue to be used, room would have to be made. The old bones were reverently removed to an ossuary, over which Saunière ultimately built a chapel dedicated to Our Lady of Lourdes. The gift to Saunière of a grave "in perpetuity" was a mark of special recognition.

Bérenger was the Saunières' second son and eldest surviving child. Of Joseph's ten other children three boys and three girls survived, four died in infancy. They lived in a solid town house in the main village square of Montazels, overlooking a pond bounded by an iron fence, and at that time decorated with tritons, mythological bronze sea creatures - now alas transported.

The family was reasonably well off. Saunière père was bailiff for the Seigneur Cazemajou and manager of the flour-mill, a position that carried with it a certain amount of prestige. The Cazemajous were cousins of the Négri d'Ablès, and the Couiza branch of the Cazemajous had inherited considerable land from Marie Négri d'Ablès' father, François.

Education in mid-19th century France was rare, unless one was rich enough to employ a private tutor. Bérenger and the next brother in line, Jean Marie Alfred, three years his junior, were sent to the local priest for lessons, who was sufficiently impressed with both the boys to recommend them to Mgr Gueneret, Superior of the Grand Seminary of Carcassonne, for training as priests. The church offered the best opportunities for employment and advancement, whether or not one had a vocation.

Bérenger became a pupil at the School of St. Louis de Limoux, graduated to the Petit Seminary, and entered the Grand Seminary in June 1874. He successfully completed the required courses in morals, dogma, philosophy and church history, and was ordained in June 1879. His brother Alfred had already been ordained the previous year, and appointed Curate at Alzonne.

Alfred hovers over the Rennes-le-Château story like an uneasy ghost. He became a Jesuit, and was appointed tutor and chaplain to the family of the Marquis of Chefdebien at Narbonne, but was dismissed for prying into their private affairs. He was credited with being the lover of the Marquise de Bourg de Bogas, accused of being an alcoholic, and was excommunicated. The portrait signed with the name of a Parisian photographer, which was assumed to be of Bérenger, has been identified in fact as being that of Alfred, so that it seems reasonably certain that Alfred at some time visited Paris. When he died in 1905 Saunière wrote to the Bishop saying bitterly "am I expected to atone for my brother's sins?" His accounts do, however, show that he received

20,000 Fr. F. from Alfred.   No question has ever been asked about where this money originated.

On 16 July 1879 Bérenger was appointed assistant priest at Alet-les-Bains, which had become an important city since the installation of the railway line which opened earlier that year, joining Carcassonne and Quillan. Here he met the painter Henri Dejardin Beaumetz, who was the same age as himself, and they became friends although their political opinions were widely different - Saunière being Royalist by upbringing and inclination, while Beaumetz was radical, and was in fact elected as Republican Deputy for the Department of the Aude from 1889 - 1900, becoming Undersecretary of State for Fine Arts.

Alet-les-Bains was Left oriented. In September 1879 it joined with the neighbouring town of Limoux to celebrate a Republican Festival which also promoted the local wine industry, and the Mayor of Limoux, Oscar Rouge, opened the Place de la République, with its central fountain, covered market and Petiet museum. While not sympathising with the politics involved, Saunière could not help but approve of the amenities and opportunities for employment that these new improvements provided.

He was studying the writings of Nicholas Pavillion, 29th Bishop of Alet, whose pastoral work had been very much directed towards promoting improvement in the conditions of the largely illiterate peasants. In particular he strongly advocated that women should be encouraged to teach the ignorant people in the countryside. They were sentiments that Saunière later endeavoured to put into practice, sometimes to his own detriment.

According to the Alet register of births and deaths, "Our Reverend Father in God, Nicholas Pavillion died on 8 December 1677. He confessed, received Extreme Unction and the Blessed Viaticum during his illness. He has been buried at the foot of the cross of St Andrew in the cemetery of this parish". There was no marker on his grave, but in the nineteenth century his influence was still being felt by Republican atheists and religious Royalists alike.

In July 1881 Mgr Felix Arsène Billard succeeded Mgr Leuillieux as Bishop of Carcassonne, and on 16 June 1882 he appointed Saunière priest in charge of the new church of Our Lady of the Assumption at Clat near Axat. It was a primitive little hilltop village devoted to rearing sheep, and a disappointing appointment for an ambitious 30 year old priest.

It was here, a little over a year later, that Saunière received news of the death of the Comte de Chambord, grandson of Charles X, the last direct heir to the throne of France. It was a shock for him, as his family had always been strong supporters of the Bourbons. Certain Legitimist committees wished to raise a commemorative monument to Chambord, and by public subscription a statue was erected at Ste Anne d'Auray which showed the Comte, dressed in coronation robes as Henri V, kneeling before the crown of France. Attended by Ste Genevieve and Joan of Arc, he appeared to be entreating Ste Anne to restore the throne to the descendant of the "Lily that had been cut down". Ste Anne remained remarkably deaf to their pleas.

For two more years Saunière had to endure his enforced isolation and inaction. But a change was coming... On 1 June 1885 Mgr Billard appointed Saunière parish priest to the church of St. Mary Magdalene at Rennes-le-Château, a small village of some 200 inhabitants in the Aude, Languedoc. The Church at that time was still administered and controlled by the State, and all appointments of clergy had to be confirmed by the local council. Saunière was duly approved, and his stipend fixed at 75 Fr. F. a month, which was average for the time. Parishioners were expected to supplement their priest's income as needed by personal gifts.

The church building, dating from around 1059, was dilapidated, the presbytery uninhabitable, vandalised by patriots during the Revolution. Saunière took up residence at a house in the village and purchased what he needed from the local store on credit.

He was very poor, and over the next sixteen months he owed a considerable sum of money to his landlady, Mme Alexandrine Marro, for board and lodging.

The summer passed peacefully enough in Rennes-le-Château, but with October came the upheaval of the legislative elections. To be Catholic was to be Monarchist, Right Wing and Conservative. The faithful could not tolerate the idea of the Church being made subservient to civil administration, and religion forcibly tied to a Ministry.

The Third Republic had been declared in 1870, but the Royalists never ceased planning for the Restoration of the Bourbons. Then in August 1883 came the shocking news that the Comte de Chambord was dead. There were still other candidates, however, and Legitimists, Orléanists, Monarchists, Bonapartists and some of the moderate Left formed an uneasy alliance in the elections of 1885 to promote the Comte de Paris as their candidate. It was not what any of them liked, but the best option they had. The Comte was the grandson of the Orléanist constitutional monarch, Louis Philippe I, who had named him heir to the throne of France when he himself abdicated and fled to England in 1840. His eldest son, the Dauphin, had been killed in a carriage accident.

On the eve of the poll of 4th and 5th October Saunière preached an anti-Republican sermon from the pulpit of St Mary Magdalene. "The results so far have been magnificent" he said, "but victory is not yet complete. The moment has come, and we must use all our efforts against the adversary". He was prompt in naming this adversary - the Republicans. "This is the devil we must conquer. They must bow before the force of religion and the baptised. The sign of the cross is the sign of victory". Also, somewhat misquoting Bishop Nicholas Pavillion, he took the opportunity to inform the women of the congregation that they must spread instruction and piety among the non-educated electorate in order to convince them to vote for the defenders of the faith, in other words the Royalists. The village erupted into ferment.

Unhappily the Republican minority triumphed, aided by the Left oriented Masonic Lodges. Their support was clearly recognised in the English edition of Karl Marx's manifesto of 1888, which also indiscriminately attacked as reactionary the Royalists, the clergy, and the French middle classes. "..In spite of their pompous talk" it proclaims, "they make themselves very comfortable, gathering the golden apples and exchanging faith, love and honour for the sordid trade of wool, sugar beet and brandy..."

Saunière was denounced to the Prefect of the Aude for inciting disorder and exerting electoral pressure. On 1 December 1885 the Council suspended him from office, which meant also the loss of his stipend. Already poor and in debt, he was left destitute. Bishop Billard was understanding. He made Saunière a personal loan of 200 Fr. and arranged for him to take up a position as Professor at the Petit Séminaire of Narbonne.

It was at about this time that Saunière received a donation of 3000 Fr. F. from the Comtesse de Chambord, reputedly paid to him through her nephew Archduke Johann Salvator de Hapsburg (not Jean-Stéphane de Hapsburg as stated by Gérard De Sède). It may have been while he was at Narbonne that he was contacted by Archduke Johann. This payment was apparently compensation for the reverses Saunière had suffered in supporting the Royalist cause in the recent elections. According to Pierre Jarnac, an expert Rennes-le-Château historian, the money was in fact paid in two instalments, 1000 Fr. F. in 1886, the year in which the Comtesse de Chambord died, and 2000 Fr. F. two years later from her estate.

Saunière remained under sentence until 1 July 1886, on which date the suspension was lifted, his salary was restored, and he was able to rejoin his parish at Rennes-le-Château.

Saunière was a man of energy and resource. In 1887, with the assistance of a grant of 1400 Fr. F. from the Council, he put in hand essential repairs to the fabric of the buildings, overseen by M. Elie Bot who was to become his Works Supervisor for the next decade or so.

From 1890 to 1891 he was given charge of the church at Antugnac as well as Rennes-le-Château, which was time consuming, as it involved constant travel between the two villages. However, from 1891 he commenced complete restoration of St Mary Magdalene, which he decorated in the popular style of 19th century French Catholicism, work which went on until c.1900.

The 19th century was to see the renaissance of the cult of the Virgin throughout France, and in 1891 a special diocesan Mission was inaugurated in Languedoc, condemning violence, and calling for the redemption of France through prayer. There had been a positive plethora of visions of the Virgin Mary during the previous decades.

In 1830 she appeared to Catherine Labouré, a nun of the Order of St Vincent de Paul's Sisters of Charity, and instructed her to make a miraculous medal for distribution to penitents - a very lucrative proposition. Now in the 21st century replicas are still being sold at the convent in Paris where Catherine's mummified body lies in state in a glass coffin underneath the altar.

In 1846 a vision of the Virgin appeared to two local children, Melanie Calvet and Maximin Giraud, at La Salette, and instructed the villagers to repent or the harvest would fail and their youngest children would die. Some of them did. There was an epidemic of cholera and infant mortality was rife in those unhygienic days, and it is certain that there was famine - potatoes were unobtainable, and phylloxera struck the grapes bringing ruin to the vine growers. Emma Calvé, the famous prima donna whose name has been linked with Saunière's, originally spelt her name "Calvet", the same as Melanie of the La Salette visitation. The fact has been noted by contemporary authors and a possible relationship commented upon, but it is difficult to see what meaning, if any, can be deduced from these coincidental patronymics.

The Virgin of La Salette was also said to have warned against the rise of the Republicans, and threatened disaster if the monarchy was not restored, but there is no contemporary evidence, and this could have been a public relations exercise by the interested parties. It was suspected that the "vision" was really Constance de la MerlièRe, an eccentric local lady who liked dressing up. She was an ardent supporter of the Legitimists, and perhaps used the idea of a divine apparition to further the cause of the Restoration. Two local priests challenged Constance, and she brought an action against them for defamation of character, which the Court dismissed. It is significant that her lawyer Jules Favre, who conveniently lost the case, was a professed Republican and a member of the Leftist Grand Orient lodge of Toulouse.

The most famous of all the apparitions at this time was the appearance of the Virgin on a number of occasions to Bernadette Soubirous at Lourdes in 1858, during one of which Bernadette, supposedly repeating what "The Lady" had said, called out "Penitence, penitence".

On 17 January 1871 the Virgin appeared to a number of children at Pontmain. In the previous September the Battle of Sedan had brought terrible losses for the French army fighting the Franco-Prussian war, and resulted in the abdication and flight of Napoleon III. Paris was under siege, and the Prussians were within kilometres of Laval, the centre of the diocese in which Pontmain was situated. A vision of the Virgin appeared over the roof of a nearby house, some neighbours joined the children, and from time to time words appeared exhorting the people to pray. The Prussian Army halted its advance at 5.30 p.m. that afternoon, and in due course retreated for no apparent military reason.

The famous black virgin at Limoux, Our Lady of Marceille, had attracted pilgrims since the 14th century. Puivert, near Rennes-le-Château, also had a miraculous virgin, but somewhat younger. In 1817 a baker from the village was in danger of drowning in a Mediterranean storm, and called upon Our Lady of Perpetual Succour for help. She not only saved him, but he saw what appeared to be a statue of her crossing the sea towards him, and vowed a replica to his native church at Puivert if he survived, a promise that he duly honoured. By 1890 the excitement at Puivert had died down, and the cult of Our Lady of Puivert fell into abeyance, until a band of energetic locals raised the money to restore her shrine and restart the pilgrimages.

Saunière coveted a similar attraction for Rennes-le-Château. He applied to the Municipal Council for permission to use the common land in front of the Church to erect a sanctuary for Our Lady of Lourdes, for whom he had a special devotion. The Council, after due deliberation, ruled that "most of the inhabitants were in favour of the project", and gave Saunière permission to proceed provided he did so at his own expense and that the land was not enclosed.

On 20 June 1891 3000 pilgrims attended the celebrations at Puivert in honour of their miraculous Virgin, and launched the Mission that was to involve all the surrounding parishes. On the following day a statue of Our Lady of Lourdes was dedicated at Rennes-le-Château. Twenty-four children received their First Communion at St Mary Magdalene and as a special treat Fr. Ferrifiat, a mission priest from the Lazarist community at Limoux, was invited to lead the procession and preach. The new statue was carried in procession round the village before being installed on the supposed Visigothic pillar, suitably inscribed "Mission 1891" with the legend "penitence, penitence", in the open-air sanctuary Saunière had created in front of his church.

Four months after the start of the Mission Saunière carved the arms of Bishop Billard and Pope Leo XIII over his church porch, thereby gaining indulgences for pilgrims who came to the church and sought the protection of Our Lady of Perpetual Succour.

1891 saw the presbytery at Rennes-le-Château once more habitable. It is here that the romantic myth of Saunière's eighteen year old housekeeper is seen to be just that. Marie Denarnaud was born in 1868, so she was in fact twenty-three when the Denarnaud family moved into the presbytery. She was the eldest child of Guillaume Denarnaud and Alexandrine Marre who lived in Espéraza where she and her brother Barthélemy, four years younger, were born. There were two more sons, Antoine born in 1878 and Jean born in 1881, both of whom survived for less than a year.

The Denarnaud family originated from Sougraigne, but after their marriage M. and Mme Denarnaud lived in Espéraza until around 1878 when they moved to a house in Rennes-le-Château at the top end of the main street. In 1990 Henri Buthion, who owned the domaine at the time, demolished the house and the site became part of the village car park. As Mme Denarnaud's given name was Alexandrine and her maiden name was "Marre" or as sometimes spelt "Marro", it is tempting to imagine that the house of "Alexandrine Marro" where Saunière was said to have lodged when he first came to Rennes-le-Château was in fact the Denarnaud household. If his friendship with the family dated from these early days, this may be the reason why he later offered them accommodation and work at the Presbytery.

Guillaume Denarnaud worked in the straw hat factory at Espéraza, where he was joined in due course by his son, and all earnings were put into the Presbytery's communal purse. Mme Denarnaud acted as housekeeper, assisted by Marie, who took over when her mother became too old for the work. It is not known how long the family remained there, but apparently they were still living there in 1917 at the time of Saunière's death. Mme Denarnaud died in 1928, and her husband in 1930, so both outlived Saunière. Barthélemy married Antoinette Fons, and they had three children. He died in 1944 and like Marie he is buried in the Rennes-le-Château churchyard.

After the Armistice in 1918 Marie was still living at Rennes-le-Château in considerably straightened circumstances. She always maintained that, whatever its origin, it was not her money. In her last years, old, tired and sick, she sold the domaine to Noel Corbu in 1946 on the understanding that she should live in Bethania for her lifetime. She became a little strange, and said that when she visited Saunière's grave she was followed by "will-o-the-wisps" which always disappeared as soon as she shut the cemetery gate.

She is supposed to have told Corbu not to worry about money, as she would one day tell him something that would be of great profit to him, but in her last days a stroke deprived her of the ability to speak. Corbu looked after her until she died in 1953, and when he was tragically killed in a car accident on 20 May 1968 he was buried in the Rennes-le-Château churchyard, where he shares the Denarnaud tomb.

Between 1901 and 1905 Saunière built the Villa Bethania, Tour Magdala, and laid out the surrounding gardens and terraces, which still exist. He organised the building of a water tower that brought running water to the village and enabled the Presbytery to be connected in 1897. He was also said to have initiated the building of the tarmac road down to Couiza as he was considering the purchase of a motor-car, but it was not completed until after his death.

When Mgr Felix Arsène Billard died in 1902 he was replaced by Mgr Paul-Felix Beauvain de Beauséjour as Bishop of Carcassonne. Mgr Billard had been well disposed towards Saunière, Mgr Beauséjour was not. Mgr Billard himself was not above suspicion for improper financial dealings. Although nothing illegal could be proved, there were allegations of mismanagement of funds and undue pressure exerted on parishioners to bequeath money to the Bishop personally instead of to the Church, and Billard was in consequence suspended for three months. He could not have been unaware of Saunière's activities at Rennes-le-Château, and the question inevitably arises as to why he took no action.

In 1905/6 church and state were separated and Saunière was asked to produce his accounts and give an explanation of his wealth. Saunière refused. He wrote to the Bishop saying "I am not obliged...to divulge the names of my donors...My brother being a preacher had numerous contacts. He served as intermediary for these generous souls". A letter to Saunière from an unnamed friend said "You have had the money...it is not right for anybody else to question your secret".

From 1910 until his death in 1917 the legal battle raged, at which time it was found that Saunière did not in fact own anything, the property being in the name of Marie Denarnaud. All Mgr Beauséjour's efforts to recover it for the church failed. Subsequently the domaine passed to several private owners until 1997 when it was acquired by an American consortium. In 1999 the local Council raised the necessary money by subscription to buy it back and the new Mayor, Colonel J. F. Huilier, Légion d'honneur, with an eye on the tourist industry, immediately put improvements in hand. Work was started on Bethania to restore the building and furnish it "in period", with life-like dummies inhabiting the redecorated rooms, and the various museums were to be integrated, with new exhibits added, and running videos about "the mystery" on tap. Those hardy pilgrims who remember Rennes-le-Château in the early '80's will, of necessity, feel somewhat nostalgic that the old village, original, decrepit and secret, is being so greatly plasticised and polished for public display, and the ghosts driven away for ever.

These are facts: Saunière was indeed the priest of St Mary Magdalene, and invoices exist to show that he commissioned, bought and paid for the various work on the restoration of the church, and the statues and pictures that embellished it. There are also invoices and letters referring to the building and landscaping of the domaine. Although he was unable, or unwilling, to give an accurate accounting of his expenditure, what he did account for was some 193,153 Fr.F. which, although not equivalent to the millions that legend attributes to him, is still a very large sum for a village priest whose salary was 75 Fr. F. a month. Also, it did not include the cost of the land or wages for the local workmen, or take into account the cost of furniture, or the quantities of expensive food and wine supplied to the Villa Bethania, for which bills exist. Moreover, Marie was said always to have been fashionably well dressed. It has never been explained where Saunière got the money to carry out such an extensive and expensive programme.

It is also a fact that in *Semaine Religieuse de Carcassonne* of 3 February 1911, the Bishop of Carcassonne published a warning to the local population against Saunière, accusing him of appropriating money paid for bespoke masses, and prohibiting him from administering the sacraments. The warning was repeated in the same publication on 3 July 1915. The interdict was lifted only "in articulo mortis" (the moment of death), and in his obituary of 27 January 1917 in *Semaine Religieuse de Carcassonne* Saunière was not described as a priest. Saunière denied the charge, maintaining that he took money only on behalf of poor priests whom he paid quite legitimately to deputise for him when he was too busy to fulfil his many pastoral obligations. According to Rennes-le-Château author Ian Campbell, Saunière was guilty of simony in offering pardons by post for 50 Fr. F. each. "Simony", named after Simon Magus (see Acts of the Apostles, Ch.8 v.11 - 30) is the sin of selling the gift of the Holy Spirit for hard cash.

There therefore can be no doubt that something very extraordinary was actually going on at Rennes-le-Château at the turn of the century. No true explanation has ever been forthcoming; Saunière had received and spent the money, the source of which he resolutely refused to reveal. Where did it come from?

Saunière's Treasure

The most popular solution is that Saunière found a treasure of vast intrinsic value - real gold, money and jewellery - or something of political or religious value, or even a secret that he was paid lavishly to confide or hide.

The gospel according to de Sède relates that when working on the renovations to the church the old altar was removed, and inside one of the supporting pillars, which was an ancient Visigothic column, were hidden four parchments. Saunière used this column to support the statue of Our Lady of Lourdes in the grotto he created in front of the church. An alternative hiding place for the documents was also promulgated. It was said that Antoine

Captier, Saunière's bell ringer, found a glass vial hidden in the pulpit containing a paper which enabled Saunière to find a tomb. The only evidence is provided by the museum at Rennes-le-Château which contains a wooden pillar in which there is a small cupboard-like receptacle, and the witness of Captier's grandson who still lives in the village.

Whether or not this is authentic, Saunière did find a tomb. His diary entry for 21 September 1891 states it as a fact, although he does not say whose tomb or where it was. The entry for 29 September adds "Vu Cros en secret". Mgr Cros was Vicar-General of the diocese, and the Bishop's immediate deputy. There is no indication of what the confidential meeting was about, but it may have concerned this discovery.

A tomb is not an unusual feature of an old church and graveyard, and the inference is that it was a tomb of particular importance - perhaps that of Marie Négri d'Ablès, which would most likely have been in the vault under the paving stones of the church rather than in the cemetery. The parish register of 1725 contains a reference to the burial place of "seigneurs" in the Rennes church, and old plans of St Mary Magdalene show there was a vault, which was sealed by the laying of Saunière's new black and white chequered floor. Marie's husband François d'Hautpoul was buried in the church of St. Martin at Limoux, so there was apparently not a special Hautpoul family tomb at Rennes, although St Mary Magdalene had once been the official chapel of the Château. There was originally another church, dedicated to St John the Baptist, in the village for the use of the local congregation, but it was destroyed during the 14th century.

The Négri d'Ablès were a rich and influential family which reached its zenith under Marie's grandfather, Jean-Timoleon de Négri d'Ablès, one of the most important men of the 17th century. In 1655 he married Marie-Anne de Cornille, daughter of a notary of Aunat. They had twelve children, and the boys all became either soldiers or priests. After his death in 1703 his eldest son, François, then a captain in the Orléannais regiment, became

Seigneur d'Ablès, Lacam, Niort, Debets and Montpie. He married Toinette de Gaychier in 1704, and Marie, born in 1713, was their only daughter.

After the early death of her mother in 1724 and her father in 1726, Marie was sent to Toulouse to finish her education under the auspices of her uncle, François de Négri of Montroux. She married François, Baron d'Hautpoul and Rennes, Marquis de Blanchefort, in 1732. Marie was 19, François, a captain in the Royal Artillery, was 43. She took to her husband the seignieurie of Roquefleuil, all the revenues of d'Ablès and its not inconsiderable property, the noble fief of Merial, and the greater part of the Niort lands, the remainder being in the hands of her Cazemajou cousins.

The marriage was an important dynastic event. They had four children. Their only son, Joseph, born in 1737, sadly lived for only two years, and with his death the Rennes branch of the family became extinct. Marie d'Hautpoul de Rennes, the eldest child, married her rich cousin Joseph-Marie, Marquis d'Hautpoul-Felines; Marie Anne Elizabeth, the second daughter who remained unmarried, was unable as a woman to inherit the title when her father died suddenly in 1753, and was known as Demoiselle de Rennes. Gabrielle, the youngest child, married Paul François Vincent de Fleury, seigneur of Caux in the diocese of Béziers. The Blanchefort lands formed part of her dowry, and the title passed to her husband who became Marquis de Blanchefort.

Rennes-le-Château, under the feudal system, had been a prosperous village. The d'Hautpouls were generous patrons, and probably donated altar furnishings of some value to the church. Fr Bigou, the priest of St Mary Magdalene at the time of the Revolution, could have hidden the church plate before he fled in 1792 to exile and death at Sabadel, Spain. It is said that when the sans-culottes invaded the church in search of loot, they found only one chalice and paten, the minimum requirements for saying mass. Saunière was said to have given an antique silver gilt chalice as a present to Fr. Graussaud of Amélia-les-Bains in 1886.

Another suggestion is that Saunière found the ancient tomb - Merovingien or perhaps Carolingian - which contained jewellery or other grave goods. If so, it is difficult to imagine how he disposed of these secretly and profitably, and he was said to have given pieces of jewellery in charity to indigent parishioners from time to time. It was the custom to bury valuables with the nobility, and the Louvre museum in Paris has a collection of beautiful golden jewellery found in ancient royal graves. The present Rennes-le-Château church building dates from the 11th century - apart from Saunière's "improvements" - but the foundations go back even earlier, to a Visigothic structure of the sixth century.

The written words

Copies of the documents supposedly found by Saunière, as given in the Dossier Secret, and deposited at the Bibliothèque Nationale in Paris in 1967, were said to be –

♦ two fragments of gospels written on both sides of one sheet of paper (1) John XII 1 - 12, and (2) Luke VI 1 - 5, Matthew XII 1 - 8, Mark II 23 - 28;

♦ a genealogy (in the form of a litany) of the descendants of Dagobert II from 631 to March 1244, when Jean II married Elisande de Gisor, sealed by Blanche of Castile, Queen of France;

♦ the testament of François Pierre d'Hautpoul, Sgr of Rennes and Bézu, bearing genealogies from 1200 to 1644 with six lines in Latin referring to Vincent de Paul, registered on 23 November 1644 by Captier, Notary of Espéraza.

In *Rennes-le-Château: Capitale Sécrète de l'Histoire de France*, Jean-Pierre Deloux and Jacques Brétigny, two journalists who were involved with the Plantard cabal and are therefore assumed to speak for the Prieuré de Sion, added a fourth document. This was the will of Henri d'Hautpoul dated 24 April 1596 in Latin, addressed to five saints (Anthony of Padua, Antony the Hermit, Sulpice of Bourges, Roche of Modeller, and Mary Magdalene), with the letters "P.S." in the right hand corner.

This last document seems to have no bearing on the story apart from its discreet reference to "P.S.", presumably to draw attention to the Prieuré de Sion, but it is perhaps worth noting that St Antony the Hermit is featured in the paintings of Teniers, the church in Paris where Saunière supposedly took the documents to be deciphered is dedicated to St Sulpice, and the Rennes-le-Château church is dedicated to St Mary Magdalene.

The longer of the two parchments (John X11. 1 - 11) reads as follows:

1.Then Jesus six days before the Passover came to Bethany, where Lazarus was which had been dead, whom he raised from the dead.

2.There they made him a supper: and Martha served: but Lazarus was one of them that sat at the table with him.

3. Then took Mary a pound of ointment of spikenard, very costly, and anointed the feet of Jesus, and wiped his feet with her hair; and the house was filled with the odour of the ointment.

4. Then saith one of his disciples, Judas Iscariot, Simon's son, which should betray him,

5. Why was not this ointment sold for three hundred pence, and given to the poor?

6. This he said, not that he cared for the poor, but because he was a thief, and had the bag, and bare what was put therein.

7. Then said Jesus, Let her alone; against the day of my burying hath she kept this.

8. For the poor always ye have with you; but me ye have not always.

9. Much people of the Jews therefore knew that he was there; and they came not for Jesus' sake only, but that they might see Lazarus also, whom he had raised from the dead.

10. But the chief priests consulted that they might put Lazarus also to death;

11. Because that by reason of him many of the Jews went away, and believed on Jesus.

The second shorter document is an imprecise translation of:
Luke VI, 1 - 4

1. And it came to pass on the second Sabbath after the first, that he went through the corn fields; and his disciples plucked the ears of corn, and did eat, rubbing them in their hands

2. And certain of the Pharisees said unto them, Why do ye that which is not lawful to do on the Sabbath days?

3. And Jesus answering them said, Have ye not read so much as this, what David did, when himself was an-hungered, and they which were with them;

4. How he went into the house of God and did take and eat the shewbread, and gave also to them that were with him; which it is not lawful to eat but for the priests alone?

(Matthew XII, 1 - 4)

1. At that time Jesus went on the Sabbath day through the corn; and his disciples were an-hungered, and began to pluck the ears of corn, and to eat.

2. But when the Pharisees saw they said unto him, Behold, thy disciples do that which is not lawful to do upon the Sabbath day.

3. But he said unto them, Have ye not read what David did, when he was an-hungered, and they that were with him;

4. How he entered into the house of God, and did eat the shewbread, which was not lawful for him to eat,

neither for them which were with him, but only for the
priests?

(Mark 11, 23-26)

> *23. And it came to pass, that he went through the corn*
> *fields on the Sabbath day; and his disciples began as*
> *they went to pluck the ears of corn.*
> *24. And the Pharisees said unto him, Behold, why do*
> *they on the Sabbath that which is not lawful?*
> *25. And he said unto them, Have ye never read what*
> *David did, when he had need, and was an-hungered,*
> *he, and they that were with him?*
> *26. How he went into the house of God in the days of*
> *Abiathar the high priest, and did eat the shewbread,*
> *which was not lawful to eat but for the priests, and*
> *gave also to them which were with him?*

The choice of these particular passages of scripture have no
obvious relevance to the Rennes-le-Château story, except that
the incorrectly written texts provide a basis for the code
transcriptions. It is, however, perhaps of interest that the longer
document deals with the story of Mary Magdalene anointing Jesus
as King, and that the shorter document tells in three slightly
different versions the story of Jesus and his disciples accused of
unlawfully plucking the corn. "Blé", the French word for "wheat"
or "corn", is also a slang word for gold - much as English modern
slang refers to money as "bread" or "dough". The two scriptural
passages taken in conjunction could be construed as the King
(Jesus) laying lawful claim to the gold (wheat or shewbread) held
in the church (the priest's house). This is the kind of "double-
talk" that would have appealed to de Chérisey's crossword-puzzle
mind.

Much has been made of the possible meaning of the bag lying
in the forefront of the Mount of Beatitudes mural in St Mary
Magdalene. Upholders of the "physical treasure" theory suggest

that the bag in the picture, like the mythical treasure of Heliodorus, is symbolic of the gold that Saunière found in his church. But there is another possible connection. One small point of interest is the "bag" mentioned in verse 6 of the longer parchment, of which Judas Iscariot, as Treasurer, had charge. In local religious processions of the time it was customary for one of the protagonists to carry "the sack of penitence", presumably for the collection of alms which would carry indulgences. At the festival of Our Lady of Puivert on 18 May 1817, three men carried "the sack of penitence" in the procession. Since Judas certainly repented and threw aside the thirty pieces of silver that were the "price of blood", does the bag in the Rennes-le-Château picture echo the theme, once again, of penitence and the need for charity?

The Dossier Secret file is signed by Henri Lobineau, the supposed pseudonym of Leo Schidlof, a reputable genealogist. The genealogies are said to prove the survival of the sacred line of Merovingian kings through Sigisbert IV son of Dagobert II, the latest scion of which Pierre Plantard claimed to be. The table included in the Dossier Secret is a copy of the one compiled by Gabriel Fournier, Professor of the Faculté des Lettres et Sciences Humaines de Clermont-Ferrand, and does indeed list Sigisbert IV as the son of Dagobert II. M. Fournier's original, however, does not show any descendants of Dagobert II. Dagobert's cousin, Thierry III, is credited with three sons, the youngest of which, Clotaire IV (718-719) has been deleted from the family tree to make a space on the page for the insertion of Sigisbert IV's name. Fr Vincent of the Order of St Francis, writing in 1701, in his history of St. Sigebert III states categorically that Dagobert II's young son died at the same time as his father, or shortly afterwards. One ancient history says that when his father was killed, the boy fell and was trampled to death beneath the hooves of his horse.

Pierre Plantard is also named in the Dossier Secret as Grand Master of the Prieuré de Sion, the esoteric society behind the Rennes-le-Château mystery. De Sède confirmed that the Dossier was deposited at the Bibliothèque by Plantard and de Chérisey, as he had checked the original deposit slip.

It is notable that there is nothing listed for the genealogies after 1644. The Dossier Secret explains the gap by claiming that Schidlof's briefcase, which contained the missing section between 1600 and 1800, was being transported from Paris to Switzerland by a courier named Fakhar ul Islam, who was to have handed it to an agent in Geneva on 17 February 1967. On 16 February Fakhar was seen at Orly airport. On 18 February he met a man called Herbert Regis, and two days later his body was found on the embankment near Melun, having fallen from the express train from Paris to Geneva. The briefcase was never found. According to the Press, Fakhar ul Islam did indeed die in this way but there is nothing to connect him with Leo Schidlof.

If a plausible reason were being sought to explain why 200 years are missing from a family tree, a lost briefcase stolen from a murdered courier is as good a reason as any. One has only to find a suitable newspaper account of a Middle Eastern deportee found dead on a railway embankment. Schidlof died in Vienna on 17 October 1966, the year before the death of Fakhar, and was therefore unable to confirm or deny the story of the theft. Schidlof's daughter denied all knowledge of the genealogies and said they were not her father's work. De Sède in the BBC "Timewatch" programme said that the Dossier Secret genealogies were false, and had been fabricated from those printed in ordinary history books, available to any schoolboy.

According to *Le Trésor Maudit*, Saunière took the documents to his Bishop, the kindly Mgr Billard, who sent him to St Sulpice in Paris to consult the Director M. Bieil, who passed them on to his nephew, Emile Hoffet, an eminent occultist and expert in linguistics, cryptography and palaeography.

St Sulpice was a good choice for anyone looking for a church with occult connections. It was built in 1645 on the remains of a Temple of Isis, and the architecture is said to conform to the "golden mean" which is regarded as the perfect proportion, whereby a line is divided in such a way that the lesser part has the same ratio to the greater as the greater part does to the whole. It is based on the progression of numbers discovered by Leonardo Fibonacci in 1202, (whereby each number is added to the preceding one, e.g. 1, 1, 2, 3, 5, 8, 13 etc.) which is the basis of the pentacle, the pattern of the DNA code, and the arrangement of natural phenomena such as the fir cone and seed pods of the sunflower.

Eliphas Lévi (born Alphonse Constant), the most important and influential occult writer of the 19th century, was an ordinand at St Sulpice and was made deacon there in 1835, although he abandoned the priesthood just before final ordination in 1836.

St Sulpice was also the home of the enormously powerful 17th century secret society, The Compagnie du Saint-Sacrement, whose members included Bishop Nicholas Pavillion of Alet, Jean Jacques Olier the founder of the Seminary of St Sulpice, and Vincent de Paul who was Confessor to Louis XIII and XIV, and Director of Conscience to Anne of Austria.

There is an interesting story about Vincent de Paul, who before the days of his sainthood was said to have set out in 1605 to visit Marseilles, and was there captured by Moors who took him to Barbary, where he was apprenticed to an alchemist. He escaped and returned to France in 1607 where he did all he could to recover letters he had written when in exile, and he always refused to speak about what had happened during his absence.

It has been suggested that his journey was not to Marseilles, but to Our Lady of Marceille, the black virgin of Limoux, a famous place of pilgrimage, and that there he had met an alchemist who took him to the Château of Barbarie (the house of "les morts", the dead), an important occult centre where Nicholas Flamel made the first transmutation into gold on 17 January in 1357. Plantard said that his grandfather Charles Plantard was the nephew of Count François III who had lived at the Château Barbarie, and that Saunière met Charles Plantard during his visit to Paris.

The Château was allegedly destroyed by Mazarin in 1659. There is no real evidence that it actually ever existed, and was anything other than an alchemical legend. However, the Society of Letters, Sciences & Arts of Nevers excavated some ruins near Nevers in 1874 which they believed were the remains of Barbarie. The stones were so overgrown that nothing could be proved except that the building had burned down.

St Sulpice contains the gnomon of the old Meridian line - the "rose line" which is construed by many researchers as Rosaline, (that is, a reference to St. Rosaline, whose statue is prominent in the church of St Mary Magdalene at Rennes-le- Château and St Sulpice, and who is sometimes equated with St. Genevieve, the patron of France). It is consistently used in geometric calculations by a number of mathematicians who apply sacred geometry to the landscape of Rennes-le-Château, near which the old meridian runs. The occult leanings of St Sulpice can also be seen by the five pointed stars over interior doorways - the pentagram being a specifically "magical" figure.

In the Chapel of St. Agnes of St Sulpice is the famous original painting by Eugene Delacroix of Heliodorus fleeing with the temple gold.

The story is told in the Apocrypha, in II Macabees Chapter 3:

At the time when Seleuces was king of Asia and all the kings did honour to the Temple of Jerusalem, the high priest was Onias, an honest man. In his charge was a vast sum of money, four hundred talents of silver and two of gold, which had been given to the Temple for the relief of widows and orphans. The Governor of the temple, one Simon, quarrelled with Onias, and in vengeance sent in secret to the King to tell him about the money, whereupon the King appointed his treasurer, Heliodorus, to go to Jerusalem and seize all the funds. Onias naturally refused to part with them, but Heliodorus insisted. The priests prostrated themselves before the altar of sacrifice, and all the women of Jerusalem, dressed in sackcloth, rushed into the streets and prayed to heaven that Heliodorus should be thwarted in his efforts to rob them. And God heard them. As Heliodorus was leaving the temple the heavens opened, and an angel of the Lord appeared before him on a terrible horse which rode against Heliodorus and smote him with its forefeet. Then two other angels arrived, one on either side of him, and scourged him so that he fell down unconscious. Onias, realising that Heliodorus was only the instrument of robbery and not the instigator of the crime, petitioned the Lord to spare Heliodorus, who promptly recovered and converted to Judaism, so that when he returned empty handed to the King, and was asked who should now be sent to get the treasure, Heliodorus said the King should consider sending only an enemy, who would thereby be justly punished by terror and scourging, "for in that place, no doubt, there is an especial power of God, and he that dwells in heaven has his eye on that place, and defends it, and he beats and destroys them that come to hurt it..."

Saunière apologists may remark that he placed over the entrance to St Mary Magdalene a quotation from the dedication liturgy of a church "This place is terrible", a reference to Beth-el in the city of Luz as "The House of God and the Gate of Heaven" (Genesis Ch.28 v.17 - 19). Saunière may well have been merely an appointee, and if he was searching for treasure on behalf of a secular power, he certainly suffered at the hands of the Roman hierarchy, and ended up with little personal profit.

In Paris Saunière was said to have visited the Louvre and bought reproductions of Poussin's painting "Shepherds of Arcady", Teniers the Younger's "Temptation of St. Antony" and an (unlisted) portrait of Pope Celestine V. He was also said to have attended meetings where he met famous occultists such as

Stephane Mallarmé, Maurice Maeterlinck, Claude Debussy, the glamorous diva, Emma Calvé, and her lover, the neo-Rosicrucian, Jules Bois. According to de Sède, on his return to Rennes-le Château Saunière destroyed the tombstones of Marie Négri d'Ablès, a copy of the two inscriptions of which are reproduced in *Le Trésor Maudit* and the *Dossier Secret*, and which are intrinsic in decoding the two New Testament parchments which provide the secret hiding place of Saunière's mythical treasure.

It is here that we come to a problem.

Tour Magdala

The Fleur-de-lys flying on Tour
Magdala for the death of the
Comte de Paris, 19th June 1999

Church of St Mary Magdalene from the ramparts of Tour Magdala

Bérenger Saunière's grave,
St Mary Magdalene churchyard

The Church porch, St Mary Magdalene

The Garden Altar, Villa Bethania

Statue of St Mary
Magdalene, the
garden grotto

Villa Bethania from the Ramparts

Villa Bethania - the living room
(restored 1999)

Side view of the Presbytery from
the ground floor windows of
Bethania

Chapter Two

"Now I will unclasp a secret book"

(Hamlet, 1.4)

NAMES AND GAMES
The Parchments

It is now agreed by the majority of researchers that the two New Testament parchments are modern, although the writers who base their theories on these texts, particularly the mathematicians and sacred geographers who use the form and layout of script rather than the meaning of the words as a basis for their arguments, maintain that if this is true of the documents in their present form, then they are copies of, or glosses on, older documents and contain valid ancient wisdom. If they are forgeries, then the forgers must themselves be initiates. This apologia is inevitable, because once the parchments are accepted as forgeries they invalidate any thesis based upon them.

The only extant copies of the parchments, so far as can be verified, are those published in books, and the copies in the Dossier Secret file lodged at the Bibliothèque Nationale in Paris. The existence or whereabouts of the originals, if they do in truth exist, is obscure. It is alleged that they may have been among the books and documents that were stolen from expert palaeographer Emile Hoffet's library when he died in 1946.

De Sède was believed to have acquired some of Hoffet's papers around 1966. A year later he published the texts of the parchments, with the code transcriptions, in *L'Or de Rennes*, later renamed *Le Trésor Maudit*, and he gave Lincoln copies which were included in *The Holy Blood and the Holy Grail*. It was said that the code was so complex as to be unbreakable even by sophisticated MI5 computers, but Lionel and Patricia Fanthorpe published their own decipherment in *Rennes-Le-*

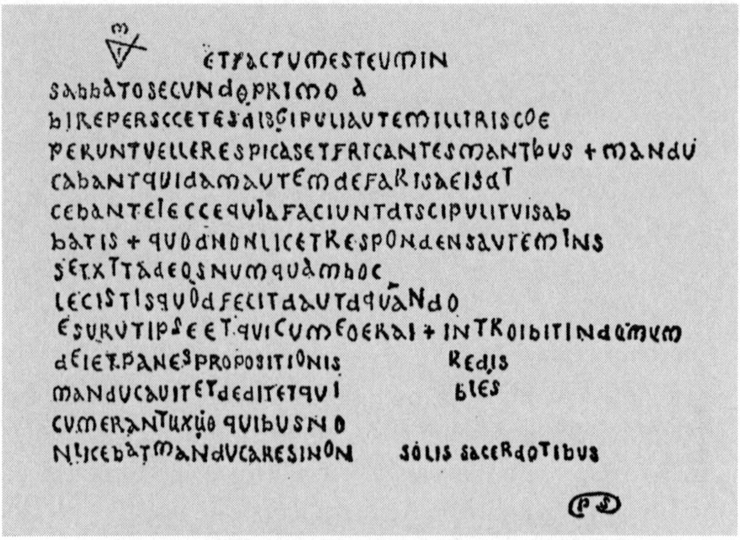

ETFACTUMESTEUMIN
SABBATOSECUNDOPRIMO A
BIREPERSCCETESDISCIPULIAUTEMILLIRISCOE
PERUNTVELLERESPICASETFRICANTESMANIBUS + MANDU
CABANTQUIDAMAUTEMDEFARISAEISDT
CEBANTEIECCEQUIAFACIUNTDISCIPULITUISAB
BATIS + QUODNONLICETRESPONDENSAUTEMINS
SETXTTADEQSNUMQUAMHOC
LECISTISQUODFECITDAUTDQUANDO
ESURITIPSEETQUICUMEOERAT + INTROIBITINDOMUM
DEIETPANESPROPOSITIONIS REDIS
MANDUCAVITETDEDITETQUI BLES
CUMERANTUXUO QUIBUSNO
NLICEBATMANDUCARESINON SOLIS SACERDOTIBUS

NO IS

JESU. MEDELA. VULNERUM + SPES. UNA. PENITENTIUM.
PER. MAGDALANAE. LACRYMAS + PECCATA. NOSTRA. DILUAS.

The two coded parchments

Château, its mysteries and secrets in 1991, and at least one member of The Rennes-le-Château Research Society has since come up with a solution.

In *The Messianic Legacy* Lincoln states that in 1981 he was told by Philippe de Chérisey that the parchments were inherited by Saunière's niece, Mme James of Montazels, the daughter of Saunière's youngest sister Mathilde, who sold them in 1965 to the League of Antiquarian Booksellers. In 1977 the Prieuré de Sion in their publication *Le Cércle d'Ulysse* alleged that the documents were deposited by Captain Roland Stanmore and Sir Thomas Frazer with Lloyds Bank Europe Ltd. in London. Lloyds Bank Europe Ltd. was subsequently absorbed by Lloyds Bank International, who in 1983 denied any knowledge of either Captain Stanmore or Sir Thomas, or of any deposit box containing the documents in question.

If Saunière did find any ancient documents which were inherited by his niece and sold by her to collectors of antiques, then the probability is that they were papers belonging to the Hautpoul family. Father Bigou, priest of Rennes-le-Château, was confessor to Marie Négri D'Ablès, Dame d'Hautpoul, who could have entrusted him with family papers and valuables before she died in 1781, and which he may have hidden in his church before fleeing to Spain a year later. He died in exile and would never have had an opportunity to reclaim them.

De Sède said that he himself had seen an antique bracelet and necklace that was part of a secret hoard hidden in the church, and also that Saunière had found two skeletons and a pot containing some shiny objects, which he declared were medals of no value, underneath an ancient stone which had been placed upside down as part of the paving of the aisle. This was the so-called "Knight's stone", now in the Rennes-le-Château museum, which is so worn that the carving is almost indecipherable. It depicts two figures on horseback, and the suggestion is that it is a carving of Dagobert II and his son Sigisbert IV. An alternative suggestion is that it is Templar, and illustrates how through vows of poverty two knights were forced to ride on one horse.

It is possible that Saunière did find some items of value which he discreetly disposed of - he was said to have sold some coins not more than a hundred years old to a goldsmith in Perpignan. None of it, however, would have been anything like equal in value to Saunière's expenditure on the church and the domaine.

ᴄhe deciphermenᴄs

As early as 1965 the decoded "Shepherdess no temptation" message was published in a so-called Prieuré de Sion document entitled *Les Descendants Merovingians* by "Madeleine Blancassall", the pseudonym of Pierre Plantard's wife, Anne.

In 1979 Lincoln was told by Plantard that the New Testament parchments were forgeries, originally created by De Chérisey in 1958 for a short television programme, but that they were based closely on originals with a few additions and amendments. According to *New Insights into Rennes-le-Château* (Cep d'Or de Pyla 1995 Volume 3) de Chérisey had offered the decipherment to *Pegasus* magazine in October 1973.

In the BBC "Timewatch" programme (17 September 1996) Pierre Jarnac, an author well versed in Rennes-le-Château history, said that in 1971 he had received a letter from de Chérisey claiming to be the author of the documents. An extract from the letter which stated that the documents were made in 1965 was included in Jarnac's *Histoire du Trésor de Rennes-le-Château* in 1984.

In the same BBC programme Jean-Luc Chaumeil claimed that Plantard had handed him two documents which were alleged to be the originals as published by de Sède in *Le Trésor Maudit*. One was in de Chérisey's own handwriting; the other had been copied and endorsed by Plantard to the effect that it was de Chérisey's work. Chaumeil said he also had in his possession an unpublished booklet of 44 pages entitled *Paper and Stone* written by The Prankster, describing how the code was constructed, and which on page 25 stated "this is the signature of the artist (signed)

Philippe de Chérisey".

Naturally those who support the veracity of the parchments insist that the information disseminated by participants in the "Timewatch" programme was, in fact, "disinformation", purposely intended to confuse the uninitiated. It is true that none of the documents mentioned was produced for independent viewing.

However, all the evidence points to the fact that the New Testament parchments were not found by Saunière in his church. Also, the famous Visigothic column in which the documents were supposed to have been concealed, which has been dismissed as a 19th century copy by archaeologists, was found to be indisputably and embarrassingly solid when it was removed to the museum from beneath the statue of the Virgin where Saunière had placed it in 1891. A great deal of speculation has been raised by the fact that the original column was placed upside-down, but there does not seem to be anything sinister about this; presumably the mason who on Saunière's instructions had chipped into its surface the legend "Mission 1891" was unfamiliar or unconcerned with Visigothic art, or the column, being second-hand, sat more firmly on the ground that way up.

The gravestones

The decoding of the documents involves the inscriptions on the two engraved stones alleged to have been carved by Fr Bigou for Marie Négri's grave.

The inscriptions as first given by De Sède are -
The vertical stone -

CT GiT NOBLe (omitting the M)
ARIE DE NEGRi
DARLES DAME
DHAUPOUL D'
BLANCHEFORT
AGEE DE SOIX
ANTE SET ANS

DECEDEE LE
XVII JANVIER
MDCOLXXXI
REQUIES CATIN
PACE

and the other, a rectangular slab at the foot of the first stone -

ET IN ARCADIA EGO
Reddis   Regis
Cellis   Arcis

The "Et in Arcadia" stone was said to have been reproduced in 1884 in a rare publication entitled *Engraved Stones of Languedoc* by Eugene Stublein, a meteorological expert; and the epitaph in *Bulletin de la Société des Études Scientifiques de l'Aude* (S.E.S.A.) Tome 17 of 1905. In a local library Pierre Jarnac discovered a genuine guide book to thermal establishments in Languedoc written by Stublein, in which his authenticated signature differed from the one in the *Engraved Stones of Languedoc*, and Jarnac therefore considered this latter book to be a forgery. The *Bulletin de la Société des Études Scientifiques* is unobtainable. As the tombstone inscriptions contained in the Dossier Secret are needed to decode the parchments, Jarnac considers that their doubtful provenance strengthens the case for the parchments also being modern inventions.

According to legend, the "Et in Arcadia" stone, from which Saunière erased the inscription, is the one broken in several pieces now in the Rennes-le-Château museum. *Le Cahiers de Rennes-le-Château* No.11 has an interesting, if somewhat untenable theory, about what happened to the other gravestone. It is suggested that the members of S.E.S.A., who copied Marie Négri D'Ablès epitaph for their Bulletin, had found the original stone thrown away in a corner of St Mary Magdalene's churchyard, which accounted for the fact that her actual burial place could not be located. The stone was broken through the middle into two pieces. *Le Cahiers* then draws attention to the surprising fact that the slab topping Saunière's grave is also broken in two across the middle, and must have been like this when placed there because the carved inscription takes account of the break:

ICI REPOSE
BÉRENGER SAUNIÈRE
CURÉ A RENNES

(break)

LE CHÂTEAU
1885-1917
DÉCÉDÉ
LE 22 JANVIER
1917 A L'ÂGE
DE 65 ANS

As the Saunière tombstone is said to measure the same as that alleged to be Marie Négri D'Ablès' epitaph stone (1.30m x .65m), the suggestion is that the two stones are one and the same.

De Sède introduces yet a third stone, which he said was found by chance buried beneath a holm-oak, lost again and then rediscovered in 1928 in a rocky hollow on Mount Coumesourde. This was supposedly commissioned by the Marquis de Fleury who married Gabrielle, Marie Négri's youngest daughter, before they fled into exile during the Revolution. Its relevance is obscure, and the Latin of the inscription is so ungrammatical as to be untranslatable.

SAE SIS
In MEDIO
LINEA UBI
M SECAT
LINEA
PARVA
P.S. PRAECUM

On the reverse side:

> CEIL BEIL
>   MCCXCII

Perhaps the initials P.S. are intended to refer to the Prieuré de Sion. The authors of *The Tomb of God* suggest that it is a geometric plan allied to the sacred geometry of the parchments, as the lettering is contained within two triangles, similar to the triangles produced on the parchments by joining specific letting, and that the M stands for the Meridian. A certain M.Cros is the only person reputed to have seen this stone and if it ever existed it has now disappeared.

It is assumed that Saunière, after deciphering the parchments and destroying the tombstones, used the solution to track down the treasure. The gaudy decorations in his church, and in particular the Stations of the Cross, are said to have been designed to illustrate its whereabouts, and the question remains as to why Saunière should wish to reveal the location in this way, when he went to such lengths otherwise to keep it secret.

In fact the examples of "bondieuserie" he installed were bought off the peg from local suppliers. The large bas-relief ("Come Unto Me" Matthew XI.28), the Holy Water stoup, and a number of the statues were supplied by Giscard & Cie of Toulouse. The Stations of the Cross, made of terracotta and painted, were also supplied by Giscard, and others very similar could be found elsewhere in the Aude - an example still exists at Mouthoumet. The total cost was 2920 Frs. and the supplier presented statues of the Sacred Heart and the Virgin and St Joseph to the church as gifts. The painting and gilding of the walls and arches was carried out by Casteix for the sum of 905.70 Frs. which Saunière settled by instalments, and the ironmongery by Charles Denarnaud, blacksmith of Alet, for 147 Frs. Altar decorations, two gold chalices and a monstrance from Fardaco of Carcassonne cost 317 Frs.

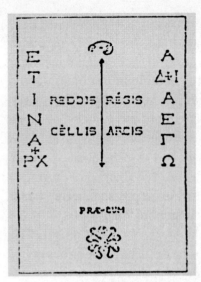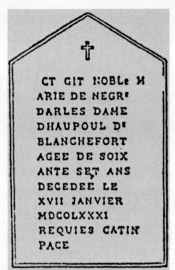

Marie Négri's two tombstones

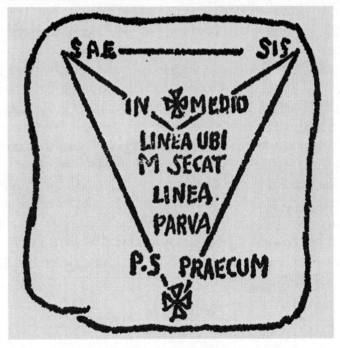

The Coume Sourde Stone

Saunière's refurbishment of his church was supposed also to be an illustration of the extraordinary book *La Vraie Langue Celtique* written by Fr Henri Boudet, priest of the adjoining village of Rennes-les-Bains, which was thought to contain certain information vital for the solving of the mystery of the treasure. The text is a series of linguistic puns and puzzles, and by an astrological code indicates twelve deposits within the local area, their position corresponding to the houses of the Zodiac beginning near the Château of Blanchefort. A reproduction of the original book was published in 1978, and in his preface Pierre Plantard adds that "not all the deposits contain anything".

Jean-Pierre Deloux, in a preface to the same edition, says "This book, that one might believe is the result of the delirious ravings of a literary lunatic, is one of the keys that provide access to the treasures and secrets that lie hidden in the ancient and savage land of Razès. Coded, enciphered, it none the less remains open to those who understand the "language of the birds" and know the cadences of the phonetic cabala...one must consult the keys of the tarot and the stars in order to travel the roads that lead to Arcadia..." Deloux goes on to declare, in obscure oracular style, "The Prince neither speaks nor dissembles: he signifies...he is privileged to untie the knot, possessing knowledge of the median and the circle, the stone and the cromlech, the lily and the roundel... By these mysteries, the thread reveals its subtle answers."

La Vraie Langue Celtique was published by M. Victor Bonnafous of Carcassonne in 1886 at Boudet's own expense, and cost 5382 gold francs. During the 28 years between then and 1914 a total of 98 copies were sold, 300 were given away including a complimentary copy to Queen Victoria, and the remainder were pulped.

So what say they?

The cipher messages, arrived at by using the misaligned letters and spelling mistakes in the two parchments and Marie Négri's epitaph, are now as well known as a television commercial.

The textual eccentricities of the epitaph inscription produce an anagram of eight letters which can be rearranged as "Mort Epée".

The solution to the longer document is based on the French alphabet of 25 letters (French does not have a "W") and achieved by using "Mort Epée" as the keyword. Out of the 140 unnecessary letters extracted from the text 128 are chosen. These are then subjected to a system of two letter substitution, and the unintelligible string of letters so resulting is deciphered by placing them on two chessboards and subjecting them to the knight's tour (moving two squares laterally followed by one square horizontally).

The result is an anagram of the 128 letters of Marie Négri's tombstone, and reads:

> *Bergère pas de tentation que Poussin Teniers gardent le clef pax DCLXXXI par le croix et ce cheval de dieu j'achêve ce daemon de gardien a midi pommes bleues Shepherdess no (without) temptation that Poussin Teniers hold the key peace 681 by the cross and this horse of god I complete (or destroy) this daemon of the guardian at noon blue apples.*

In the shorter document, the message obtained in clear from the raised letters, reads:

> *A Dagobert II roi et a Sion est ce trésor et il es la mort To Dagobert II King and to Sion belongs this treasure and he is there dead (or: it is death).*

By superimposing a triangle on a portion of the document it is possible to obtain Et in Acadia Ego. Also from the last letters of the last four lines of the document the word Sion occurs vertically.

Sacred geographers use not only the deciphered messages of the two parchments, but also the physical format of the texts. By placing geometric figures on the actual writing they pin-point certain local places on the map which they believe hide, or are clues to the hiding place of, Saunière's secret hoard.

A modern expert on old parchments comments that if, as de Sède suggests, the two New Testament extracts were printed on both sides of one skin parchment, it would not have been possible to see through them and put the two pieces of writing in juxtaposition, as some cryptanalysts have suggested. The authors of *The Tomb of God* (Richard Andrews and Paul Schellenberger), who were pilloried by the BBC for stating that the coded message of the parchments had led them to the body of Jesus buried under Pêche Cardou, admitted that in order to arrive at the solution they had to transfer the texts onto transparencies which they then read by superimposing one upon the other.

In the manner of Chinese boxes, the solution merely confounds the problem. It is cryptic beyond belief, and its meaning is further confounded by lacking punctuation, but the inventors left certain clues.

Poussin and the two Teniers (father and son) were renowned painters. Poussin twice painted the shepherds of Arcady leaning upon a tomb on which is inscribed "Et in Arcadia Ego", the motto, according to Pierre Plantard, of the Prieuré de Sion. The initials P.S. appear in the inscription on Marie Négri's tombstone, and the rectangular slab actually includes "Et in Arcadia ego". It was therefore assumed that Poussin referred to Nicholas Poussin.

Poussin was born in 1594 at Les Andalys near Gisor, France. This is the first tentative link with the Prieuré de Sion, whose archives were supposedly stored from the 16th century at Gisor castle, an important fortress from the time of the crusades.

Gisor is the setting for an extraordinary little historical anecdote. In 1188 Henry II of England and Philip II of France, each with their train of knights, met in a once-sacred field near Gisor castle with a view to negotiating a peace treaty. The day was hot, and the English took refuge under a gigantic elm tree, said to be more than eight hundred years old, which stood in the centre of the field. The French expressed their fury at such behaviour in violent action; though whether they considered the English occupation of a sacred site to be blasphemy, or whether they just objected to the English hogging all the shade, is uncertain. The English, thinking discretion the better part of valour, retreated to Gisor castle. The French, in frustration, cut down the tree, and Philip returned to Paris, saying he had not come to Gisor to play the woodcutter. This little episode, which has come to be known as "the cutting of the elm", remains ambiguous. The story as it stands is patently absurd - "1066 and All That" history, like King Canute telling the sea to go back, or Alfred burning the cakes - but the fact that it persists seems to indicate that something of significance occurred at that time and in that place.

In the Dossier Secret the "cutting of the elm" is explained as the act of severing connections between the Prieuré de Sion and the Templars, the Prieuré being the esoteric higher grade that was responsible for founding the Templars as an exoteric "outer order".

Gisor was occupied by the Germans during World War II, but was evacuated when the Allies invaded Normandy. In 1946 a workman named Roger L'homoy claimed to have found an underground chapel with nineteen stone sarcophagi and thirty metal boxes containing documents, but red-tape prevented any excavation until 1962, when André Malraux, the then French Minister of Culture, authorised further investigation. Nothing of significance was found, although L'homoy insisted that he did find his way back to the chapel, and that the archives had been removed.

The inference is that if Poussin was native to the area where the Prieuré was active, he could have early come under their influence.

In 1612 Poussin went to Paris to study painting and sculpture, where he received various commissions, including drawings for Ovid's "Metamorphosis" from the poet Marino. In 1623 he went to Rome where through Marino he came to the notice of Cardinal Francesco Barberini and his secretary Cassiano dai Pozzo, who became his patrons. Poussin's interest lay in mythological subjects, rather than the biblical studies more popular with painters of the time, and it was between 1638 and 1639 that he painted the Shepherds of Arcady. In 1640 he was recalled to Paris by Louis XIII, but the type of work offered him, including superintending the decoration of the Grande Galerie of the Louvre and commissions to design various altar pieces, made little appeal and two years later he escaped back to Rome. Here he abandoned his former somewhat austere classicism for a more poetical and imaginative approach, and by 1650 had achieved European renown. He remained in Rome for the rest of his life, and died there in 1665. His tomb is surmounted by a marble relief plaque of the Shepherds of Arcady.

In *The Holy Blood and the Holy Grail* Lincoln gives a long dissertation on Poussin's possible political affiliations, and quotes a letter from Abbé Louis Fouquet written to his brother, Nicholas Fouquet, Superintendent of Finances to Louis XIV of France, in which he describes his meeting with Poussin, and says that they discussed certain things which would provide his (Fouquet's) brother with untold secret advantages. Rennes-le-Château mythographers take this to mean that Poussin knew the secret of the treasure which Saunière may - or may not - have discovered. It is a fact that Nicholas Fouquet, Vicomte de Mélun et de Vaux, Marquis de Belle-Isle, was later arrested for embezzlement, and imprisoned for life in the fortress of Pignerol. There is a legend that he may have been the original "Man in the Iron Mask", so valuable a captive that he could not be put to death until he had disclosed the knowledge that his gaolers needed, but too dangerous to risk being identified or allowed to speak to outsiders. Inevitably the advocates of the Rennes-le-Château mystery affirm that this secret and essential knowledge was the identity of the treasure.

Enthusiastic researchers claim that the background of *The Shepherds of Arcady* is identical with the view of Rennes-le-Château seen from the neighbouring village of Arques, and there was, up to a few years ago, a tomb similar to the one in the painting in the appropriate place, but without the famous "Et in Arcadia Ego" inscription. When the Rennes-le-Château mystery landslide started the then owner of the land, reputedly connected with the American Embassy, demolished the tomb in 1988 in order to preserve his privacy and sanity.

According to Pierre Jarnac the tomb dated from around the beginning of the century. The land was owned by Jean Galibert, a mill-owner from Pontils, and in 1903 the Galibert family had commissioned a stonemason from Rennes-les-Bain to work on the tomb, though whether this was to restore an existing structure or start from scratch is not clear. When they moved to Limoux the estate was acquired by Louis Bertram Lawrence, a soldier who had stayed on after World War I and started an electrical and chemical business at Ille-sur-Tet. Lawrence apparently buried his mother and his wife in the tomb, and when Lionel and Patricia Fanthorpe visited the area in 1970, they removed part of the broken top and photographed two decayed coffins which were deposited at the bottom. The photograph is reproduced in their book *The Holy Grail Revealed*.

There is no indication that Poussin ever visited Languedoc, though he could, of course, have gone to Rome from Paris by sea via Marseilles, which might have taken him into the Arques area. The local countryside certainly bears some resemblance to the backgrounds in several of Poussin's paintings - but so also does the countryside around Rome where he lived.

David Teniers, the second painter mentioned in the longer document, was fond of painting the temptation of St Antony, and there is only one picture, St Antony and St Paul in the Desert, in which St Antony is not being tempted. It is not at the Louvre, but was in the collection of Lord Palmerston until acquired by Edwina Ashley, Countess Mountbatten, in 1942. Teniers the Younger - his father was also a painter of some distinction although not much is known about his life - had a very long career, as he started painting at the age of eight, and lived to be eighty. His output tops the one thousand mark. Although mentioned in the deciphered parchment, he appears to have no active role in the mystery.

There is no mention in the parchments of Pope Celestine V, although Lincoln includes a portrait by an unidentified artist among the paintings Saunière was said to have purchased in Paris. Celestine V was an obscure pope (1209 - 1296) who was elected in despair in 1294

when the papal throne had been vacant for twenty-three months.
Born Pietro del Morrone, a simple peasant from Calabria, while still
a teenager he entered a Benedictine house, being drawn to the
contemplative life. He was hailed as the "angel Pope" and it was
hoped he would rejuvenate the prestige of the papacy which had
fallen into some decline. He wished only to return to solitude at
Marrone, but was detained by force at Castle Fumone, near
Ferentino, where he died of an infection at the age of 87. He was
canonized by Clement V on 5 May 1313 as a confessor, and his feast
day (no longer observed) was 19 May.

There was apparently a painting of the Coronation of Celestine
V by an anonymous 16th century artist in the Celestine monastery
of Marcoussis until the order was dissolved during the French
Revolution. The authors of *The Tomb of God* (Richard Andrews
and Paul Schellenberger) discovered a very old negative in the
archives of the Louvre, and reproduce the painting in their book.

Could it be that the portrait Lincoln mentions is not intended to
be Celestine V, who seems to have little relevance to the Rennes-
le-Château story, but Clement V, the Pope who was pressured
by Philippe-le-Bel of France into destroying the Knights Templar?
Clement V was formerly Archbishop of Bordeaux, one Bertrand
de Goth, son of Ida Blanchefort, and Lincoln suggests that Clement
may have known a secret that was entrusted until the 18th century
to the Blanchefort family, including Marie Négri D'Ablès (Marie
de Blanchefort) whose confessor was Fr Bigou, the priest of
Rennes-le-Château. Some people believe that the cipher
documents found by Saunière were composed by Fr Bigou, and
that he also carved Marie's tombstones in such a way as to include
the necessary keyword.

Sceptics have pointed out that no reproductions of paintings were
available from the Louvre until 1901. In all fairness it must be pointed
out that Lincoln does not say that Saunière bought reproductions
from the Louvre. He says he visited the Louvre and bought
reproductions. He could have visited the Louvre merely to check
the references, and bought the reproductions from one of the many

art shops in Paris. Before the days of ubiquitous cameras and photocopiers, it was common for struggling artists to live by making copies or engravings of masterpieces.

There remains the enigma - what is the common denominator of these three very different works of art? Guy Patton in the *Rennes Observer* (No.25 December 1999) suggests that the reason for the choice of these three painters lies is their connection with heresy. Pope Celestine was adamant in attacking Pelagianism and Nestorianism, both condemned by Rome as heretical. St Antony was a fourth century Egyptian hermit who fought vigorously against the temptations of the Gnostics with whom he shared his desert retreat. Poussin may have acquired an interest in the heretical doctrine of Jansenism through his friend and collaborator, Philippe de Champaigne. Jansenists were Stoics, and their rather gloomy intellectual philosophy is aptly summarised in the enigmatic phrase "Et in Arcadia Ego", used by Poussin in his two Arcadian paintings. Languedoc has a long history of so-called heretical associations, and Patton's theory is that whoever or whatever is behind the Rennes-le-Château mystery, be it the Prieuré de Sion or another, could be part of this secret, and continuing stream with which Saunière may have been familiar.

Sacred geographers settle for the fact that a pentacle can be superimposed upon the structure of Poussin's second version of the Shepherds of Arcady, and that this or other associated geometric figures can then be transferred to a map of the Rennes-le-Château region to produce proposed treasure sites. Schellenberger and Andrews demonstrate that pentacles can also be traced in the paintings of St. Antony and St Paul in the Desert, and the Coronation of Pope Celestine V. Artists since the time of Pythagoras have regarded the golden mean as the ideal measurement of proportion, and it is the geometric basis for erecting the pentacle. Martin Kemp, a reputable art historian, maintains that a similar underlying pattern could be attributed to almost any painting, because it is simple enough to superimpose any geometric figure on a flat surface, and that no significance should be given to the claim that these three paintings use the "golden section" as their infrastructure.

In occult symbolism the pentacle with one point upwards represents the human body, but with two points upwards it is regarded as diabolic. It is also a glyph for the pagan horned god - goat, bull or stag - all symbols of virility and the life force. The god of the old religion inevitably becomes the devil of the new. The "devil" that supports the holy water stoup in Saunière's church is an example of the horned god, and the Christianisation of "Old Nick". He has retained the esoteric symbols of the four elements - himself as earth, the salamanders that top him as fire, the basin for water, and the four angels above as air.

The ancient fertility religion has strong roots in this area of France, and is still celebrated in the Carnivals of Limoux, Alet, Couiza, Espéraza and Quillan, when the mummers, dancing through the streets for Mardi Gras, recall the revels of Saturnalia.

Franck Marie in *La resurréction du Grand Cocu* describes the scene:

> *"...Firstly it can be seen afresh that the trance-like ecstasy of the dancers is comparable only to sacred dance. All day, all night... above all, the glimmer of torches and the perfume of resin, drifting with smoke in the wind, conjure up even more strongly archaic ritual, and the mystery of ancient superstitions..."* and adds *"It was not until 1972 that women could be seen taking part in the Carnival at Limoux. The antifeminism of the Carnival was, and remains, one of its main social characteristics...everywhere else, where it survived, it remained traditionally all-male".*

It is only the identification in the parchment of "Poussin" as Nicholas Poussin the famous 17th century painter that ties Saunière in with the visit to the Louvre, or indeed with Paris at all. The proof put forward that he visited St Sulpice because he said mass there is not valid, because contrary to some mythographers' belief, his name cannot be found in the mass book. Marie Denarnaud, however, insisted that he did visit Paris, and he may well have done so, but for quite another reason, as will be seen in due course.

No mention is made of Marie Négri's tombstones until Saunière's return from Paris. If he took the parchments to St. Sulpice to be deciphered, how was the decipherment done without access to the keyword contained in Marie Négri's epitaph, since this is an integral part of the solution? If Saunière could not read the documents, he would not have known in advance about the keyword contained in the epitaph, and the need to take a copy of the tombstone inscriptions with him. The sequence of events does not bear logical examination, but de Chérisey, as a novelist, was writing an entertaining story and not an analytical thesis. As will be seen, however, it is possible for experts to decipher documents without the keyword, given certain parameters.

Who hides may find

As soon as written language was invented, the need arose for a way to make the contents incomprehensible to those for whom it was not intended - hence the invention of codes and ciphers. Technically a cipher is a system of substitution of letters, numbers or symbols for those of the clear message, and a code is the substitution of a pre-arranged word or phrase meaning something quite different from the clear text. A code cannot be broken without the key, which must be known to the recipient of the message. The parchments and tombstones are in cipher, the solution, if there is one, is in code.

A partial guess at the code meanings might be deduced in view of the association of Poussin with the artist of that name, and references in the documents to the inscription "Et in Arcadia Ego", but phrases like blue apples could in fact mean anything. Solutions for this have ranged from suggestions of the sun shining at mid-day through stained glass in Saunière's church to create blue coloured circular patterns on the chequerboard floor, to grapes as the source of wine symbolising the blood and body of Christ. De Chérisey himself said blue apples was an "in" joke associated with Scottish Rite Masonry.

It is possible to break a cipher based on the substitution of letters, numbers or symbols for those of the clear message without knowing the key, provided the cryptanalyst knows the language in which the original document has been written. This is done by the frequency method.

Two or more documents are chosen, of similar length and in the same language as the document to be deciphered. The occurrence of each letter or symbol is counted in all the chosen "control" documents, and a table of percentages of frequency computed. A similar analysis is then applied to the cipher document, and a comparison made whereby the letter that occurs most frequently in the control documents is substituted for the letter or symbol occurring most frequently in the cipher document, and so on throughout, by matching the percentages of frequency. Once a skeleton is made in this way, the cipher document is subjected to known eccentricities of language. For example, "e" is the commonest letter in English. If there are a number of words ending in "e" something, the "something" will possibly be "d", as "ed" is a very common ending for past tenses in English. Similarly double letters that look like vowels will be "e" or "o" because they are the only vowels in English that double. Expert cryptanalysts have an intimate knowledge of such eccentricities of language, and it is possible to break a cipher by the frequency system even if more than one alphabet is used.

Using only one alphabet was too easy to break, even with the addition of a keyword. Mary Queen of Scots used a mono-alphabetic cipher for her secret correspondence. A letter containing details of the Babington plot, which planned to assassinate Queen Elizabeth I and place Mary on the English throne, was captured and deciphered by Elizabeth's spymaster Walsingham, thereby ensuring Mary's trial and execution.

Seeking better security, cryptographers started to use more

than one alphabet, alternating between them during encrypting a message. Blaise de Vigenère, a French diplomat born in 1535, achieved the ultimate in multi-alphabetic ciphers, using twenty-six alphabets.

The alphabet was written out 26 times, each succeeding line starting one letter later:

Plain: a b c d e f g h i j k l m n o p q r s t u v w x y z

1. b c d e f g h i j k l m n o p q r s t u v w x y z a
2. c d e f g h i j k l m n o p q r s t u v w x y z a b
3. d e f g h i j k l m n o p q r s t u v w x y z a b c
4. e f g h i j k l m n o p q r s t u v w x y z a b c d
5. f g h i j k l m n o p q r s t u v w x y z a b c d e
6. g h i j k l m n o p q r s t u v w x y z a b c d e f
7. h i j k l m n o p q r s t u v w x y z a b c d e f g
8. i j k l m n o p q r s t u v w x y z a b c d e f g h
9. j k l m n o p q r s t u v w x y z a b c d e f g h i
10. k l m n o p q r s t u v w x y z a b c d e f g h i j
11. l m n o p q r s t u v w y z a b c d e f g h i j k
12. m n o p q r s t u v w x y z a b c d e f g h i j k l
13. n o p q r s t u v w x y z a b c d e f g h i j k l m
14. o p q r s t u v w x y z a b c d e f g h i j k l m n
15. p q r s t u v w x y z a b c d e f g h i j k l m n o
16. q r s t u v w x y z a b c d e f g h i j k l m n o p
17. r s t u v w x y z a b c d e f g h i j k l m n o p q
18. s t u v w x y z a b c d e f g h i j k l m n o p q r
19. t u v w x y z a b c d e f g h i j k l m n o p q r s
20. u v w x y z a b c d e f g h i j k l m n o p q r s t
21. v w x y z a b c d e f g h i j k l m n o p q r s t u
22. w x y z a b c d e f g h i j k l m n o p q r s t u v
23. x y z a b c d e f g h i j k l m n o p q r s t u v w
24. y z a b c d e f g h i j k l m n o p q r s t u v w x
25. z a b c d e f g h i j k l m n o p q r s t u v w x y
26. a b c d e f g h i j k l m n o p q r s t u v w x y z

It will be seen that in this way the top line is in clear, and there will also be an alphabet in clear down the left side.

A keyword is chosen, for example "kingdom" which is then written as many times as is necessary under the message to be encrypted, so that each letter in the message is associated with a letter from the keyword. For example:

PUT BAG IN THE SAFE
k i n g d o m k i n g d o m k

To encrypt, take the first letter "p" of the text to be encrypted and find the equivalent keyword letter, in this case "k". This means the alphabet line starting "k" must be used, which in fact is line 10 of the Vigenère square which is:

Plain: abcdefghijklmnoPqrstuvwxyz
10.   klmnopqrstuvwxyZabcdefghij

The intersection of letter "p" from the plain alphabet with the corresponding letter on line 10 gives "z" which is the first letter of the enciphered text.

The second letter of the text is "u" which means using the line of the Vigenère Square starting with "i", which is Line 8:

Plain: abcdefghijklmnopqrstUvwxyz
8   ijklmnopqrstuvwxyzabCdefgh

In the plain alphabet, U corresponds with C, which becomes the second letter of the enciphered text.

The same system is continued throughout and the message reads:

ZCG HDU UX BUK VORO

To scramble further, the letters are run together: ZCGHDUUXBUKVORO, or broken up to choice: ZCGH DU UXBU KVO RO To decipher the encrypted message, the process has only to be reversed and the letters sorted into intelligible words.

The need for the recipient to know the keyword, and the rather lengthy system involved, meant that the Vigenère Square was not as popular as its security warranted, but it was still considered to be the ultimate in secrecy until the nineteenth century, when an eccentric gentleman called Charles Babbage cracked it in 1834 as an intellectual exercise. Babbage's true claim to fame is that he invented the first automatic calculator. Struggling one day with some navigational tables, he exclaimed "I wish these figures had been executed by steam", and immediately started on a project to build a machine capable of doing accurate mathematical calculations. Supported by Government funding he produced two very practical machines, and although he lost interest before they were completed, his work has remained the reason and basis for the development of the modern calculator, and cipher machines which are mathematically oriented.

In 1918 a German inventor, Arthur Scherbius, created a cipher machine called Enigma. The sender and recipient had to agree in advance how the cables were to be plugged into the machine, which then scrambled the message. This gave such an enormous range of possible alternative readings that Enigma was considered impregnable. As late as 1926 British Intelligence was intercepting Enigma messages which were still indecipherable. One of the problems was that Enigma was continually being updated which made all previous break-in attempts invalid. The cryptanalysts each time just had to start all over again.

During the 1930's Rejewski, a Polish cryptanalyst, infiltrated the current Enigma code, but by 1938 the German cryptographers had further re-scrambled Enigma to the extent that it was again totally baffling. Rejewski's work had, however, indicated that Enigma could be broken, and it finally was, by Alan Turing.

A young mathematical genius, in 1930 Turing invented what was in fact the blueprint for the modern programmable computer, but technology was not sufficiently advanced at that time to enable it to be built. He was a Cambridge don, enjoying a quiet University life and freedom to practise his sexual preferences, when in 1939 he was co-opted as a cryptanalyst for the Bletchley Government Code and Cipher School.

From then on his work was specifically code-breaking. Pressured by Churchill, who foresaw the urgent need to penetrate German Intelligence if the Allies were not to lose the Battle of the Atlantic, Turing joined the Bletchley "think tank", his aim being to find alternative ways to attack Enigma. Using his previous academic research for the Turing computer and analysing Rejewski's work on the early version of Enigma, Turing came up with a machine that in fact finally broke the Enigma code. Security denied him recognition for his incredible achievement. In 1952, while reporting a burglary to the police, he inadvertently revealed his homosexuality. He was arrested, tried and convicted of gross indecency. His security clearance was withdrawn, he was forced to consult a psychiatrist, and to undergo hormone treatment that made him impotent and fat. Two years later at the age of forty-two, severely depressed, he committed suicide by eating an apple dipped in cyanide.

The breaking of the Enigma code seriously worried the Americans when they entered World War Two. The only really secure method that remained to them appeared to be by writing the message in an unknown language. They therefore employed Navajo Indians to translate secret communications into their tribal language before being encrypted. It certainly fogged the Japanese Intelligence interceptors, because outside the actual Tribe there were reputed to be only half a dozen Navajo speakers in the World. This meant having both a Navajo recipient as well as a Navajo sender capable of coping with the difficulties of translation and encipherment, and one of the problems was that the Navajo language has no words that equate with the terms of modern warfare. Aircraft therefore had to be classified according to size and function as birds - for example, hummingbird for fighter, owl for observation plane - and ships as fish, shark for destroyer, frog for amphibious vehicle etc. And there was still the risk that the Japanese might recognise Navajo, which however rarely spoken is an existing language in contemporary use.

The Elizabethans had an almost spy-proof solution. Dr John Dee, Astrologer Royal to the Queen, mathematician, navigator, writer, lens maker, metallurgist, linguist, alchemist and magician, was also one of Walsingham's agents. He travelled throughout Europe ostensibly as a visiting lecturer to Universities and Royal Courts, and was in fact collecting information about Philip of Spain's plans to invade England.

Dee was the original 007, and signed his reports OO > (the eyes and ears of the Queen). He invented a complete language known as Enochian, with its own grammar and vocabulary, which he said was dictated to him by the angels through the medium of the crystal. It was totally unbreakable, since even if the message were intercepted and deciphered, nobody spoke Enochian. One of his successes was the discovery of a plot by the Spanish to suborn the charcoal burners to burn down the Forest of Dean. The forest was, and still is, composed of golden oaks which was the wood used to build the English fighting ships. The destruction of Dean would have been equivalent to the damage inflicted on the Germans by the RAF bombing of the Ruhr during World War Two.

Compared with Enochian and the Enigma codes, the Rennes-le-Château parchments are comparatively simplistic. Ciphers are breakable because they have an underlying pattern. Codes, however, have no compulsion to relate to the clear message; provided the sender and recipient both know the code, the actual words can mean anything. For example, a code message reading "Ring Aunt Phyllis tomorrow" could equally mean "fly the country immediately" or "beware your wife knows all" or even "congratulations you have won the lottery"! An analysis of the actual words of the code message will reveal nothing.

From the misinformation so carefully leaked by the early authors, however, the wording of the Rennes-le-Château coded parchment is apparently meant to have some logical relationship to the clear meaning. Popular speculation has taken Poussin to refer to the painter, "681" to refer to the year Sigisbert IV arrived in Languedoc - if he ever did - and "the horse of God" to mean the Knight horse-headed chess-piece whose tour of two boards reveals the cipher solution.

De Chérisey maintained that the message was a word-game: "Poussin" (little chicken) was a pun on "Hautpoul" (big chicken), and "cheval de dieu" (horse of God) was a sound play on the words "cabal de Chérisey". "Shepherdess" referred to a local legend about a young shepherd boy who fell into a cave and found a hoard of gold, "681" was the year of Dagobert II's death (except that it was actually 679), and the "cross" near the railway embankment was the one referred to in *The Tomb of God*, though de Chérisey does not explain its significance.

Richard Andrews and Paul Schellenberger worked out an entirely different set of meanings for the code words. They believe that "Bergère" (usually translated as "shepherdess") can also be a type of armchair, and here refers to the Devil's armchair, a strange rock formation on a hillside to the East of Rennes le-Château. "681" they take to mean the height of the nearby Col de Espinas; and "cheval de dieu" to be the slang term for a cricket, in turn a slang word for a square pillar, which they equate with the support of a railway bridge, here located on the Espéraza line. They identify the cross as a crumbling 17th century monument on the north-western side of the railway, on the base of which is an inscription reading -

> IMPVLSVS EVERSVS SVM
> VT CADEREM
> ET DXS SVSCEPI TME

"Thou hast thrust sore at me that I might fall: but the Lord helped me." (Psalm 118 verse 13).

The cross surmounting this stone, of more recent date, reads

> RESURRE-
> XIT
> 1801 - 1876

By using these geographical locations and complicated mathematical calculations Andrews and Schellenberger declare they have located Saunière's secret treasure - the body of Jesus buried under Pêche Cardou.

What else can we deduce from the code text?

Regarding de Chérisey's story of the young shepherd, there is another more appropriate local legend in Auguste de Labouisse Rochefort's book *Voyage to Rennes-le-Château* (1832) about a young shepherdess, who when tending her sheep early one morning saw, on a neighbouring hillside near Blanchefort Castle, the devil with all his gold spread around him. Terrified she ran home, but when the villagers went to look, both the devil and his gold had disappeared. This story ties in nicely with the Demon Guardian of the code message, and of course the gold would be no temptation to the little shepherdess, because all good children know that fairy gold in the light of day next morning turns into dead leaves.

681 by Gematria (the ancient Greek system of letter/number substitution) can be made to read "pax". Peace was certainly an object of the 1891 Mission, which advocated the cessation of war and violence, and a small point of coincidence is that the neo-Visigothic pillar on which 1891 was carved was upside-down. If turned the right way up, 1891 becomes 1681. Marie Négri's tombstone gives the date of her death as MDCOLXXXI, which is 1681, whereas she actually died in 1781. There is no '0' in Roman figures. There is also another way to arrive at the attribution of 'peace' to 681: by adding the numbers together $(6 + 8 + 1 = 15 = 6)$ we arrive at 6 which in Cabala is the number of Tiphareth, the central Sephirah of the Tree of Life, which stands for harmony, balance and peace.

The eminent numerologist, Neil Hudson Newman, points out that the letters of the epitaph on Poussin's tomb, "Et in Arcadia Ego", number 2 2 7 3, and three times 227 is 681. 227 is the 50th in the series of prime numbers, and 50 is an important occult number.   Jason's ship, Argo, was said to have had 50 oars. Argo's figurehead was made of wood from the oracular oaks of Dodona, was able to speak, and guided the Argonauts on their quest for the mysterious treasure known as the Golden Fleece. "Argo" is a gloss on the word "argot" meaning jargon (language peculiar to a specific class or sect).   Dodona was sacred to Diana of the black doves, so that her oracles naturally used an esoteric vocabulary - "the language of the birds".

In *The Rennes Observer* No.25 (Dec.1999) researcher Larry Dean offers an alternative cross, the Calvary near Antugnac, the village where Fr Saunière acted as locum from 1890-91 while they were awaiting the appointment of their new priest.   In *The Tomb of God* the Calvary is used as a vital pointer to the burial place of Christ.

It is inscribed

> IN
> RI
> 1830
> B.D

Dean suggests that B.D. could stand for ...Bis Domine (twice God), taken from Non Nobis Domine, the opening lines of Psalm 115, a phrase that also equates in Gematria with 681. The opening verses of this Psalm read:

> *"Not unto us, O Lord, not unto us:*
>   *but unto thy name give glory, for thy mercy,*
>   *and for thy truth's sake.*
>   *Wherefore should the heathen say:*
>   *Where is now thy God?...*
>   *Their idols are silver and gold, the work*
>   *of men's hands.*
>   *They have mouths, but they speak not,*
>   *eyes they have, but they see not...*

An interesting allusion to secret treasure?

There is also, of course, the Calvary that Saunière put in his open-air sanctuary in front of the church. On the base of this are carved the letters:

A.O.M.P.S.

This is taken to represent the popular pious text "Christus a omnipotens defendit" (Christ Almighty Defender), but could it mean something else?

And yet another contender might be the cross, dedicated to the Magdalene, that once stood on the high point of the Rennes-le-Château hill, now the site of the Magdala Tower.

Michael Gabriel in *The Holy Valley and the Holy Mountain* says that the valley of Rennes-les-Bain was known in the 18th century as the Valley of the Cross. This does not refer to the remains of the many Celtic crosses that litter the area, but to a cross marked out by sacred geography, delineated by "various features, such as springs, ruins, peaks, churches and castles, aligned to it in order to highlight some memorial in the calendar that is superimposed upon it. This cross holds the knowledge that is more precious than material treasure, and reveals to the initiate the Gold of Wisdom. The secret was known to Fr Boudet, and is incorporated in his book *La Vraie Langue Celtique* ".

The somewhat incoherent language of the coded message is necessitated by the linguistic straight-jacket self-imposed upon the author by the necessity to use 128 specific letters, in order that the result should be an anagram of Marie Négri D'Ablès' epitaph. This juxtaposition has no apparent practical purpose, serving merely as an elaboration of the games plan, but shows remarkable ingenuity by resulting in the approximation of a coherent message. Amateur cryptographers are apt to ignore the bits that will not fit in very comfortably with their theses.

As an intellectual exercise it is possible to create a personal interpretation of the ambiguous coded message:

"Shepherdess no temptation". There is the legend about the shepherdess seeing the devil counting his gold. For her it was certainly no temptation.

"Poussin and Teniers hold the key". Assuming they used the golden section, which is the basis of the pentagram. Michelangelo uses the pentagram as his divine plan for the human body.

"681" being the supposed date of Sigisbert IV's arrival at Razès. The Merovingians were "divine magician kings" who ruled but did not govern.

"blue apples". The apple is the symbol of wisdom, sacred to the goddess (feminine principle) because cut crosswise it provides a five pointed star. Mary Magdalene is sometimes regarded as a personification of Sophia, divine wisdom. Blue is the colour of the Virgin.

In Greek mythology, Pegasus, the winged horse of the Muses, is the inspiration of poetry. His kick caused the soul-inspiring waters of Hippocrene to spring from a mountainside. To be mounted on Pegasus is to be engaged in original writing. By stretching the imagination a little, therefore, it might be argued that the creation of the parchments, and their poetic form, is the "demon guardian" that conceals the secret, and the kick of inspiration is needed to release it from its hidden source.

As a hypothetical construe: how about -

Gold is no temptation. Life's quest is knowledge gained through the eternal wisdom of the feminine.

OR

Gold is worthless. The key to life is the divine plan and the object is renewal (or resurrection) through the divine child.

Saunière had a special devotion to the divine child. There is an entry in his personal notebook at the beginning of the year 1891, accompanied by an illustration taken from the journal *La Croix* which shows a baby being taken to heaven by three angels. Below this is a picture of the Three Kings of the Epiphany, beneath which is written:

Melchoir: Reçois, O Roi, l'or, symbole de la royauté.
(Receive, O King, gold, the symbol of Royalty)
Gaspard: Reçois, la myrrhe, symbole de la sépulture.
(Receive myrrh, symbol of the tomb)
Balthasar: Reçois l'encens, o toi qui es Dieu.
(Receive incense, thou who art God)

The legend of the Three Kings is orthodox enough, if apocryphal, but it is perhaps not insignificant that Sigisbert IV, the supposed fountain of the revived Merovingian line, which plays such a large part in the Prieuré de Sion legend, was considered a "royal divine child", and so also was the Comte de Chambord, the last legitimate heir to the French throne, who was a posthumous child and regarded by loyal monarchists as "miraculous". To the Legitimists it was not considered heretical to regard the Bourbons as ruling by divine right.

Saunière may, or may not, have been familiar with Masonic and Martinist practices, or the occult symbolism that can be read into his choice of somewhat esoteric decorative schemes, but he was no stranger to the more obscure means of communication.

According to de Sède the following cryptogram was found among Saunière's papers after his death:

```
YENSZNUMGLNYYRFVHENMZFP.S
OT+PECHEUR+A+L'EMBZ
VOUCHURE+DU+RHONE,SONZ
UPOISSON+SUR+LE+GRIL+F
LDEUX+FOIS+RETOURNA.UD
RN+MALIN+SURVINT+ET+XH
RXV+FOIS+LE+GOUTA+.CUZ
TIT.,IL+NE+LUI+RESTA+QV
KUE+L'ARETE.+UN+ANGE+T
NVEILLAIT+ET+EN+FIT+UQ
YNPEIGNE+D'OR.B.S,CURH
OVTSVKYRMSTIJPZCKPFXKA
```

It has apparently not yet been deciphered. As with the New Testament parchments the original is missing, and there is no proof of authenticity, but if this is another of de Chérisey's games it is difficult to see the reason for it, and it is hardly ever mentioned in the Saunière legend. This may account for the lack of interest by cryptographers in trying to crack it, but on the other hand, it may perhaps be impossible to break because it has been created at random with no basic cryptic logic.

This cipher follows the pattern of that used in *The Beale Papers*, a fascinating little tale of a vanishing cowboy's buried treasure, contained in the Simon Singh's *The Code Book* published by the Fourth Estate, London. This story parallels so closely that of the Rennes-le-Château mystery as it has come down from de Sède, that the inevitable conclusion arises that Pierre Plantard and Philip de Chérisey used it as their model when creating the original Rennes-le-Château myth.

In 1885 a pamphlet was published anonymously stating that a fabulous hoard of gold, silver and jewels had been hidden by one Thomas Beale an itinerant cowboy, details of which were contained in three coded documents. These consisted of several pages of columns of figures.

The story as given was that in January 1820 Beale arrived at the Washington Hotel, Lynchburg, Virginia, where he stayed until the following March. In January 1822 he returned, and again spent the winter at the Washington Hotel. On leaving he entrusted the proprietor, Robert Morriss, with a locked iron box containing important papers. Morriss put it in his safe and forgot about it until four months later. On 9 May 1822 he received a letter from Beale from St Louis which said that he was off West on a hunting trip, and in case of catastrophe Morriss should open the box after ten years. He added that the box contained papers which were unintelligible, but that he had left a sealed letter addressed to Morriss with a reliable friend which would reveal everything, and that it would be delivered in June 1832.

Beale never returned to Lynchburg, and the promised letter never arrived. By 1845 Morriss felt he should take some action. He broke open the box and found it contained three documents written entirely in numbers. It also contained a letter to Morriss explaining that in April 1817 Beale and twenty-nine companions had journeyed across America to Santa Fé. They then headed north, hunting buffaloes. When some 250 to 300 miles north of Santa Fé, they had just made camp when one of the party discovered what looked like a seam of gold in the nearby rocks. With the aid of the local tribesmen they mined the area and accumulated a great deal of gold and silver which Beale transported East, but finding it cumbersome to carry on a horse, he buried it. He then went back to the mine, and returned after eighteen months with a further load which was added to the secret hoard. He had been asked by his companions to leave a memorandum of the treasure with some reliable person in case of accident, and this was contained in the papers in the iron box.

The first document gave the location, the second was a list of the contents of the vault, and the third stated the names of those who were entitled to share in the treasure.

In 1863 Morriss, at the age of eighty-four, felt that he should take action if Beale's wishes were to be carried out. He confided the problem to "a friend", identity unknown, who being unwilling to assume the responsibility decided to make the whole matter public. Withholding his name, he wrote down everything he knew in *The Beale Papers*, and asked a respected member of the local community, the county's road surveyor James B. Ward, to act as his agent and publish the pamphlet anonymously.

The author did, however, reveal that he had deciphered the second document with the aid of a "book code", using the Declaration of Independence as the key. The resulting solution said that the hoard was buried in the county of Bedford, about four miles from Buford, six feet down in an underground vault that was roughly lined with stone. Packed in covered iron pots, it consisted of 1014 pounds of gold and 3800 pounds of silver, deposited in November 1819; and 1907 pounds of gold, 1288 pounds of silver and some jewels which had been bought to facilitate transport, deposited in December 1821, the total being valued at $13,000 (approximately $20 million by today's standards). The document concluded with a statement to the effect that document one described the exact location of the vault "so that no difficulty will be had in finding it".

The unknown friend who was reputed to hold the key was never identified, and documents one and three have proved unbreakable, in spite of strenuous efforts that have continued up to the present time.

In 1912 two treasure-hunters, George and Clayton Hart, thought they had found the solution. They excavated their chosen site using dynamite, but achieved nothing but a very large hole. Professional code-breakers from organisations such as the U.S. Cipher Bureau have had no better luck. In 1960 the Beale Cipher and Treasure Association was founded to encourage interest in the mystery, but in spite of continued professional and amateur efforts documents one and three remain unsolved. The opinion of experts is that Beale was using a "one-off" unique key text which he probably wrote himself, and without the key the cipher might never be broken.

An alternative suggestion is that the author purposely scrambled the figures in his published pamphlet which would prevent the holder of the key from personally deciphering the documents, finding and sticking to the treasure; but that it might encourage him to come forward. The author would then produce the true text and together they could decipher the documents and share the proceeds.

It is always possible, of course, that the treasure was accidentally found by someone long ago and quietly appropriated.

Sceptics believe that the most likely solution is that the whole Beale mystery was a hoax, that Beale never existed, that the author of the pamphlet made it all up and wrote the coded documents himself, and that only document two could be deciphered because documents one and three were composed of random figures that meant nothing. As evidence they quote that the letter in the iron box, supposedly written in 1822, contained words such as "stampede" which were not in use until 1834.

Believers in the truth of the mystery maintain that the two indecipherable documents do, none the less, show specific underlying patterns in the figures which point to their being genuine codes, even though no-one has yet been able to discover what they mean.

In his book *Beale - History of a Mystery*, published by Hamilton's, Bedford VA, 1997, local historian Peter Viemeister states that Beale did exist, at least several Thomas Beales born in Virginia are listed in the 1790 census. He adds that a Cheyenne legend tells of a vast amount of gold and silver that was moved East and buried in the mountains there. According to the postmaster's records, a man called Beale passed through St Louis in 1820, which fits in with the claim made in the pamphlet that Beale went to St Louis in 1820 after he left Lynchburg to travel West.

Modern treasure-hunters are still looking for Beale's treasure. In February 1983 Joseph Jancik and Marilyn Parsons, with their dog Muffin, were charged with "violating a sepulchre" after being caught digging up a grave in Mount View Church cemetery in the middle of the night. (Does that sound familiar?) Mel Fisher, who salvaged the gold from the Spanish galleon "Nuestra Señora de Atocha" off Key West Florida in 1985, believed that the Beale gold was buried at Graham's Mill in Bedford County, Virginia. He bought the site, but after a lot of digging found nothing.

The author of the pamphlet warned the reading public that they would be wasting their time, money and efforts. "Never, as I have done" he says "sacrifice your own and your family's interests to what may prove an illusion...", but adds "...when your day's work is done, and you are comfortably seated by your good fire, a short time devoted to the subject can injure no one, and may bring its reward." Another version of bedtime stories?

Literary hoaxes are not uncommon. The 18th/19th century was the golden age, and the deceptions were usually harmless public relations exercises. For example, Horace Walpole maintained that *The Castle of Otranto* was not his original work but a translation from the Italian. It was only after its success and publication of the second edition that he admitted his authorship.

On occasion the lies went wrong. The most famous case was the young genius, Thomas Chatterton, who assumed the persona of a certain Thomas Rowley who had lived in Bristol during the 15th century. At the age of twelve Chatterton wrote *Elinoure and Juga* and other pieces in praise of Bristol which he passed off as Rowley's work, ageing his manuscripts by rubbing the parchment with yellow ochre and scraping them along the dirty ground. The poems were much praised until it was recognised that he wrote in heroic couplets which did not exist in the 15th century. Reviled as a forger, he committed suicide by taking arsenic. He was seventeen years old.

There was also the case of Moses Wilhelm Shapira who likewise came to an unfortunate end. He was born in Kiev in 1830 of Jewish parents, but went early to Jerusalem where he converted to Christianity. He became a dealer in both fake, and occasionally real antiques that he bought from the desert Bedouins. In 1882 he acquired a bundle of parchment scrolls alleged to be unknown sections of Deuteronomy some 2000 years old. He sent them to Dr Konstantine Schlottmann, Professor of Old Testament Studies at the University of Halle, who rejected them as rubbish, although similar scrolls reputed to be parts of the Pentateuch, which had been found at the same time, were regarded as genuine. Shapira accordingly took his scrolls to London where they were authenticated by Dr Christian Ginsbury, an expert on Old Testament texts, and put on show at the British Museum to whom Shapira hoped to sell them for a million pounds. Ginsbury then changed his mind and said that the scrolls were a forgery, compiled by a consortium of Polish, Russian and German Jews. In March 1884 Shapira shot himself. The provenance of the scrolls was never settled, and there is now some idea that they may have been genuine.

James McPherson, on the other hand, was also a literary liar but a successful one. In 1760 he published *Fragments of Ancient Poetry collected in the Highlands, translated from the Gaelic and Erse Languages*, followed two years later by *Fingal, an Ancient Epic Poem in six books, composed by Ossian, son of Fingal, the story of a third century chief written in heroic language*. McPherson had no evidence of the authenticity of this work, and there were no Gaelic texts. Dr Johnson said the poems were fake, and a committee was set up to investigate. Eight years later they decided McPherson had "embroidered what was genuine" (it will be recalled that Plantard maintained that de Chérisey did likewise with the coded parchments). McPherson had already admitted as much in the preface to his work, and although the provenance of the poems was never settled, his work was highly regarded, and he was buried in Westminster Abbey next to Dr Johnson!

One of the best contemporary literary hoaxes is *The Final Solution* by Stephen Knight (published in 1994) in which the author presents a very plausible case for the identity of Jack the Ripper. Knight's contention is that the Whitechapel murderer was not just one man, but a group of high-up Government officials and Master Masons. Between 31 August and 9 November 1888 five women were found in a small area of the East End of London with their throats cut and their bodies mutilated, and although there have been endless theories about the reason and the perpetrator, the crime was never solved. Theories might proliferate, but nobody was brought to trial.

Knight's story revolves around Prince Albert Victor Edward, Duke of Clarence, Queen Victoria's grandson. His thesis is that Prince Eddy, as he preferred to be called, met Annie Elizabeth Crook at the studio of the painter, Walter Sickert, in Cleveland Street, and fell in love with her. Annie worked at a tobacconist's shop nearby, where her fellow assistant was Mary Kelly, the

Ripper's last victim. When Annie became pregnant Eddy married her, and in due course a daughter, Alice Margaret, was born. Annie's friend Mary Kelly was engaged as the child's Nanny.

When news of the marriage leaked out, Annie was taken at the instigation of the Prime Minister, Lord Salisbury, to Guy's Hospital where she was confined as a mental case, subjected to brain surgery, and thereafter spent the rest of her miserable existence between workhouses and insane asylums. Eddy was forcibly removed and detained under strict supervision at St James's Palace. Mary Kelly, however, escaped with the child, and went to ground in Whitechapel.

Had she kept quiet, she would have survived. However, the story was too good to keep to herself, and she confided in three or four of her closest friends among the local prostitutes. Threats of blackmail percolated, and Salisbury was faced with the problem of dealing with the incipient scandal. His choice of instrument fell on Sir William Gull, Queen Victoria's Physician in Ordinary. Both Salisbury and Gull were Freemasons of high standing, and the Masons were all powerful with the Throne and the Government. Gull was entrusted with the job of removing not only Mary Kelly, but her associates, and in ritually killing the women he fulfilled his mission, but somewhat exceeded his licence. He had a history of violence and mental instability. Almost immediately after the death of the last victim, Gull disappeared from society, and his death was announced in 1890, though he may in fact have been in a mental institution at that time, and did not die until later.

The account, as presented by Stephen Knight, is sufficiently convincing to warrant belief in the accuracy of his accusation. It just happens that it is not true. Knight himself, before his early death from cancer, admitted that the book is romantic fiction, an elaborate edifice built upon the flimsiest foundation of conjecture and circumstantial evidence. It became, and still is, a well-deserved best-seller, and is a very entertaining detective story, as well as being remarkably believable.

In fact, Prince Eddy's visits to Cleveland Street were for quite a different reason. Number 19 Cleveland Street was the location of the infamous male brothel, where delivery boys from Mount Pleasant Telegraph Office were in the habit of supplementing their income, being willing to oblige the wealthy clientele for ten shillings or so a session.

Eddy was second in line for the Throne, the eldest son of Edward, Prince of Wales (later Edward VII) and the beautiful Danish Princess Alexandra, daughter of King Christian IX. He was born on 8 January 1864, a sensitive and delicate boy, whose inclinations and talents were artistic, rather than being directed towards shooting, hunting and womanising like his Royal father, who inevitably disliked him. He was his mother's favourite child, adored and spoiled by his sisters, and understandably in the circumstances, homosexual.

He was probably taken to Cleveland Street by Lord Arthur Somerset, one of the Prince of Wales's Equerries, and a major in the Royal Horse Guards. The scandal broke in September 1889, when one of the disgruntled telegraph boys went to the Police. Homosexuality was illegal and carried the possibility of a long prison sentence. Although Somerset was identified as a regular visitor to No.19, the idea of an aristocrat, the Prince's trusted servant, and a serving officer in "The Blues", being involved in homosexual practices was too shocking to be entertained. He was granted leave of absence from his duties, and quietly disappeared. Charles Hammond, the brothel keeper, fled to the Continent, and later, with money given to him by Somerset, to America. Lord Salisbury himself let it be known that he did not consider the case worth pursuing. In fact, the whole affair was hushed up.

The most important move now was to get Prince Eddy married. The Royals' first choice was his second cousin, Princess Alix of Hesse, and Eddy dutifully proposed, but the lady was serious-minded and turned him down. His own somewhat erratic fancy fell upon Princess Hélène d'Orléans, daughter of the Comte de

Paris, pretender to the French throne. Exiled in 1886, the Orléans family were living at Richmond, England, and nineteen year-old Hélène regarded the Heir Apparent as a romantic figure. She also fancied being Queen. The Royal Family, however, regarded her as totally unsuitable. They had recognised Napoleon III as Emperor of France, and Hélène, moreover, was a Roman Catholic and legally barred by Parliament from the British throne. A compromise was reached and in December 1891 Eddy was betrothed to Princess May of Teck, who was only half-royal being the daughter of a morganatic marriage, but otherwise suitable. He died, however, of influenza on 14 January 1892 before the marriage could take place, and a replica of his bride-to-be's bouquet of orange blossom was laid on his coffin. Queen Victoria, who was fond of her grandson, remarked tartly "May never really loved poor Eddy". The Princess was duly passed on to George, the next brother in line, and in due course they reigned as King George V and Queen Mary.

ꜰᴀᴄᴛ ᴏʀ ꜰᴀɴᴛᴀsy?

Whether or not the whole Rennes-le-Château mystery is a fabrication, the question remains - why? What prompts someone, apparently otherwise sane, to spend energy, time and money, imposing a false premise on persons unknown.

The answer must lie in the psychology of the hoaxer. We all have weaknesses, a fantasy, an obsession, ambition, a blind spot or prejudice, although we do not all necessarily publicly indulge them to the detriment of society. These are, however, the raw material of a hoax.

There is inevitably a measure of self-deception and some self justification on the part of the initiator. Hoaxers have a taste for intrigue, aspirations to greatness and a liking for public attention, they enjoy being lionised, and are often bullies who like to dominate those they consider weaker, and sometimes more fortunate, than themselves.

The motive may be for gain, fame, fun, mischief or out of sheer boredom. Most commonly it is for money. It may involve a taste for revenge, not necessarily on an individual but on life in general, a feeling of not receiving due and proper recognition or reward.

Deceit is the means of operation, and promotion is the secret of success. Victims must be made receptive, and the groundwork carefully prepared by the careful dissemination of misinformation. There has to be an element of plausibility.

Pierre Plantard, self-styled descendant from the true Kings of France, certainly had both social and political ambitions. De Chérisey seems to have been a natural practical joker who enjoyed intrigue for its own sake, and unlike Plantard he did not seek the spotlight or look for social or political advantage. Perhaps he did not need to, for according to Jean-Luc Chaumeil, de Chérisey genuinely came from minor nobility, and was by profession an actor known as "Amadée", which may account for a lot. His was the crossword puzzle brain that allegedly created the coded parchments, and it seems he took a wicked delight in stirring up such a storm of misapprehension.

Both de Chérisey and Plantard presumably hoped for some financial gain from exploiting the Rennes-le-Château mystery, even if it was only royalties from the book they failed to get published, and the gradual leakage of information about the Prieuré de Sion's part in the story certainly roused considerable public and media attention. There were enough verifiable factors to ensure plausibility. It is perhaps ironic that in the end the original progenitors of the mystery received less reward than the subsequent researchers, writers and promoters, and they could hardly have foreseen the prestige and profit accruing to the village itself from the consequent tourist boom.

Fr Saunière's gold seam has had an unprecedented spin-off in the books, films, TV, postcards and photographs, talks and tours that exploded from de Sède's modest beginnings. But all the ink and paper, the conferences and lectures, the theories and theses, have failed to come up with the answer: did Saunière find treasure, and if so, what was it?

Aʟʟ ᴛʜᴀᴛ ɢʟɪᴛᴛᴇʀꜱ....

It is difficult to imagine what Saunière might have found that could be converted into the sort of money that he admitted spending, even allowing for the amounts for which he would not, or could not, account. The popular assumption is that he found a fabulous treasure: real valuables, gold and silver, money or jewellery; antique artefacts that would attract collectors; legendary or mythical objects; a secret that he could be paid to reveal or conceal.

The originators of the story, Gérard de Sède, and Lincoln, Baigent and Leigh, make no commitments about Saunière's actual findings. De Sède is content merely to report the Abbé's discovery of documents in the church which led him to "discover a tomb" which may - or may not - have contained treasure, but as a second string, mentions the genealogies that "prove" the survival of the royal Merovingian line. *The Holy Blood and the Holy Grail* goes a step further in that the authors suggest that Mary Magdalene was the wife of Jesus, the true King of Israel, that their descendants married into the Merovingian dynasty, and that this secret knowledge was sufficiently shocking to warrant Saunière's selling it, either to the Vatican, or to the Hapsburgs, who were affiliated with most of the ruling European royal families.

This would hardly have been a particularly lucrative story to auction in 19th century France. The Roman Catholic Church had been abolished by the Convention in 1792, re-established briefly by Napoleon I in 1799, and finally separated from the State by the Commune in 1870. By the time that Saunière was appointed to St Mary Magdalene at Rennes-le-Château, the Royalists' efforts were concentrated on restoring the Bourbons to the throne of France, and the Monarchists dreamed of a third Empire. Moreover, the Government elections of 1885 had resulted in the return of the Republicans to power. The country was exhausted after the Franco-Prussian war, there was high unemployment and industrial unrest. There would have been little interest in the restoration of a Merovingian king. The analogy might be for a candidate claiming descent from Saxon King Harold to try to usurp the throne of Elizabeth II during the World Cup Final.

The concept of a "hidden king", however, is one that has a strong psychological appeal. The "Sacred Bloodline" features in countless myths and legends, such as the stories of the *Keepers of the Grail*. It is all part of the ancient wisdom that has survived from the time of the Magi of the Nativity, via religion, mythology, ritual and poetry, channelled underground through esoteric organisations to initiates, astrologers, alchemists and mathematicians throughout the ages.

Among modern writers, the idea of a religious secret connected with Rennes-le-Château includes locating the burial place of Jesus on the assumption that (a) he survived the Crucifixion, or (b) his body was later brought to France; or alternatively the discovery of the tomb of Mary Magdalene. The legend that Mary came with her sister Martha and brother Lazarus to the little seaside town of Les Stes. Maries de la Mer in the Languedoc is nothing new, and her bones and her ointment pot are listed among the possible "treasures". Other sacred objects that have been named are the Ark of the Covenant, the Emerald Tablets of Hermes, Moses' Stone Tablets of the Law, the Urim and Thummim, the Philosopher's Stone, the Elixir of Eternal Life, the Spear of Longinus, and the Holy Grail. None of these would have been very easy to market for a poor priest in a remote French village.

Among the "real" treasure suggested, the most important is that of Solomon's Temple at Jerusalem, including the great golden seven-branched candlestick, which was looted first by the Romans after the destruction of the Temple in 70 AD, taken to Rome by Titus, re-looted by the Visigoths in the fifth century, and carried with them when they invaded Septimania. The royal treasure was stored at Toulouse, but the most powerful magical and religious symbols of the nation were taken to Carcassonne. Some of this hoard was later pillaged by the Saracens and taken to Toledo.

The Roman Empire was well established in Southern France, and another possibility is that the "treasure" was gold imported to pay the local Roman legionaries, or alternatively mined by them in the area. Languedoc and Provence are littered with Roman remains, and bits of pottery, statues, and coins still turn up today among the furrows of the farmers' ploughed fields. Other contenders for the honour of being the "treasure" are: cash-boxes belonging to the Templars, never found when the Order was dissolved by Philippe-le-Bel in 1307; the Cathar (unspecified) treasure, removed from Montségur before the citadel fell in 1244; and the gold provided by Blanche of Castile (Louis IX's daughter) to pay her invading army in Languedoc, and ransom her son "El Desdichado".

The purveyors of sacred geometry, including Lincoln who started the cult in his book *The Holy Place*, claim to have found extraordinary ancient relics in the landscape around Rennes-le-Château, connected with local tombs, temples, churches, menhirs, and mountains, including a Temple of Isis, a Temple of Time, and cryptic messages left by Atlantean refugees, descendants of the Pharaohs, and visiting Aliens. Rennes-le-Château is regarded as a "power point", like Glastonbury and Chartres, a place of cosmic force, where the time warp is operative and the veil between the seen and the occult is thin. Elizabeth van Buren, in her book *Refuge from the Apocalypse* says that when Armageddon comes, Rennes-le-Château will be the place of survival for the initiates, though it is not clear whether this will be the "other world" (in which case the initiates will, like Enoch, cease to be) or the entrance to some kind of hollow world space.

In his Preface to Boudet's book *La Vraie Langue Celtique*, Pierre Deloux, possibly speaking for the Plantard cabal, states that it was Henri Boudet, priest of Rennes-les-Bains, and not Bérenger Saunière who held the secret of the treasure. When the book failed to gain the expected readership, Boudet planned to illustrate it by restoring the church of Rennes-le-Château in such a way that it provided clues to the hiding places. He supervised the work and paid for it, but Saunière was not privy to the secret, which he only learned when he attended Boudet on his deathbed in 1915. It was then too late for him to benefit by the revelation, as he himself died only two years later.

Deloux maintains that the only secret that Saunière found was contained in the genealogies he discovered in his church, which detailed the Plantard family's legitimacy as the descendants of Sigisbert IV, son of Dagobert II, and the first of the Merovingian Kings to adopt the name of Plant-ard (Living Branch). The guardian of the "Lost King" and custodian of the "treasure" is the Prieuré de Sion. "Without the Merovingians the Prieuré de Sion would not exist", he says, "but without the Prieuré de Sion the Merovingian dynasty would be extinct". Deloux does not, however, deny the existence of the "treasure". He lists the various possible sources: Roman, Visigothic, Cathar, Celtic, Templar, and maintains that certain families, which include Blanchefort, Hautpoul and Fleury (names familiar from their association with Marie Négri d'Ablès, she of the two phantom tombstones), were in possession of the secret. This they shared, by decree, with certain members of the Church: Abbé's Delmas, Bigou, de Cayron, and latterly Henri Boudet. Their task was to make the best use of such part of the "treasure" to which they had access, but without disclosing anything to their superiors. It was Boudet who donated a large sum of money for the restoration of the monastery of Prouille, a foundation dedicated to St Vincent de Paul, for the relief of the unfortunate.

Pierre Plantard, in a Preface to *La Vraie Langue Celtique*, also emphasises that Boudet was the originator of the Rennes-le-Château church decorations, the "Grand Master" of the operation. According to Boudet's account books, found after his death on a nearby rubbish heap and saved on account of their lavish leather bindings, from time to time Boudet gave considerable sums of money to Marie Denarnaud to pay for the work that Saunière was undertaking on his behalf, but once this was completed, the payments stopped. No money was ever paid direct to Saunière.

Plantard says he met Marie in 1938 when she invited him to stay at Villa Bethania on the occasion of her 70th birthday, and she described the two priests to him. Abbé Saunière appeared to him "to be a man full of good life, unpolished and shrewd, having at his disposal a sketchy education without any inclination to the intellectual ardour and passion-to-know that drove his colleague at Rennes-les-Bains".

Plantard in the Preface also mentions his grandfather, Charles, who was invited by Saunière to visit him in June 1892. Among the other guests were Boudet and Elie Bot, who was the overseer of Saunière's building work. Charles described Saunière as a tall, well set-up dark young man, who held forth on the merits of the local wines. He seemed to overshadow Boudet, small, slim, with lavender-blue eyes, who would drink only water, but it was the latter who "emanated a aura of great learning". Invited by Boudet to supper at Rennes-les-Bains, Charles was entertained with a simple meal beautifully served, and afterwards was shown the priest's library and photographic laboratory. In spite of his modest way of life, Boudet appeared to be sufficiently wealthy to indulge his chosen pleasures.

Henri Jean-Jacques Boudet was born to an impoverished family on 16 November 1837 at Quillan in the Aude. He was precociously intelligent, and came to the notice of Abbé Emile de Cayron, who financed his education. Boudet was ordained priest on Christmas Day 1861, and in 1872 M. Billard, Bishop of Carcassonne, appointed him priest-in-charge of Rennes-les-Bain, where he lived with his mother and sister. He had one brother, Edmond, who lived at the neighbouring village of Axat.

From 1872 until 1880 Boudet walked his parish, becoming acquainted with his flock and learning the countryside, which he loved. He was particularly attracted to the austerity of the winter scene, where "the stones were not hidden by too much vegetation". By 1880 he had finished writing *La Vraie Langue Celtique* and decided to publish it anonymously, at his own expense. He appointed as printer François Pomies of Carcassonne, who in due course was superseded by Victor Bonnafous, Bookseller, who also agreed to undertake the marketing. Boudet was not satisfied with the proofs, and made so many corrections it practically meant a reprint. This lasted until 1886, and 500 copies were made, at a cost of 5382 gold francs. 98 copies were sold. Boudet is also credited with having written a small book of prayers, called *Lazare veni forus*, but as it was not printed until 1915 at Toulouse, the provenance is doubtful. He died on 27 January 1917, and although legend has inevitably raised doubts about it, his cause of death was registered as cancer of the intestine. At his own request he was buried at Axat, next to his brother Edmond, and not with his mother and sister in the churchyard at Rennes-les-Bains. His now very neglected tombstone still shows the little closed book that he had requested should be carved on it, which bears on its cover

IXOIE

There has been considerable speculation by various cryptographers about the meaning of this inscription, and the fact that the book is closed and not open, as usual on graves. A closed book is a simple symbol of an ended life, and the inscription is not actually very esoteric. It is probably the early Christian acrostic: "Jesus Christ, Son of God and Saviour", and there is a similar tombstone of the same period with the same closed book, in no way connected with the Rennes-le-Château story, in Montparnasse cemetery in Paris.

There seems to be no doubt that Boudet was the prime mover in whatever was going on in that corner of Languedoc during the late 19th century. He had access to funds, and because his life style was more modest than Saunière's, it has escaped such close scrutiny. His patron, Abbé Emile de Cayron, also spent considerable amounts of money on his church, without disclosing its origin. Yet another poor parish priest with access to seemingly unlimited cash. The suggestion inevitably is that he knew the secret of the treasure and passed it on to Boudet.

ᴄhe scales and ᴄhe sword

Saunière always refused to reveal the source of his wealth. Isolated in a small village on the summit of a high rocky hill, he lived in considerable affluence, and spent lavishly on extravagant personal projects. His life style could not help but raise curiosity and envy in the breasts of the ecclesiastical authorities, and when Mgr de Beauséjour took possession of his Bishopric in 1902, it was inevitable that questions would be asked. On several occasions he asked the Abbé for an explanation, and received no replies. By law a priest's accounts were open to public scrutiny. Saunière refused to produce anything, or to meet and provide a verbal report. The Bishop's increasingly furious orders were ignored.

In 1909, the Bishop attempted to bring this troublesome, if farcical situation to a conclusion by removing Saunière from the parish of Rennes-le-Château and appointing him Priest in charge at Coustouge in Haute Corbière, a move which he had every right to instigate. He hoped by this means to get control of the Saunière property. Saunière refused to go. He replied stating that, with the greatest deference, he considered that whatever spiritual advantages there may be, he was not required to neglect material ones. "I tell you, Monseigneur" he wrote, "with all the firmness of a respectful son, No, Monseigneur, I will never go..."

Saunière resigned from the parish on 1 February 1909, beating the Bishop's sentence of suspension by one day. His successor, Abbé Marty, arrived to find there was no living space for him in Rennes-le-Château, the Presbytery being leased by the Council to Saunière. He therefore remained in residence at Céderonne, and Saunière continued to say his masses at his private altar in the greenhouse chapel of Villa Bethania, to the unavailing chagrin of the Bishop and the gratification of the villagers.

Thwarted of his revenge, in 1910 the Bishop moved officially against Saunière. No longer having any direct control over him, he took the only course open and resorted to legal action. The only crime of which he could accuse Saunière was taking money for masses which he did not perform. The first citation from the Court said "...in view of M. Saunière's inflated expenses it is feared he is enriched by the fees from masses he has not said...", and summoned him to appear before the examining Tribunal on 16 July. Saunière refused to attend, but he was allowed to appoint a proxy to plead his cause. He appointed Doctor Huguet who agreed to act for him without charging fees, asking only for reimbursement of expenses. Huguet was an eminent theologian, and also an accomplished musician. Born in 1863 at Barbaste (Lot-et-Garonne) he was educated at the Séminaire St. Sulpice in Paris, where he was ordained, and later became a Canon. He made a special study of ecclesiastical law, and was well known at the Vatican. "L'Affaire Saunière" dragged on, and involved several trips to Rome, so that even on an expenses only basis, Dr. Huguet was well recompensed.

The Tribunal duly convened, but Saunière did not appear. He was recalled for 23 July and again did not attend. Accused of traffic in masses, disobedience to his Bishop, excessive expenditure and non-justification of the accounts, Saunière was judged in absence and suspended from Divine Office for one month. Further, he was ordered to repay the fees received for masses not said, the amount non-determinable as no accounts had been submitted. Saunière ignored this sentence.

Summons to appear before the Tribunal continued to be issued at roughly monthly intervals, with demands that Saunière should present his accounts. Saunière continued to do nothing. On 5 November 1910 he made his one and only appearance before the Tribunal and was sentenced to proceed within the next two months to make a ten days' Retreat to a local monastery. Saunière's reply to this was that he was unwell, he continually procrastinated, and on 5 March 1911 he furnished a Medical Certificate from Dr. Roche stating that he was unable for reasons of health to undertake spiritual exercises at present. Allowing for excuses, it is possible that Saunière's health was now beginning to break down, and the sentence was temporarily allowed to fall into abeyance.

The Bishop's patience, however, was exhausted. He said that if Saunière was too ill to attend the Tribunal, he was authorised to send the accounts by post. If he failed to do so by 16 March 1911, he would be suspended indefinitely from all priestly functions.

Saunière replied by letter dated 13 March 1911:

"*Monseigneur,*
You have sent me an order from the Bishopric dated 9 March asking me, under threat of suspension, to give you an account of my expenditure. The only balance sheet I can offer you is the one that you already have. There can be no question about its validity, since it explains the expenditure I have had to make. Further conclusive evidence is provided by the Certificates from the Mortgage Registry that I am attaching to this letter. As far as expenses are concerned, I have dutifully submitted receipts to justify these. Not all the receipts are included, for the simple reason that I have lost some of them, and since most of them involved routine expenditure, after two years I considered it was no longer necessary to keep them. I am sending all those in my possession. I hope you will take great care of these documents, 81 altogether, and when you no longer need them I would be grateful if you would return them to me. They are indispensable to my personal financial security.
I have the honour to inform you that I had intended to start my ten days' Retreat from the beginning of Lent. My health forced me to change my plans, but if it improves I am planning on making the Retreat at the Grand Séminaire at Carcassonne, trusting they will be able to accommodate me, to carry out the prescribed exercises during the ten days preceding Easter.
Accept, Monseigneur, my obedient and respectful sentiments, etc. B. Saunière".

The documents in question were never returned. Presumably the Grand Séminaire was not accommodating, and the Retreat was finally made at the monastery dedicated to St. Vincent de Paul at Prouille, from 25 April until 3 May 1911. From there Saunière wrote daily letters to Marie Denarnaud in the form of a diary, giving her a detailed account of his activities. In the first he lists the programme for each day, which started at 5.30 a.m. and consisted of meditation, church services, and sermons, interrupted only by mealtimes and three half-hour "free periods", until bedtime at 7.30 p.m. He addresses her as "Bonne Marie", "Ma bien chère Marie" and once as "Ma petite Marinette" and signs himself "ton Bérenger" or "ton devoué et affectionée Bérenger", so whatever their relationship, there was obviously affection between them. He had after all known her for twenty years.

At first Saunière's secret prayer was to be allowed to abandon his incarceration at Prouille and return at once to Rennes-le-Château. He was worried about leaving his parish and "the work he had to accomplish there", but once settled for the time being at least he accepted the situation, in spite of the austerity of his surroundings, so different from those to which he was accustomed. In his letters to Marie he methodically records his views about the monastic life, both as a man and as a priest. As a man he regretted the solitude, he disliked eating alone, and was pleased when a novice arrived who could share his meals. He liked food, and took pleasure in sending details of the monastery menus to Marie who was an accomplished cook. As a priest who had never rejected the smallest part of his religion, he was conscious of the special occasions and hallowed places he daily encountered at Prouille. But above all, he was worried about what was going on at home, who was looking after the rabbits and his pets, which included geese, ducks, birds, dogs and a monkey. From the seven letters that still exist, Saunière can be seen as a man of strong and resolute character, as someone who always needed to be in charge.

The question arises - what was "the work that needed to be accomplished there" that he was so concerned about during his absence from Rennes-le-Château? He had officially relinquished his duties as parish priest some two years earlier. Why was he determined to remain there after his resignation? Then there was the matter of the letters which he left with Marie to post when he went travelling, which were intended to show that he was still there. All small pointers, easily overlooked, that suggest there was some clandestine activity in which he was involved - a commitment which he felt in duty bound to fulfil.

Meanwhile, increasingly irritated letters continued to arrive for Saunière from Jean Saglio, the Vicar General, asking for further details of his accounts.

The figures that Saunière had supplied were as follows:

Summary of invoices for the estate, paid or owing, supplied to the Commission of Enquiry:

Purchase of land	1550.00
Siburce Caminade, architect	2800.00
Elie Bot for:	
Masons	10305.61
(there was still 1205.61 Fr. outstanding)	
Workmen	220.00
Masons	50.25
Elie Bot for personal work	250.00
Joseph Fabre (roof)	412.50
Denarnaud (ironmongery)	3109.30
Oscar Vila-Idrac (carpentry)	2324.35
Duchesne (wallpaper)	434.70
Tisseyre (plasterwork)	1140.47
Castex (inscription)	32.50
Laffon (painter)	941.19
Ste Chaux et Ciments d'Albi	1935.10
Cimenteries Berthelot, Grenoble	300.80
Taillefer (tiles)	<u>602.50</u>

26417.27 Frs.

Saunière listed the cost of the estate as follows:

Land	1550.00
Villa Bethania	90000.00
Tour Magdala	40000.00
Terraces and gardens	19050.00
Interior decoration	5000.00
Furnishing	10000.00
	165600.00

This leaves a discrepancy of 139,583 Fr.

The cost of the restoration of the church was listed as 16,200 Fr., for which invoices were supplied to the value of 6200 Fr. The Calvary was said to have cost 11,200 Fr. and there were bills for only 1000 Frs. This leaves approximately 154,200 Fr. unaccounted for, but as Saunière says, he did not keep all the invoices.

The Credit Account supplied by Saunière was as follows:

1. Payment for 30 years of ministry	15000.00
2. Family living in, earning 300 Fr. a month carried over 20 years	52000.00
3. Madame X by brother	25000.00
4. 2 Families of the parish of Coursa	1500.00
5. Madame Lieusere	400.00
6. Pères Chartreux	400.00
7. Mgr Billiard (a personal loan)	200.00
8. La Comtesse de Chambord	3000.00
9. Madame Labatut	500.00
10. Parish collections	300.00
11. Revenue from the church	500.00
12. Bequest	1800.00
13. Gifts from father	800.00
14. M.de C.	20000.00
15. Almsboxes, 1200Fr. per year for 15 years	18000.00
16. Lottery run in Parish	1000.00
17. Through Brother	30000.00

18. Postcards, 60 Fr per month for 5 years	3600.00
19. Postage stamps (antique)	3000.00
20. Articles & copies of letters	1000.00
21. Sale of wine, 1908 & 1909	1600.00
22. Antique furniture, pottery & oddments	4000.00
23. Superannuation fund	800.00
Brought forward	184400.00
24. Two anonymous donors	1000.00
25. Personal work by M. l'Abbé 5 years, 3 Fr. per day	3750.00
26. Voluntary donations and tips	4000.00
	193150.00

A draft letter from the Commission, undated but certainly written after 19 March, requested an explanation of income, based on the figures Saunière had supplied:

1. Regarding the 52,000 Fr. received over 20 years from "the resident family": when did the family become resident, how many members did it consist of, and how were they able to earn such large sums of money as 300 Fr. a month?
2. How was it possible regularly to obtain 1200 Fr a year from the alms-boxes?
3. When was the lottery held?
4. What was meant by 3600 Fr. for the sale of postcards - were they new ones? To whom were the antique postage stamps sold for 3000 Fr? What was the origin of the furniture, porcelain and oddments which were sold for 4000 Fr?
5. What was meant by "Articles and copies of letters"? How are the two receipts (Art.25 & 26) accounted for?

The letter concludes "We would be grateful to receive your answers to these points before Saturday. We await your clarification in order to complete our work on the audit. Yours etc."

Saunière replied on 25 March 1911:

"M. l'Officiél -

Here is the information that I am able to provide in reply to the various questions you ask:

Firstly, twenty years ago I took into my home a family composed of father, mother, and two children. The father and son were earning 300 Fr. a month. All our funds were put into a common purse. Hence the amount of 52,000 Fr. The family worked in the hat trade.

The alms boxes were there for visitors who, having heard my talks about Rennes-le-Château and accepted my hospitality, repaid this by donations in the form of tips. There are a lot of visitors who come to take the baths at Rennes-les-Bains, which explains why they are generous.

The lottery took place around 1887.

My brother, being a priest, had many connections and he acted as an intermediary for gifts.

The postcards are views of Rennes-le-Château. There are 33 of them, priced 10 centimes each. All the Bathers took a complete set. These postcards were so successful I could hardly provide enough of them. They are new and they are my property.

My collections of old stamps amount to about 100,000. They are perfect and for sale. I stick to the accepted prices, and collectors are so happy to have the opportunity to buy them that they don't try to bargain.

The antique furniture, porcelain and oddments I search for around the neighbourhood. Their sale pays for my travels and enquiries.

The articles are written for newspapers and prospectuses for young people. They like what I do, and pay well.

Why shouldn't I credit the balance sheet with the free transport I get, and with my own personal work? Doesn't this represent a real contribution by me?

Here, M. l'Officiél, very truthfully are the explanations
that I am able to give in reply to your enquiries.
Please accept my very respectful compliments etc.
B. Saunière"

According to official records, M. Guillaume Denarnaud worked
at the hat factory from 1894 - 1907, and his son Barthélemy
from 1895 - 1909, an overall total of 15 years. Their combined
wages for this period was 22,796 Fr. F., which is 29,204 less
than the 52,000 quoted by Saunière for 20 years. Saunière
inflated the figure he provided by adding an extra five years' work
for each of them, and included hypothetical earnings for Madame
Denarnaud and Marie.

On 4 April Canon Carpentier wrote to Saunière again on behalf
of the Commission of Enquiry:

M. l'Abbé ,
We must inform you of our astonishment that you have
replied to our enquiries in such an incomplete and
evasive fashion. In particular -
1. We asked what documents or receipts you have to
support your statement of an annual regular income of
1200 Fr. from the alms boxes, and to send these to us.
You have not replied.
2. We asked you for the dates on which you received
the most important donations through the intermediary
of your brother (Art.3, 14, 17). You have not replied to
this either.
3. We have examined your expenses account: this is
not an account, it is a collection of vouchers and they
are incomplete, because the total sum amounts to
around 36,000 Fr. whereas you have yourself submitted
expenses of nearly 200,000 Fr. You do not include any
payment for purchase of land, or for the very extensive
excavating and building work which you have initiated.
It is absolutely essential that by the end of this week

*you send us a true account giving us details of the total
expenditure, and not only of a small part of your
payments.*
Accept our sentiments etc."

Saunière replied to this by stating that he had been careful to
provide information that was as precise as possible. He explained
that Rennes-le-Château had an interesting history which he would
relate to visitors, and because these were "very correctly behaved
people", they did not like to tip him, and instead would put
donations in the alms boxes. He did not record the takings in a
ledger, but had estimated the average annual amount of these
donations.

The donations from his brother extended over the years 1895
- 1903. (It is possible that the 20,000 Fr. F. from M de C (Art.14)
was obtained by Alfred from M. de Chefdebien when he was
employed by him).

He considered the Certificates from the Mortgage Registry
justified the balance between income and expenditure. He could
not be any more categorical and explicit than this.

He pointed out that there had not previously been any question
about the cost of land or building. The land in any case had been
acquired by the family living with him.

As to being evasive, he begged to point out that he was not "an
entrepreneur or a salesman". He was acting on his own behalf
and responsibility, and was content to keep notes that were
sufficient to ensure that he did not run into trouble. He regarded
detailed accounting, such as practised by business men or banks,
was unnecessary in his case.

The Commission merely repeated that they were acting on
behalf of the Bishop, and requested a meeting with Saunière as
soon as possible, to which Saunière replied that his last meeting
with them had damaged his health, and he must decline.

The Commission then wrote yet again on 9 May asking for an
explanation of the expenditure of almost 200,000 Fr. for which

only 36,000 Fr was accounted. Why could he not obtain duplicate receipts for those lost or destroyed?

Saunière's reaction to this was to repeat that as he had already explained, his meeting with the Vicar General the previous November had resulted in a scene that had made him ill, and he considered it imprudent to take such a risk again.

The Commission angrily replied that this did not answer their questions and again requested details of Saunière's accounts.

On 2 June Saunière wrote to the Commission saying "at any cost you demand documents which I do not have". He had given them what existed, and he was not prepared to embarrass friends by asking for duplicates of receipts. "Like impatient and frustrated creditors", he says, "you demand to be assured that I am not threatened with bankruptcy. God be thanked, that is not the case." He added that he intended to appeal to Rome against the Commission's sentence suspending him from Divine Office.

Canon Saglio, writing on behalf of the Commission, once more requested an accounting. Saunière repeated his excuses about not asking for duplicate receipts, particularly with regard to the workmen paid in cash, which would "arouse suspicion and distrust", and again stated that the Dénarnaud family paid for the land from their personal resources. (Since Saunière had already said that all the Dénarnaud's wages were put into the communal purse, where did they get the considerable sums of money they were alleged to have spent?).

He denied receiving any financial benefit from payment for masses, and maintained that none were left unsaid. There was no point in the Commission continually insisting on his producing receipts he did not have. Their attitude was undermining his health, and he was confined to his bed. He finished by stating he was awaiting a decision from Rome.

The Commission ignored all this, and wrote again asking for the cost of the land, the buildings erected on it, and the refurbishment of the church.

In a final letter dated 27 November 1911, Saunière sent the following:

"1.Purchase of land. 1550 Fr.   I think you should remember that this was not acquired by me.

2.	*Restoration of church*	*16,200*
	Cost of Calvary	*11,200*
3.	*Construction of Villa Bethania*	*90,000*
	Tour Magdala	*40,000*
	Terrace and gardens	*19,050*
	Interior fittings	*5,000*
	Furniture	*<u>10,000</u>*
		191.450 Fr

I trust that this information will serve to terminate the affair that has caused me such trouble, and so badly affected my health during the past months".

As a result of this correspondence, the Commission made a report to the Bishop stating that they were not satisfied with the explanations given. M. Saunière had refused to meet them, and claimed illness through stress for not doing so.

They emphasised that the most important point to be noted was that the land was not in Saunière's name, and under the freehold laws he therefore did not own any of the structures on it. They admitted that they had in their possession a document from Joseph Fabre of Dourgne, recording having received from Mlle Denarnaud, landowner of Rennes, through the agency of M. Caminade, Architect of Limoux, the sum of 41,250 Fr. for supplying and placing the roof of Villa Bethania. They also possessed copies of Marie Denarnaud's seven Certificates entered in the Register of Mortgages at Limoux.

The affair was followed by a new series of summons made to Abbé Saunière to present himself before the Tribunal, starting on 30 October 1911. When he failed to comply, the Commission condemned him for embezzlement and misappropriation of church funds, and sentenced him to suspension from Divine Office until he had "made restitution". Saunière appealed to Rome. The Bishop in fact, under ecclesiastical law, was not empowered to suspend a priest for more than six months, and the Congregation of the Council at Rome upheld the appeal. Mgr Beauséjour had to lift the suspension, but he never reinstated Saunière as a priest.

None of which helps to solve the problem. Only one thing becomes obvious from the proceedings: Saunière received and spent a considerable amount of money, and was adamant that its origin should never be disclosed. And it never was. This secret was apparently more important to him than any personal animosity he might encounter, any damage he might suffer, or any rewards he might receive.

It is interesting that from the documents that Saunière provided, it may be inferred that, whatever its source, the money did not come direct to him. Large sums were received via Saunière's brother Alfred, and others dispersed via Fr Boudet of Rennes-les-Bains. Mgr Billiard, Bishop of Carcassonne, was incredibly blind to what was going on in his diocese, and himself received generous donations from Fr Boudet for his charitable causes. Marie Dénarnaud was the general "cut-out" for payments made.

What part did Fr Gélis, the old priest of Coustassa who was mysteriously murdered, play in the charade? Abbé Jean Antoine Maurice Gélis, born on 1 April 1827 at Villeseque (Landes), was a good and pious priest, who enjoyed alike the esteem of his fellow clergy and the affection of the parishioners whom he had served for forty years.

On 5 November 1897 "La Semaine Religieuse of Carcassonne" reported that during the night of the previous Sunday/Monday the Abbé had been found, beaten to death, in the kitchen of his presbytery. The extraordinary thing about this gruesome murder was that apart from three great pools of blood, the whole place was in perfect order. There had been no break-in, nothing was stolen, although there was almost 1000 Fr. F. in gold and notes in various drawers and cupboards. There were no foot or finger prints. The body was laid out tidily in the centre of the room, hands crossed on his breast, "like an effigy on a tomb". The only slight disturbance was in the bedroom, where the locks of a travelling bag containing papers had been forced, but if anything had been taken it was not apparent.

There was no obvious motive. The only clue, if clue it was, was provided by a packet of cigarette papers, with the trademark "Tzar", floating in one of the pools of blood near the window. On one of the papers was written in pencil the words "Vive Angelina". The Abbé not only did not smoke, but hated the smell of tobacco, and was adamant about not allowing anyone else to do so in the presbytery. Jacques Rivière in *The Fabulous Treasure of Rennes-le-Château* says that "Vive Angelina" represented the cry of a particular ideology. He does not, however, explain what this ideology was.

Gélis was an elderly, nervous man who lived quietly by himself, but that evening he must have received a late visitor who was known to him, whom he admitted to the house. Whom did his demise profit? His only relative, a nephew, was the obvious suspect, but he had an unbreakable alibi, it being proved that he was away at Luc-sur-Aude that night. The police arrested him, but he was released for lack of evidence. There were no further enquiries. The funeral took place at Coustassa, attended by Mgr Cantegrill on behalf of the Bishop, and most of the local clergy: Saunière, Boudet, the Curé Doyen of Couiza, and priests from Arques, Montazels, Luc-sur-Aude and d'Antugnac.

The crime was never solved. It was committed by someone who was familiar with the surroundings, appeared to be premeditated, and the aim was not money, but perhaps a search for evidence. Was Gélis involved in whatever was going on in that place at that time? Coustassa is only 2 km from Rennes-le-Château, and Saunière recorded in his diary on 21 September 1891, the day that he had his confidential meeting with M. Cros, that he also saw Gélis, Carrière and the Curé of Nevian. Was Gélis party to a secret that was too much for him, and had spoken out of turn? Was it necessary to make sure of his silence, not only by killing him, but by recovering incriminating evidence? The savage way in which the old priest was killed, and the respect shown in the careful way the body was laid out, seems to indicate that the murderer was intent upon making a specific statement - perhaps it conveyed a warning? A deed committed of necessity, not of choice?

There is yet another priest in the Saunière saga who appeared to have access to inexplicably generous funds: Abbé Cayron, who was Henri Boudet's sponsor, and paid for his education. In his obituary of 3 January 1897, written by "an unnamed friend of the deceased", Emile François Henri Geraud de Cayron, Abbé of St. Laurent near Montferrand, is described as "a much loved, good and pious priest, and something of a recluse, St Laurent being a rather solitary place." He was born on 11 December 1807, and appointed to St Laurent on 10 November 1834, where he remained for fifty years. At his own expense he restored his church, reconstructing and lavishly redecorating it in Gothic proportions and style. He said that the money was given to him by a local family who had survived the Revolution. The Diocesan authorities tried to move him, ostensibly for his advancement, but Cayron refused to go. At the age of seventy-eight he retired in December 1885 to Toulouse, and died there a year later.

Apparently a convocation of priests in the Aude valley, Languedoc, were in the late 19th century involved in something which perhaps brought them material gain, but what else? What was the thread that held them together, and who was behind it all?

Chapter Three

'By my life, they are a sweet society of fair ones.'

Henry VIII 1.4

THE ONCE AND FUTURE CABAL
The Secret Custodians

In *Le Trésor Maudit*, Gérard de Sède makes no mention of the Prieuré de Sion, and only hints at the idea of a Rosicrucian sect that inspired Saunière's extraordinary style of ecclesiastical decoration.

He does, however, say "...not only hidden gold, but hidden blood becomes a dynastic treasure, and revives a myth whose political role, at various moments in French national history, has been far from negligible: the myth of 'le roi perdu'". He quotes two books published in Geneva: *Genealogy of the Merovingian kings and origins of various French and foreign families of Merovingian roots according to Abbé Pinchon, Dr Hervé and the Abbé Saunière's parchments* by Henri Lobineau (1956), and *Merovingian descendants or the Visigothic Razès enigma* by Madeleine Blancasall (1963). Both books are concerned with the survival of Dagobert II's son, Sigisbert IV, and the Merovingian bloodline.

The author's names are clearly pseudonyms: Henri Lobineau, who is listed as also having compiled the genealogies in the Dossier Secret, was first identified as the reputable genealogist Leo Schidlof, but his daughter categorically denied that her father was involved. Madeleine Blancasall was probably Pierre Plantard's first wife, Anne Lea Hisler, who died in 1971. "Madeleine" parallels St Mary Magdalene, the dedication of the Rennes-le-Château church, and "Blancasall" is a combination of the names of two local rivers, the Blanque and the Sals. Madame Hisler, under her own name, was responsible for a number of contributions to the Prieuré's "house magazine", *Circuit*. In the light of subsequent revelations, it is reasonable to suppose that both books were the work of the instigators of the Plantard myth.

It is really Henry Lincoln who propagated the Rennes-le-Château mystery. He had read *Le Trésor Maudit* as early as 1969, and met de Sède in Paris some sixteen months later, in order to discuss with him the idea of using the Rennes-le-Château story for two BBC TV "Chronicle" programmes. During the course of his research, Lincoln visited Rennes-le-Château and talked to Henry Buthion, the then owner of the Saunière domaine. There were hints about the Prieuré de Sion, but Lincoln's main interest at that time was in clues to the "treasure", and the origin of Saunière's fortune.

When the BBC decided to make a third film, "The Shadow of the Templars", they commissioned a Paris-based journalist, Jania Macgillivray, to find out more about the Prieuré de Sion. The first clue was the name "Plantard" on the back of photographs that Lincoln had obtained for his "Chronicle" programmes. Also, de Sède had shown Lincoln the Dossier Secret as lodged at the Bibliothèque Nationale in Paris, and subsequently carefully leaked to him various titillating bits of disinformation.

Jania Macgillivray duly tracked down Pierre Plantard and arranged for him to meet Henry Lincoln in Paris. At this meeting Plantard admitted that the coded parchments were "confections" created by Philippe de Chérisey, but said that they were an amended version of good originals. Plantard was duly photographed with his son Thomas, and filmed during an interview at Madame Chaumeil's art gallery. It was at this interview that Plantard claimed that he was the "lost king", the latest descendant of the Merovingian dynasty.

There were further meetings, culminating in the publication of *The Holy Blood and the Holy Grail* (1982) and *The Messianic*

Legacy (1986) in collaboration with Michael Baigent and Richard Leigh. Lincoln's final, and very entertaining, dissertation on the trials and tribulations of the author researcher are reported in *Key to the Sacred Pattern* (1997), in which he gives a lively account of his connection with Rennes-le-Château, and goes on to propound his theories about sacred geometry. He is careful always to say that as a journalist he merely reports, it is up to the reader to draw conclusions.

So what are we to believe? The gospel, as set forth in the books of Henry Lincoln, says that there is some historical evidence that there was an Abbey, founded in 1099 on the ruins of a Byzantine basilica on Mount Sion north of Jerusalem, known as "Sainte Marie du Mont Sion et du Saint Esprit". The occupants were an order of Augustinian canons who according to a 17th century historian took the name of "Chevalier de l'Ordre de Notre Dame de Sion".

The Prieuré maintains that King Baudouin I of Jerusalem, "who owed his throne to Sion", in March 1117 negotiated the constitution of the Order of the Temple at the site of Saint Leonard of Acre, which was a fief of the Ordre de Sion. The Knights Templar had been active since 1114, perhaps as the military arm of the Ordre de Sion. The inference is that the Ordre de Sion was the "Inner Circle", while the Templars were the exoteric group. It was the Templars that flourished, rapidly gaining wealth and prestige under the patronage of Bernard of Clairvaux, the most influential religious figure in 12th century Europe.

In 1152 ninety-five members of the Ordre moved to France. Sixty-two entered the large priory of Saint Samson at Orléans, which had been donated by Louis VII. Seven enrolled in the ranks of the Knights Templars, and twenty-six entered the small priory of the Mount of Sion at Saint Jean le Blanc, outside Orléans. The charters establishing the Ordre de Sion by Louis VII at Orléans still exist in the municipal archives of Orléans, and there is also a Papal Bull of 1178 confirming the Ordre de Sion's possessions, which include properties and land in Picardy,

Lombardy, Sicily, Spain, Calabria, and a number of sites in the Holy Land, including Saint Leonard of Acre. There also exists a charter whereby the small priory donated land in 1239 and 1244 to the Teutonic Knights. There appears to be no doubt, therefore, that there was a religious community known as the Ordre de Sion, and that it was both wealthy and powerful. There is no evidence that this community was ever known as the Priory of Sion.

In 1177 Jerusalem was taken by the Saracens, and the Dossier Secret alleges that the remaining members of the Ordre de Sion returned to France. In 1187 there was dissension between the Ordre de Sion and the Templars, supposedly connected with Sion's anger at the ineptitude of Gérard de Ridefort, Grand Master of the Temple, in losing Jerusalem, and the two organisations separated. The segregation occurred at Gisor, and is the true origin of the legend of the "cutting of the elm". The two communities no longer shared the same Grand Master and administration, and it was in 1188 that Sion adopted its new title of the Prieuré de Sion, with "Ormus" as a subtitle.

"Ours" in French and "ursus" in Latin means "bear", a totem animal of the Merovingians. Ormus was also the name of an Egyptian magus, and was regarded by the Gnostics, and subsequently by the Masons, as the "principle of light". According to tradition, Ormus conferred on his initiates a red or "rose" cross, as later adopted by the Rosicrucians. The Prieuré de Sion also used the title of l'Ordre de la Rose-Croix Veritas. It is alleged that in spite of the "divorce", Sion continued to hold a watching brief on the Templars, and may have been instrumental in giving them warning of King Philippe-le-Bel's act of suppression. The Grand Master of the Prieuré at the time is given as Guillaume de Gisor, who is named in the actual records of the Inquisition as a colleague of Guillaume Pidoye, one of the King's men. It is hinted that Guillaume de Gisor may have been a double agent, and so in a position to leak the King's intentions and allow some of the Templars - and their gold - to escape.

Apart from what looks like a very hypothetical list of Grand Masters of the Prieuré, there appears to be no historical evidence that the Ordre de Sion, whether or not this was the origin of the Prieuré de Sion, survived beyond the 13th century.

It may be interesting here to look at the list of alleged Grand Masters, or as the Prieuré itself entitles them, Nautonier, meaning helmsman or navigator. They were all named, or took the name of, Jean or Jeanne, which was a dynastic title like Pharaoh, and the office was open equally to men and women:

Jean de Gisor	1188-1220
Marie de Saint Clair	1220-1266
Guillaume de Gisor	1266-1307
Edouard de Bar	1307-1336
Jean de Saint Clair	1336-1351
Jeanne de Bar	1351-1366
Blanche d'Evreux	1366-1388
Nicholas Flamel	1388-1418
René d'Anjou	1418-1480
Iolande de Bar	1480-1483
Sandro Filipepi	1483-1510
Leonard de Vinci	1510-1519
Connetable de Bourbon	1519-1527
Ferdinand de Gonzague	1527-1575
Louis de Nevers	1575-1595
Robert Fludd	1595-1637
J. Valentin Andreae	1637-1654
Robert Boyle	1654-1691
Isaac Newton	1691-1727
Charles Radclyffe	1727-1746
Charles de Lorraine	1746-1780
Maximilian de Lorraine	1780-1801
Charles Nodier	1801-1844
Victor Hugo	1844-1885
Claude Debussy	1885-1918
Jean Cocteau	1918- 1963

Jean Cocteau died in 1963, and Pierre Plantard said he became Grand Master on 17 January 1981. Who acted as Grand Master between these dates is not stated.

Among the Grand Masters are at least nine who had occult interests: Nicholas Flamel was an alchemist; Robert Fludd was a doctor who turned magician; Johan Valentin Andreae, cabalist, wrote the Rosicrucian manifestos; Isaac Newton and Charles Radclyffe were involved with the Royal Society, cradle of Freemasonry; Nodier was an esoteric novelist; Victor Hugo and Debussy were prominent figures in the 19th century French occult revival; and Jean Cocteau's opium dreams expressed in his writing, plays and films, are material evidence of his occult interests. Secret societies, and "occult" actually only means "occluded", by their very nature inevitably have a mysterious appeal, and frequently involve some form of religious, mystical or magical ritual. Their exoteric aim is to offer spiritual uplift: their esoteric to exert power, often politically.

Sons of the Widow

It is the usual practice for such societies to claim an ancient origin. Masonic mythology claims that Freemasonry started with Hiram Abiff, "the son of the widow", of the tribe of Napthali, who "was filled with wisdom and understanding, and cunning to work all works in bronze". (Chronicles 3:9).

When Solomon decided to build a temple to house the Ark of the Covenant, he called Hiram from Tyre to Jerusalem, and commissioned him to design and make, among other ritual objects, the two great bronze pillars, Jachin and Boaz, to mark the entrance to the sanctuary. These pillars were hollow, and housed documents of religious and national importance. Hiram was killed by three envious workmen who struck him on the head with a mallet, and buried his body at midnight in a pile of rubble on the top of Mount Moriah (the Temple Mount). Hiram, however, heard them plan to mark his grave with a sprig of acacia and escape across the Red Sea to Ethiopia, and he rose up and denounced his murderers. The story is used as an admission ceremony for Master Masons, in which the candidate suffers the mock death and resurrection which is the common practice in all initiation rituals.

The idea of "ancient wisdom" had been revived by the scholars of the Renaissance, and was widely propagated by the 17th century Rosicrucians who used Hermetic teachings and the Cabala as a basis for political propaganda, but what was different about Freemasonry was that it provided an element of cohesion, and offered a universal esoteric movement based on strong central direction.

Although some branches of Freemasonry claim that their foundation dates from the 15th century or earlier, it was not until the 18th century that the Freemasons were firmly established in Britain and France. James VI of Scotland (James I of England) was reputedly initiated at Perth in 1601; and Elias Ashmole, co-founder of the Royal Society of which Charles II was President, recorded in his diary that he was initiated at Warrington, Lancashire, in 1646. However, the Grand Lodge was not established in London until 1717.

The first French Lodge, "Brotherhood and Friendship", is believed to have been started at Dunkirk in 1721, and a Lodge, whose members were mainly aristocratic and Catholic, was founded by Charles Radclyffe in Paris in 1725. Radclyffe was an ardent supporter of the Stuarts, fought for "Bonnie Prince Charlie" in the 1745 rebellion, and paid with his life - he was executed at the Tower of London in 1746. In 1742 Radclyffe had possibly initiated Karl Gottlieb von Hund, although Hund always maintained that his initiator was Prince Charles Edward Stuart himself.

Hund was a native of North-Eastern Saxony, where he owned considerable lands. He was instrumental in introducing the Strict Observance rite which, he said, was confided to him by "unknown superiors", and had been taken to the Isle of Mull by the Templars when they fled there between 1307 and 1314. A brilliant organiser, he funded the new Lodges by charging fees for admission to the various degrees. The real attraction of the new Masonic Templarism which Hund invented was its devotion to "ancient wisdom". Initiates studied alchemy, and Hund claimed to have found the elixir of life. He also had hopes of finding the lost treasure of the Templars. When he died in 1776 he was buried in the costume of the Provincial Grand Master of the Order which he had himself designed.

French masonry was not recognised by the English Grand Lodge until around 1743. The Grand Lodge in Paris was founded in 1756, suffered an early political split, and was reassembled in 1771 by the Grand Duke of Luxembourg. A year later it was reconstituted on radical terms as the Grand Orient of France. The leader of the movement was the Duc d'Orléans, who changed his name to Philippe Egalité and sided with the revolutionaries against his cousin, Louis XVI. His sister, the Duchess of Bourbon, was Grand Mistress of the women's lodges.

The first Lodge in the United States was established in 1720. Members were by no means radical in their outlook, and George Washington, who was associated with the Grand Orient of France, was offered the status of King. American Masons were apt to regard an independent America as an ideal hieratic political structure, rather like an extension of the Lodge itself.

In 1738 Pope Clement XII declared Freemasons excommunicated, but as the Papal Bull was not recorded by French Parliament it had little effect. By 1789 twenty-six French Lodges were presided over by priests. However, during the period leading up to the French Revolution, politically there was a general move towards the Left, and by the late 19th century the majority of Freemasons were supporters of the Republic, and Freemasonry came into serious conflict with the Catholic church. As Saunière discovered to his cost during the 1885 elections.

In 1785 there is no doubt that the aim of the majority of the French Lodges was to discredit the aristocracy, and Queen Marie Antoinette in particular. It is here that we come to the mysterious tale of the diamond necklace. History relates that the Court jewellers, Baszange and Bohmer, made a fabulously valuable diamond necklace which they hoped to sell to the Queen. She was certainly anxious to acquire it, but being unpopular for her extravagance and frivolity, she was unwilling to appear as a principal in the transaction. She therefore persuaded Cardinal de Rohan to acquire the necklace on her behalf, and guarantee payment for it.

The Cardinal, already unpopular because of his known opposition to the French-Austrian alliance, saw this as a simple way of gaining credibility at Court. The go-between in the business was Countess Jeanne de la Motte, a young adventuress who claimed Valois blood, being a descendant of a bastard of Henry II, and who had been trying unsuccessfully to obtain a pension from the Government. Through her agency a meeting was arranged between the Cardinal and the Queen in the Royal Gardens, but the Queen did not keep the tryst. She sent in her place a notorious prostitute, Demoiselle d'Oliva. Somewhere in the course of these negotiations the necklace disappeared, and the jewellers complained publicly and very loudly that they had been robbed of both jewels and payment.

In August 1785 the Cardinal was arrested and charged with using the Queen's name to procure a valuable necklace without payment. He in turn accused Jeanne de la Motte, whose letters of authority appeared to be forged. Jeanne was tried, found guilty, and sentenced to flogging, branding and imprisonment for life in the Salpetrière. Nine months later she escaped, probably with the Queen's help, and fled to England. The Cardinal was acquitted, but unable to face the scandal he retired to a religious house for the rest of his life. The diamonds were never found.

Altogether it was a very unsavoury business. The Cardinal was a peer of the realm and a member of one of the three great houses of France. The Queen's enemies, who never ceased accusing her of every kind of immorality, and even published a series of scurrilous pamphlets about her which were circulated at

Court, hinted that she had bribed the Cardinal with the promise of sexual favours and then refused to honour the pledge. It was never discovered who in fact did have the diamonds, whether the Queen received them and then, fearing further adverse publicity at such monstrous extravagance, denied all knowledge of the transaction and let Jeanne take the blame, or whether Jeanne stole them when they were entrusted to her for delivery. "What became of the Queen Marie-Antoinette's diamond necklace" became a popular historical "who-dun-it" comparable with mysteries such as was Queen Elizabeth I married, was Perkin Warbeck really Richard, Duke of York, the younger of the two little Princes who disappeared from the Tower of London - or where did Abbé Saunière really get his money.

At her trial Jeanne, who may have been made the scapegoat and out of loyalty would not betray her sovereign, named Count Cagliostro as her accomplice. As a result of his supposed involvement in the diamond necklace affair, Cagliostro is seen by historians as a sort of shabby-genteel con-man scratching a dishonest living on the fringes of 18th century Paris society, but this is far from the truth. Alessandro, Count Cagliostro, was born Guiseppe Balsamo in Sicily in 1743, and as a young man adopted the name of his godmother, Countess Cagliostro, who was a relation of his mother. His family, although somewhat impoverished, were minor Sicilian nobility. He was nominally a Roman Catholic, but early became interested in theosophical studies, and was instructed in alchemy and magic by no less a person than the Grand Master of the Knights of Malta.

In 1776 Cagliostro and his wife, Serafina, went to London where in 1777 he was admitted to the Esperance Lodge. Soon after this he acquired a manuscript purporting to give details of an early form of Egyptian masonry, with which he became obsessed. He introduced new rituals into Lodges based on these rites, in the form of a higher grade open only to those who were already Freemasons.

Cagliostro was primarily an occultist. His interests were prophecy, Hermetic philosophy and ritual magic. He practised conjuration, and was believed to own a copy of the Necronomicon (the Book of Secret Names), a very sinister grimoire apparently originating from the East around the middle of the ninth century. He was not particularly interested in making money - he always seemed to have plenty of his own - and he never took payment for his services. It was naturally assumed he possessed the alchemical secret of making gold, and he was also credited with the ability to find hidden treasure. He loved mystery and had a habit of travelling under false identities, which inevitably led to the suspicion that he had something to hide. Using a child to scry for him he experimented in clairvoyance, and as a good psychologist this, combined with shrewd intuition, earned him an enviable reputation for brilliant divination. People travelled long distances to consult him; wherever he went there were demonstrations of almost hysterical adulation. He had a natural ability for healing and achieved some genuine cures, particularly with illnesses of psychosomatic origin. The medical profession naturally hated him, and he stood in danger of indictment for practising medicine without a licence. The Church also was wary of his reputation: what he was doing was very close to heresy.

Nonetheless, Cagliostro continued to prosper, and his fame grew. He travelled extensively in Europe and was received at the Courts of Frederick II of Prussia and Stanislaw of Poland. His connection with the French Court was through Cardinal Prince Louis de Rohan, whom he cured of asthma. He is also said to have restored to health Rohan's uncle, Maréchal de Soubisse, who was dying.

Marie-Antoinette was more fool than knave, and it is probable that she was set up as a target by the left-wing antimonarchists, prompted by the French Masons, using Cagliostro as their tool. By very cleverly using the Cardinal's desire for Court favour, and Jeanne de la Motte's obsession with being recognised as of the "blood royal" and greed for financial security, the instigators of the plot not only achieved their political objectives in traducing the Queen and weakening the position of the monarchy, but they at the same time acquired a very nice contribution towards the funds that stirred up social unrest, and finally erupted in the bloody horror of the Revolution.

Cagliostro, disillusioned and discredited, wandered around Europe for a time, but in 1789 applied to the Vatican and obtained permission to visit Rome, where he and his wife took a house in Piazza Farnese. Pope Pius VI promptly rescinded the permit, and Cagliostro was arrested by the Inquisition, accused of demonic sorcery, heresy, fraud, sacrilege and plotting to overthrow royalty, and sentenced to death. The Pope commuted the sentence to life imprisonment, and Serafina was sent to a convent. Cagliostro spent the last six years of his life chained to a wall, in solitary confinement, in the fortress of San Leo near Urbino. He died there - or some say was murdered - on 6 August 1795, and was buried in an unmarked grave.

The legend persists. What was he? Charlatan or saint? Healer, magician, or petty crook? Cagliostro was said to have lived for 2000 years, and been present at the Crucifixion. One day will someone appear claiming to be the enigmatic Count? And will he, like so many lost kings or heroes whose ends are obscure and whose bodies disappear, be of necessity a fraud?

One of the precepts of Freemasonry was that within the Lodge all men were equal. It preached a middlebrow, non-class, commonsense ethos, and provided the amenities of the gentleman's club without the snob value. This, however, was the Age of Enlightenment, and during the early part of the 18th century there arose a comfortably-off middle class that included merchants, teachers, and clerks, who aspired to upper-class status. Such social advancement was normally not available in ordinary life, but perhaps it might be attained through the Lodge.

The idea of "Knightly" Orders was introduced in 1736 by the Chevalier Ramsay, a Scottish Catholic Jacobite, who was secretary, and later literary executor, of the French writer Fénelon,

Knight of the Order of St Lazare. The Masonic manifesto was based on the craft worker in stone, but Ramsay created a fictitious provenance by suggesting that some medieval stone-workers were also knightly warriors who had taken part in the Crusades, and that the secret signs of recognition practised by the Brotherhood originated in those used by Crusaders in order to distinguish each other from any Saracens who might have infiltrated the Crusading ranks.

The patent absurdity of these allegations did not meet with any immediate success, but the seed was sown. It hinted at the idea of a handing-on of practices that involved esoteric knowledge, and suggested the institution of higher grades of a Chivalric Order. Solomon's Temple was already an integral part of Masonic myth. It was a short step from there to acceptance that the Templars had played a part in Masonic tradition. The contention was that the Templar Grand Masters were in possession of special spiritual illumination learned from the Essenes, who in turn had received it from Hiram Abiff at the time of the building of Solomon's Temple. This secret wisdom was passed on through the Canons of the Holy Sepulchre at Jerusalem to the Knights Templar then in residence. The murder of Hiram, embedded in orthodox Masonic lore, became equated with the death by burning of Templar Grand Master Jacques de Molay at the hands of King Philip IV. The parallel acquired political value by encouraging antagonism against the contemporary French monarchy. It is said that as Louis XVI's head fell beneath the guillotine, a voice from the crowd cried out "Jacques de Molay, now thou art avenged".

Knights and Crosses

Who - or what - were the original Knights Templar? Their true origin is lost in antiquity, but according to Guillaume de Tyre, a Frankish historian writing between 1175 and 1183, the Templars were founded by Hugues de Payen, a member of the cadet branch of the Counts of Troyes, and a vassal of the Count of Champagne. Around 1118 Hugues and eight companions organised themselves as the Poor Knights of Christ and the Temple of Solomon, with the declared intention of protecting pilgrims travelling to the Holy Sepulchre. With the permission of King Baudouin I of Jerusalem they took up residence in part of the Palace said to have been built on the site of Solomon's Temple. Their accommodation at least was very comfortable, and they each owned three horses, for which special stables were built.

The new Order, constituted under the auspices of the Canons of the Church of the Holy Sepulchre, lived by the Rule of St Augustine. The members were laymen, vowed poverty, chastity and obedience, wore no special religious garb, and relied on the Patriarch of Jerusalem for their subsistence. In an early letter Hugues speaks of their resentment at being regarded as servants, unrecognised as a religious Order, without benefit of the prayers of fellow Christians, since their work involved shedding blood rather than succouring pilgrims. It would appear that in the aftermath of the First Crusade, when many of the volunteers had taken their loot and gone home, there was a serious shortage of trained soldiers, and the Poor Knights were being used for military duties rather than for charitable purposes. They were on the point of giving up, but were saved by obtaining the patronage of Bernard of Clairvaux.

In 1126 Hugues travelled to Europe in search of funding and support. In 1128 he met Bernard at a Church Council at Troyes, and very shrewdly asked him to write a constitution for the Order, now calling themselves the Knights Templar after their place of residence. Troyes was Hugues' home-town, and interestingly had possessed a school of Cabala since 1070. It was also the cradle of the Grail romances, and in "Parsifal" Wolfram von Eschenbach (c.1220) names the Templars as the Guardians of the Holy Grail.

Bernard liked the concept of a reformed military religious Order, and not only gave the Knights Templar a new Rule based on his own Cistercians, but granted them autonomy whereby they were to be responsible directly to the Pope. His reputation ensured the Templars of acceptance by the highest dignitaries of the Church. In a papal bull of 1139, "Omne datum optimum", Pope Innocent II consolidated the status of the Templars as a Religious Order. They adopted a white mantle, and a few years later Pope Eugenius III granted them the privilege of emblazoning their surcoats with a red cross patte. "Béauseant", (perhaps derived from baucent, i.e. piebald) their black and white banner, bore the legend "Non Nobis Domine". Hugues de Payen was named Grand Master.

The knight as an idealistic, loyal and chivalrous nobleman is largely the invention of 19th century romantic literature. The popularity, and much of the success of the Templars, was that they conformed to the existing feudal system. Knights were mainly from obscure families who practised war as a profession, rather than from the upper nobility, and below the upper echelon of a small number of military elite there was a large section of sergeants or esquires, clad in brown or black mantles, and below them again the servant brothers who performed essential menial duties. These lower grades were mainly peasants, illiterate and often ex-criminals. St Bernard stigmatised the knights of the Crusades as formed from men guilty of serious crimes who "took the cross" as a way of purging their sins.

In 1147, just prior to the Second Crusade, a chapter of 130 Templars was held in the presence of King Louis VII and the Pope. They had achieved star status. From then on, donations of land throughout Europe and the Middle East, money and goods were showered upon them. Recruits queued up to join and endow them with their patrimonies. Individual Knights were supposed to own nothing but their clothes, weapons and eating utensils, but the Order became extremely rich. To facilitate the administration of their extensive properties, and transmit funds to the Holy Land, the Templars set up a banking system whereby cash could be invested and kept safe. They organised loans, and invented the first cheque, so that money could be paid into a specific Commanderie, and on production of a receipt, drawn out at any other. This gave them enormous prestige and power, since even Kings were their customers.

During the next hundred years the Templars became a political entity to be reckoned with: they were a strong, disciplined force, and owned the only standing Army in Europe: they were involved in top level diplomacy between kings, statesmen and the church: the Master of the Temple regularly attended Parliament: they were involved in international finance, and became a clearing house for new ideas, new knowledge, science and technology. They had good relations with their neighbours in the Middle East, and kept in close contact with Islamic and Judaic culture and ideas. They possessed their own harbours, shipyards and ships, were the first sailors to use the magnetic compass, and were expert in navigation. They developed surveying, road building and map-making. They understood the need for cleanliness and hygiene, had their own teams of physicians and surgeons, and owned their own hospitals. They were glamorous and successful, the wonder and envy of their contemporaries, friends and enemies alike. Perhaps not surprisingly, such incredible achievement brought its own nemesis: Templars grew complacent, and increasingly brutal, arrogant and corrupt.

In 1185 King Baudouin IV of Jerusalem died, and in the ensuing dynastic upheavals, Gérard de Ridefort, the current Grand Master, broke all his promises to Baudouin, and brought the European community in the Holy Land close to civil war. He antagonised the Saracens, and the long-standing truce with them failed. In 1187 Saladin crossed the Jordan and captured Tiberias.

Ridefort rashly decided to attack the Saracens who were entrenched on the Horns of Hattin. It meant the Christian Army had to cross a waterless plain; thirsty and exhausted, they suffered a disastrous defeat. The Templars, in the rear, were surrounded, unable to advance or retreat; two hundred and thirty were killed, and another hundred were taken prisoner. Secular prisoners were sold into slavery, knights were beheaded. Only Ridefort was spared. Two months later Jerusalem fell. The Holy City, recaptured by the Crusaders nearly a century earlier, was again lost to the Christians.

During the following century the situation became steadily worse. By 1291 the Saracens occupied almost all the Holy Land, and in May of that year the last city, Acre, was captured. The Templars evacuated to Cyprus, but felt circumscribed in their new headquarters. They looked with envy at the Order of Teutonic Knights, who presided over their own independent principality stretching from Prussia to the Gulf of Finland. The Templars too desired a homeland in a more congenial area. Their eyes turned towards Languedoc, virtually independent, separated from Norman France by its traditions and language, and the long-established haven of foreigners, refugees, and dissidents.

The Templars already had a foothold in Southern France. They maintained good relations with the Cathars; wealthy local landowners, Cathar themselves or Cathar sympathisers, donated land to the Templars. During the Albigensian Crusade, the Templars in theory remained neutral, but they seem on occasion to have helped Cathar refugees, and offered them safety within the Templar ranks, where neither church nor state could touch them. It is not outside the bounds of possibility that they were influenced by Cathar thought. Their long association with the Middle East, and particularly with Islam, would have familiarised the Templars with unorthodox and Gnostic doctrines, so that Cathar beliefs would not have come as strange to them.

King Philippe-le-Bel certainly did not relish such a powerful and prestigious organisation sitting on his doorstep. In addition, he owed them money. According to Guillaume de Plaisian, the King's Minister, in 1305 one Esquinas de Floyran, a Templar "of humble condition", denounced his colleagues firstly to the King of Aragon, who ignored him, and secondly to the King of France. Two other Templars, names unknown, also made denunciations; a dozen secret agents were infiltrated into the Order's ranks, and subsequently confirmed the accusations.

Having carefully prepared a list of accusations, Philippe issued sealed orders to all his seneschals throughout France which were to be opened simultaneously and executed immediately. In the early morning of 13 October 1307 the King's men moved against the Templars, arresting all they could get their hands on, on suspicion of heresy. It differed from normal procedure in that, although authorised by the papal Inquisitor in France, the arrests were effected by the King and not by the Church. Those taken included the Grand Master Jacques de Molay, the Visitor-General, the Preceptors of Normandy, Aquitaine, and Cyprus, and the former French Royal Treasurer.

In addition to heresy the charges against the Templars included worshipping idols, witchcraft, blasphemy, and sexual perversion. Specifically they were accused of adoring Baphomet in the shape of a bearded head, which "it was believed could save them"; making gold, and causing the land to germinate; of denying Christ; and during initiation of spitting or urinating on the cross, bestowing obscene kisses on the posterior, navel and mouth of Brothers, and promising to practise sodomy.

The prisoners were treated abominably. Used to community living, and the mutual support that it provides, they were segregated in solitary confinement, humiliated, denied all legal aid, and barbarously tortured. Many Templars, including the Grand Master, confessed. However, as the Order was, at least in theory, under the jurisdiction of the Pope, it was not possible to pass sentence. Clement V was a weak man, the King's nominee, and living on French soil, but he realised that unequivocally to endorse Philippe's actions would seriously jeopardise Papal authority, so he prevaricated. Any heretic who had confessed and then withdrawn his confession was regarded as lapsed, and in 1310 fifty four lapsed Templars were illegally condemned to be burned alive. In spite of a mild protest from the Pope to the Archbishop of Sens, the sentence was carried out on 12 May.

By 1311, although nothing had been proved against them, Philippe pressured Clement to agree to the dissolution of the Order.

Their property was to be passed to their rivals, the Hospitallers of St John of Jerusalem, but in effect a considerable part of it ultimately passed into royal hands. On 18 March 1314 the Grand Master, Visitor-General, and the Preceptors of Normandy and Aquitaine were brought before a commission including French cardinals and clergy for final sentence. They were condemned to perpetual imprisonment. The Grand Master and one of the Preceptors withdrew their confessions, and asserted the religious orthodoxy of the Templar Order. The two men were handed over to the secular authorities, and burned to death the same day on the Ile de France in the middle of the Seine, opposite the Royal Palace.

Although Philippe was undoubtedly motivated by jealousy and greed, there were other contributory factors in his move against the Templars. He was committed to the idea of a crusade against the Byzantine Empire, a project opposed both by the Pope and the Templars, for which he needed money. He regarded himself as the Church's Vicar in France, and it was common practice throughout Europe for monarchs to collect taxes on behalf of the Pope as a crusading tithe. Much of this disappeared on one pretext or another into royal treasuries. Philippe's efforts to get control of the Templar revenues fell within this policy, but he was finally forced to hand over what he had collected to the Hospitallers. He was also a strong supporter of the move to merge the Templars and Hospitallers which would have provided royal access to redundant properties, a proposal that the Templars vigorously opposed.

Nor was his religious zeal entirely fictitious. This was the time of universal witchcraft hysteria. So-called witches practised "natural" magic; they were concerned with divinations, spells, love philtres and herbal medicines, some of them occasionally poisonous. All these were certainly heretical, but directed mainly against individuals, which made witches less dangerous than magicians, who supposedly defied the Church, conjured by the blasphemous use of divine names, had liaisons with devils, and whose actions could affect whole communities.

The accusation of witchcraft against the Templars had no foundation, but they could, in effect, have been regarded as magicians, since there is evidence, even if it is circumstantial, that they were versed in the ancient lore of Cabala. Cabalism was believed to have originated in the Fertile Crescent at the time of Abraham, and offered an alternative version of the Creation. The creative powers of God were set out in the Tree of Life, a glyph involving ten sephiroth which were concepts of godhead, superimposed upon two pillars of opposing force, one white male and one black female, coalescing in a central red pillar of balance. Mankind being subject to human limitation, each sephiroth was envisaged as a particular icon. At the head of the central pillar was Kether, the first remote idea of divinity, the image for which was a bearded head seen in profile, because God, being transcendental, was always half hidden. Cabala was familiar to the Hebrews and Merkabah, the innermost teaching of cabalistic mysticism known as "The work of the Chariot", is symbolically described in Chapter I of the Book of the Prophet Ezekiel. No-one was allowed to study Merkabah, which contained atom-splitting power, before the age of thirty, when the initiate was considered sufficiently mature to deal with its dangerous potential. The medieval Church regarded Cabalism as the work of the devil, although like the Old Testament it can be adapted to Christian theology. Baphomet may be a combination of the Greek words "baphe" and "metis" meaning "absorption into wisdom". As an icon of God, he would certainly be capable of any degree of creation. He is sometimes depicted as androgynous, with two faces and a long silver-grey beard, which resembles the figure of the Red King in alchemical symbolism; or as an oracular head of copper that answered questions.

Another explanation of Baphomet is that it was the Turin Shroud, which the Templars were said to have owned, and which when folded would show just the head of the supposed imprint of

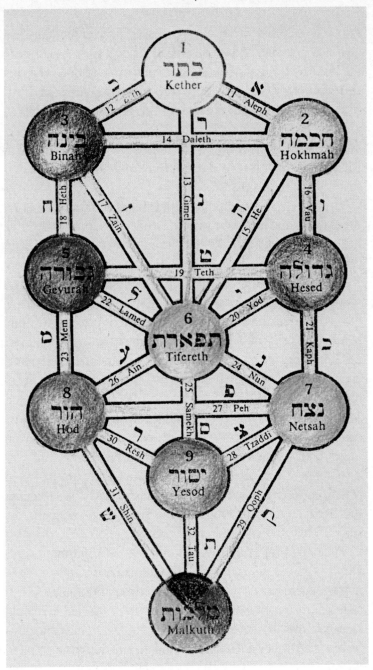

The Tree of Life

the body of Christ, They also possessed a silver reliquary in the shape of a woman's head, which had inside it either a skull or two leg bones. The emblem of a skull and crossed bones has been found in Templar churchyards, and was adopted by the Freemasons, although apart from being a symbol of mortality, its arcane significance is obscure to the uninitiated. It has been suggested that the reliquary contained bones of either Mary Magdalene or John the Baptist, both of whom were specially revered by the Templars.

There has been a continuing belief among schismatics that John the Baptist, and not Jesus, was the true Messiah, and the Jewish historian Josephus actually states that John was a political danger to Herod. The gospel account of John's death (Matthew 14, verses 1 - 13) is ambiguous. It tells how John denounced Herod's marriage to Herodias as illegal, and in consequence Herodias plotted his death, getting her daughter Salome to ask for John's head as the price of dancing for the King. This as it stands is an unlikely story, like much of the New Testament as edited by the early Church fathers, which resulted in a very slanted piece of journalism. Herod may have lusted after his step-daughter, but John was popular, with a large public following, and to put him to death in such circumstances and for such a perverse reason would undoubtedly have been a major political error on Herod's part. The gospel story also has more the aura of a parable than an actual happening. The 17th century alchemist Michael Maier said that John the Baptist "makes gold from rods and gems from stones", but alchemists always speak in jargon.

The shedding of the seven veils that left Salome naked to Herod's gaze sounds more like a fairy story or the making of a myth than an actual report. In "The Epic of Gilgamesh" - the oldest story extant in the West - Ishtar, entering Hell in search of her lover, discards seven veils, thus shedding divinity and power. Seven is an important magical number, and the seven colours of the rainbow that arch over Ezekiel's chariot are the seven colours of the lower sephiroth of the Tree of Life, the seven concepts of godhead and gates to paradise.

Moreover, the head was brought to Salome, the arch priestess, in a dish. The cult of the head is a very ancient one; primitive tribes took their enemies' heads after battle believing that they would thereby absorb the virtues and attributes of their adversaries. In *Peredur*, an early Welsh version of the Quest story, the grail is described as a bleeding head in a dish; and in the *Mabinogion* Bran the Blessed, who is sometimes equated with Brons, the brother-in-law of Joseph of Arimathea, is mortally wounded in battle, and tells his followers to cut off his head, which continues to entertain them for fourscore years before being buried on Tower Hill to protect Britain from invasion. The knights who guarded the head were called the Assembly of the Wondrous Head. And in the *High History of the Holy Grail* King Arthur is healed of an incurable wound by the severed head of the Black Knight.

The charges of denying Christ and defiling the cross might be attributable to Gnostic doctrine, which like Muslims regarded Jesus as a holy prophet but not divine, and the cross as an instrument of Roman torture beneath contempt. The infamous kiss was not a very serious allegation: men often kissed each other on the mouth in salutation, and the kiss of peace was regularly exchanged between royal visiting celebrities. Homosexuality was probably as common among the Templars as in any other exclusively male community, and while regarded as profane by the Church, is a fact of life. The ancient Greeks regarded the emotional bond between their young warriors as an important contribution to their bravery. No soldier would risk being shamed in battle before his lover. The same was perhaps true of the Templars.

It cannot therefore be asserted with total conviction that they were not literally guilty of some of the accusations brought against them, although their moral culpability is certainly questionable. There always have, and always will be, those who seek for an alternative mode of thought, consciousness and expression. The stream of ancient wisdom refuses to be dammed.

The Templar mythmakers insist that however much of their vast wealth was dissipated to other Orders of Chivalry or disappeared into private and State coffers, a large part of it not only survived, but is still hidden. Hughues de Chalons, the nephew of the Templar Visitor to France, Hughues de Pairaud, escaped abroad and took his Uncle's wealth with him. According to some German Freemasons, Jacques de Molay confessed that the two pillars, Jachin and Boaz, that guarded the entrance to the Paris Temple, were hollow and contained Templar treasure. Also, that on the day before he died de Molay sent his nephew, the Count de Beaujeu, to a crypt in Paris which was reserved for burial of the Grand Masters. Here de Beaujeu found a large silver casket containing the secrets of the Order, including the crown of Jerusalem, Solomon's golden Menorah, and four golden statues of the Evangelists from the Church of the Holy Sepulchre. He wrapped the casket in a voluminous shroud set aside for de Molay, and spirited it away. None of the fabled Templar treasure has ever been found, and inevitably the hidden gold has been interpreted by occultists as the alchemical gold of spiritual enlightenment, and not material valuables.

The secret art of alchemy embraces the physical application of primitive chemistry and physics, running parallel with which is a system of ritual and spiritual exercises, the whole expressed in pictorial language which has no single vocabulary, and which defies logic. The exoteric object was to create the philosopher's stone which could cure all ills and grant eternal life, while the esoteric aim was to reach spiritual perfection.

One way of externalising both these objectives was to turn base metal into gold, considered to be the ultimate expression of purity, being incorruptible. It was believed that as all physical matter had a common basis (as has been proved by modern nuclear physicists) which would permit its transmutation, so the imperfect human body contained a soul which was capable of achieving salvation.

The most favourable time to start the Great Work was in the Spring, and the astrological sign for Aries was also used as a symbol of the prima materia. What prima materia actually was has never been revealed. The quest was a lifetime dedication, and there is no evidence that anyone succeeded, although Nicholas Flamel supposedly made the first transmutation during the 14th century, and Dr John Dee, Astrologer Royal to Queen Elizabeth I, cut into two the warming-pan which she had sent to him, and returned one half to her turned into gold. He presumably knew how to gold-plate on copper!

Dee was not only a magician and alchemist but also a scholar, expert in the practical disciplines of mathematics, optics, linguistics, astronomy, and navigation - he invented the instruments and charts used by Drake and other sea-faring adventurers on their voyages of world discovery. He also seems to have discovered some form of laser projection. When he invited the Queen and her attendants to his laboratory at Mortlake, and demonstrated the art of scrying, his magic diary records that the visitors saw figures outside, not within the crystal.

Dee himself did not scry, but employed a rather dubious character called Edward Kelley as a medium. Many historians believe that Kelley was a charlatan, but Dee was no fool to be taken in by a con-man, and the extant accounts of their scrying sessions seem to indicate that Kelley's visions were at least in part genuine. Protected by royal patronage, Dee narrowly escaped burning as a heretic. His contemporary Italian magus, Giordano Bruno, did not, and was burned alive as an impenitent heretic on the Campo de Fiori, Rome, on 17 February 1600.

In simplistic terms the alchemical prima material was subjected to various procedures involving heat, moisture and distillation, which were intended finally to result in the production of the philosopher's stone. Running parallel to this process was a system of study, meditation and visualisation aimed at the raising of consciousness and attainment of wisdom. The moral is simple and universal: life, death, resurrection/renewal, as prescribed by every mystery cult since the dawn of time. The end is always beyond human comprehension, and in the Grail romances out of all who seek only the perfect knight achieves success. The journey is more important than the goal, and those who strive are at least allowed to approach the threshold of revelation. Intention is all.

ᴄʜᴇ Ρᴇᴏᴘʟᴇ ᴏꜰ ᴄʜᴇ Ðᴏᴠᴇ.

The Oxford Dictionary explains heresy as "opinion contrary to orthodox Christian belief or accepted doctrine". On this basis, the Templars may have been heretics, the Cathars certainly qualified.

There have been many books written about the Cathars; most of them based on conjecture, and some of them nonsensical. We do not actually know very much about their beliefs, and they have over the years acquired an extraordinary aura of mystique. They were a secret people, and if they ever committed their doctrines to writing, these perished with them in the 13th century holocaust. All that survived are the Inquisition records of interrogation, which is like reading Jewish history as compiled by the Nazis.

One fact is clear. The Cathars wanted no part of the pomp and circumstances of the established Catholic church. They rejected its theology, practices and hierarchy, thus undermining its power, privilege and revenue. They lived in small peaceful communities on inaccessible mountain-tops. Property appears to have been held in common, but overall they were not poor. The ruins of the Cathar castles - Montségur, Queribus, Peyrepertuse - are evidence of rich and powerful overlords, princes in their own right.

By the middle of the twelfth century Catharism was already well established in Languedoc, and in 1174 Bernard of Clairvaux preached against the Cathars at Toulouse. In 1204 Pope Innocent III attempted unsuccessfully to enlist the aid of Philip Augustus of France against them, and a year later an itinerant Spanish monk,

Dominic Guzman, founded the Dominican sect which was to become the Holy Inquisition. In 1208 the Pope called for a crusade against Catharism and the civil war, which lasted forty-six years, was on.

In theory the Cathars were pacifists and had no army. They were, however, not opposed to accepting the military protection of the Counts of Toulouse and Foix, backed up by King Pedro II of Aragon. Like other religious wars, it rapidly became a political conflict - the North against the South. Under Simon de Montfort, Languedoc was ravished by the land-hungry Norman barons, and thousands of its inhabitants, Cathar and Catholic alike, were slaughtered. De Montfort's command to "Kill them all, God will know his own", is almost certainly apocryphal, but very apposite.

In 1213 King Pedro was killed at the battle of Muret, and in 1215 Toulouse fell. Count Raymond died in 1226, and his son, Raymond VII, yielded in 1229, promised to extirpate the heretics, and married the niece of the King of France.

The war was virtually over, but persecution dragged on. In 1244, after a ten months' siege, the holy citadel of Montségur surrendered, and two hundred Cathars, men, women and children, walked down the hill and into the fires. They had asked for a delay of two weeks to prepare for death, which was surprisingly granted. During that time three men were lowered down the western face of the cliff and passed through the enemy lines to safety in the caves of Ornalac. It was said they took with them the treasure of Montségur.

The writer, Arthur Guirdham, who claims to be a 20th century reincarnation of a Cathar, states that the treasure consisted mainly of precious documents including copies of lost gospels, as well as money. The amount of books and coin transportable silently down a steep precipice in the middle of the night is questionable. The Cathars had no sacred vessels of gold and silver. What then was the treasure that it was so important to preserve?

The personal survival of the refugees seems to have been of vital importance, and it was arranged for a beacon fire to be lit on

Bidorte, the mountain opposite Montségur, to signify that they had reached safety. If they in fact carried some sort of material treasure it has never been traced, although attempts have been made to find it for more than seven hundred years.

After the fall of Montségur Catharism lingered on for a time. Queribus fell in 1255 at the instigation of Blanche of Castile, but when the invaders entered the castle, it was found to be empty. As late as 1320 a lawyer named Guillaume Belibaste was burned as a Cathar at Villerouge Termenes.

A great deal of emphasis has been laid by modern writers on the belief that Cathars regarded the material world as the creation of Satan, and that sexual intercourse was to be avoided since it perpetuated the body, a manifestation of evil materialism. Also that they did not believe in Christ's humanity, as God would not consent to inhabit corrupt human flesh. They did not in fact deny the Incarnation, but were concerned more with the Christ force, the mystic Word as depicted in the first chapter of St John, rather than the earthly Jesus of the synoptics. As Guirdham points out, it is a misconception, a misreading of the small print.

The Cathars believed that it was everyone's duty to aim for spiritual perfection, but they preached chastity rather than abstinence. Cathar communities grew and thrived. Rejecting Catholic liturgy, they resented the Church's claim to exclusivity in the matter of marriage. They had their own civil ceremony of hand fasting, which prompted hysterical Catholic denunciation of supposed sexual deviations, and equally hypothetical repressive Puritanism.

So far as we know, the only sacrament Cathars recognised was the Consolamentum, of which two forms survive - the Rituel de Lyon, written in Langue d'Oc, and the Rituel de Florence in Latin. These give details of the ceremony which consisted mainly of the officiating minister touching the aspirant with the gospel of St John, and bestowing the kiss of peace. It was a beginning rather than an end in itself, a kind of baptism, confirmation and ordination all in one, requiring a period of study, meditation and training. Emphasis was on self purification. After bestowal of the Consolamentum the Parfait was required to abstain from sexual congress, eating meat, to observe the prescribed fasts, and to keep the faith. In this the tenets do not vary much from any monastic requirements, and monasticism was very popular in the twelfth and thirteenth centuries. St Bernard was the "pin-up" of all Europe, and monasteries and convents proliferated.

It was unusual for the Consolamentum to be given before years of discretion were reached, and indeed was most commonly bestowed on the deathbed so that, like Extreme Unction, it provided a passport for the soul to higher regions. Most aspirants were middle-aged couples who had brought up their children and were ready to give up family life and manual labour in favour of the equally hard, but more rewarding work of teaching and healing. The Lady Esclarmonde, sister of the Count of Foix, who was instrumental in founding the Cathar community at Montségur, herself became a Parfaite after presenting her husband with six children.

On an exoteric level this is a credible assessment of Catharism. But there was more to it than that. Guirdham mentions "secret gospels". The favourite exoteric gospel seems to have been St John, but esoteric Catharism may also have included the study of The Revelation of St John the Divine, which has a very close affinity with the book of Ezekiel, and Maaseh Merkabah. Was the secret book of the Cathars a Christian version of Cabalism?

Cabalism was the inner mystical teaching of Judaism, codified by Ezekiel in his vision of the Chariot, a glyph of creation alternative to that described in Genesis. In brief, En Soph, the transcendental eternal creator, manifests in the ten sephiroth of the Tree of Life, which are concepts of ten aspects of divinity. From these arise the four elements, which in turn create the physical universe, the shorthand symbols of which are the twenty-two letters of the Hebrew alphabet. The Tree of Life itself is a pattern or plan which can be used as a filing system, and can be applied equally to any kind of theology. Christian mystics adopted it with enthusiasm, and use it as a mandala for meditation to "rise on the planes", or in other words to raise consciousness to higher levels. The ultimate object is union with the godhead. The basis of Cabalism is a doctrine of two opposing forces - not good and evil, but dark and light, positive and negative, male and female, spiritual and material - and achieving the balance between. In this sense it can be said to be dualistic.

We now pass into the realm of myth and legend. It has always been accepted by the Church, without foundation, that the beloved disciple was John-bar-Zebedee. In fact, it was far more likely that Lazarus was meant. No mention of the beloved disciple is made until we come to the raising of Lazarus, who was the only adult ever to be restored from death to life. (The two other instances mentioned in the New Testament were teenagers: the widow's son in the cornfields at Nain, a straight gloss on a fertility ritual, and Jairus' daughter, of whom Jesus is reported as saying she is not dead, but sleeps, which may literally have meant just that). The raising of Lazarus has all the hallmarks of an initiation. Jesus delays his return to Bethany for three days, he calls Lazarus from the tomb, and tells the women who are weeping for him to loose him and let him go. It was customary to shed tears for the sacrifice, and initiation ceremonies inevitably include symbolic death. Ezekiel, writing as late as 500 BCE mentions that women wept for Tammuz at the north gate of the Temple: the women of Jerusalem wept for Jesus on the way to Calvary, and Mary wept for him in the garden.

The Gospel of St. John (11.5) says "Jesus loved Martha, and her sister and Lazarus", and when the women sent to Jesus they said "He whom thou lovest is sick" (11.2), and again when Jesus reached the tomb, he himself wept, and the Jews said "Behold, how he loved him" (11.35.36). Whether one believes that Lazarus was literally raised from the dead or went through an initiation is irrelevant - it is obvious that on this occasion he was given some special grace. Was it, perhaps, the apostolic succession, and that the true church was committed to the care of Lazarus, while the exoteric church was put in charge of Peter? There is a strong esoteric tradition that the inner teaching was given to the Beloved Disciple.

From gospel accounts, it would appear that Bethany was the nearest Jesus had to an earthly home. The house obviously belonged to Martha, and the early church identified her with the woman with the issue of blood, which would have made her ritually unclean according to Jewish law, and would account for her being apparently unmarried, unusual for a woman of her age and social standing. She appears in the gospel as a rather bitter, jealous person, which is unfair. It was the woman's job in the home to look after guests, Mary would in common courtesy have been expected to play her part, and one cannot but sympathise with Martha who always seems to be left with the washing-up. It is, however, to Martha that Jesus gives the first dogma of faith - at the raising of Lazarus he says to her "I am the Resurrection and the Life" and "Said I not unto thee that if thou wouldst believe, thou shouldst see the glory of God."

The Golden Legend, written by Jacobus de Voragine (1229-1298) equates Mary of Bethany with Mary Magdala who anointed Christ as king and sacrifice, the woman taken in adultery, and the penitent from whom Jesus cast out seven devils. Inevitably the early Church fathers who were both terrified and fascinated by women and sex, regarded the devils as sexual sins. The cult of the Magdalene was so strong it almost exceeded that of the Virgin herself. Where Mary the Mother of God was sanitised to the point of being a-sexual, the Magdalene, with her flowing hair and flask of perfume, could be stigmatised without any evidence as a reformed whore, and gloated over. But the seven devils have another connotation. The "Zohar" describes the way to union with God as through seven gates, seven regions and seven palaces, each of which has attendant devils which must be conquered with the aid of the appropriate angels. And Sophia, Holy Wisdom, built her house on seven pillars, which are the seven lower sephiroth of the Tree of Life, embracing seven attributes of manifestation.

When Mary sat at the Master's feet and was taught, was this the gnosis that was given to her?

There is a legend that after the Crucifixion Mary, Martha and Lazarus came to Southern France. Lazarus went to Marseille, where he founded his own church and became the first bishop; Mary, after making a number of converts and doing a few miracles, retired to a hermit's cave in the mountains where she spent the rest of her life in prayer. She eschewed food and clothing and was nourished only by heavenly bread. The Sforza *Book of Hours* has a picture of her being raised up on a flying carpet by four angels, modestly clad in a kind of furry rug of her own hair. Martha, true to her vocation, cared for the sick and needy, and at Tarascon conquered a dragon, like St. Margaret, by binding it with her girdle. Mary and Martha are often regarded as the two kinds of religious devotees - the contemplative and the active.

Without real reason, but that it seems poetically right, it is tempting to suggest that the doctrines of Lazarus, Martha and Mary were the foundation of the Cathar faith. It was said they brought to France with them the Holy Grail - and Montségur has been described as the Grail Castle. Was the secret Christian doctrine, based on ancient Cabalistic mysticism, and handed by Jesus to the Beloved Disciple and his sisters, the treasure that had to be carried in person in the minds and hearts of the three chosen Parfaits who escaped the flames? At least it is believed they took with them from Montségur, in some form, the Holy Grail.

According to the academics, the grail derived from much earlier pagan sources, being originally Ceridwen's cauldron of plenty. The first genuine grail romances originated in the 12th century with Crétien de Troyes' *Perceval*, which was written in 1180 for Count Philip of Flanders. Wolfram von Eschenbach produced his own version, claiming that his source was Kyot the Provencal, who had it "of a Jewish astrologer from Toledo called Flegetanis". They were all written at the turn of the century over a period of some fifty years, and as copyright had not yet been invented, it was quite usual for writers to use each other's plots and then attribute the origin to ancient lost manuscripts. Each author told his own version of the story, adding and adapting to taste. It was a time of great creativity: Magna Carta, St Francis and St Dominic, the building of the great Gothic cathedrals, and the founding of universities.

What exactly the grail is, is left obscure, although it is usually accepted that it is the chalice used by Jesus at the Last Supper, or the cup in which Joseph of Arimathea caught Christ's blood and sweat during the Crucifixion. We are told "...it was not of wood, nor of any manner of metal: nor was it in any wise of stone, nor of horn, nor of bone..." It shines with its own light. It is carried by a beautiful maiden, or glides along without visible support, and is accompanied by heavenly music and the sweetest perfume. It provides everyone present with the food most desired. A. E. Waite, the 19th century religious occultist, suggests that it was a phial of Christ's blood, and that the sustenance it provided was spiritual not physical, analogous to taking Holy Communion. Wolfram's grail is a type of philosopher's stone, a scrying crystal capable of flashing divine messages, although it also provides food and drink, can prolong life, and promises peace and prosperity. It was kept at the castle of Monsalvatsch, which has been taken to be Montségur, and was guarded by Red Cross Knights, identified by the faithful as "Templars".

Crétien saw the grail as a chalice in which the host was carried. The anonymous *High History of the Grail* has five transformations of the grail, though we are not told what they are: "The grail appeared at the sacring of the Mass in five several manners that none must tell". Internal evidence suggests these were: spear, cup, child, stone and dish. In the *Didot-Perceval*, an amalgam of the works of Robert de Boron, Geoffrey of Monmouth and various anonymous sources, the grail is described as a "vessel" and is carried by a boy. The grail procession usually includes in various forms a cup, a spear that bleeds, a sword and a dish. These four symbols are repeated in the suits of the Tarot minor arcana.

Another suggestion is that the grail is a stone that fell from Lucifer's crown when he plunged down from Heaven. Neil Hudson Newman, author of *Pathways of the Gods*, suggests the grail stone is the zircon, heaviest of the semi-precious jewels. The zircon is also technically called the jargon, and has a tetragonal crystal structure. The triangle is a basic figure of sacred geometry, and the Oxford Dictionary describes jargon as "language peculiar to a class or profession etc., barbarous or debased language". One might perhaps class ciphers and codes as jargon.

The Quest of the Holy Grail, known colloquially as the "Cistercian version", was probably written by Walter Map, an archdeacon of Oxford, based on the work of an unknown monk. He aims to Christianise the story, which had hitherto retained a number of pagan elements, and his hero is Galahad, the stainless knight, who is as near to being an icon of Christ as he could come without being blasphemous. The original grail winner is Perceval, the holy fool, son of the widow, who is so innocent that he knows nothing, not even his own name. When he first sees a knight in armour he thinks that the man was born like that, enclosed in a hard carapace like a tortoise. Throughout the quest Perceval retains his simplicity, that at times becomes plain stupidity, but succeeds at last by an intuitive understanding of the divine. The third grail seeker is Bors, a prudent man who wins through hard work and common sense. The three winners might be considered as different aspects of the same person: Perceval is justified by faith, and Bors by good works, the two Pauline channels of grace. Galahad needs no justification, he is already elect.

The interesting point about both Perceval and Galahad is that they are of the family of grail keepers, which presupposes that the grail involves not only a sacred quest but also the inheritance of a holy blood line. Pierre Plantard, self-declared descendant from the Merovingian priest-kings, would have regarded himself as eligible to be a grail winner, and the Prieuré de Sion claims to be the guardian of the sacred treasure. It is easy to see how the legend of royal/divine descent grew, could become plausible, and finally convincing to the adherents of a neo-chivalric Order. The Nazis, obsessed with their own conception of the Holy Grail, and chasing the illusion of racial purity, were similarly deluded. A team of German investigators excavated in Rennes-le-Château during the Second World War in search of the treasure, but found nothing.

In 1890 Jules Doinel, the librarian at Carcassonne, established a neo-Cathar church, and appointed himself Bishop of Mirepoix. He was the Secretary of the Society of Arts and Sciences, of which both Saunière and Boudet were members. Doinel was succeeded as bishop by Dr Gérard Encausse (Papus of Tarot fame) who was Grand Master of the Martinists, a mystical-Christian sect devoted to the work of the 18th century Unknown Philosopher, Louis Claude de St Martin, whose writings and dogma are concerned mainly with Cabala. Doinel was reported to Rome, and although the Vatican expressed disapproval of an attempt to revive Catharism, they took no action, choosing to regard Doinel's church as yet another minor literary society, and his activities as the work of a crank.

Martinism, however, became an important factor in the 19th century French occult revival, and Saunière may have been a member, in common with a number of other priests. He is believed to have belonged to the Lyon lodge, and he may even have organised his own branch lodge at Rennes-le-Château. His bookplate bore two interlocking triangles, one white and one black, the Martinist logo.

The church at Rennes-le-Château is dedicated to Mary Magdalene, and the painting under the altar, attributed to Saunière himself, or at any rate executed at his instigation, shows her outside her hermit's cave with an open book beside her, which it is tempting to identify as the secret gospel. The devil holy water stoup incorporates the four elements - the horned god as earth, the salamanders that are fire elementals, the basin of water, and above the four airy angels making the sign of an equal-armed cross, the Cabalistic sign of equilibrium. "The Sermon on the Mount" mural is strewn with roses, and Guirdham says roses, with a chalice and dove, are Cathar symbols. The twenty-two petalled rose of the Hebrew Alphabet (3 mother, 7 double and 12 single letters) is also a Cabalistic mandala.

The Invisible Brethren

When the inventors of the Rosicrucian Brotherhood chose the symbol of the rose cross for their emblem, they were reaching deep into the human psyche. For Christians the cross means the sacrifice on Calvary, but the four branch equal-armed cross goes back beyond that, to primitive civilisations who regarded it as a conjunction of the male and female principles. In Cabala it is the symbol of four-fold creation - four holy creatures, archangels, elements, compass points, seasons, divisions of the day, fixed stars, cardinal virtues - and at the centre is the world-axis, the point of perfect balance, order, justice and mercy. Here, we may say, dwells the power and the glory, Jehovah or Christ the King. In mundane terms, the shape of the cross is regarded as the plan of man, and represents Adam Kadmon, the first conceptual human being. When God decided to create mankind as a projection of himself, he drew a veil across his face to shield his shining. His image was reflected upon the curtain, and this was Adam Kadmon, the archetype of humanity, both male and female. After the Fall physical life split into the two sexes, but the initiate still looks at the vision that is both God and Mankind, and strives to reach the ideal that it represents. In the veil that is a two-way mirror, man sees God in his own image, as God made mankind in his.

The rose has always been regarded as a symbol of perfection, of completion and consummation. Its attributes are feminine: the bride in Solomon's *Song of Songs* is the Rose of Sharon; the Virgin is the Mystic Rose, her chaplet of prayers a rosary. The Litany of Loreto says of her:

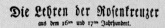

The title page of
*"Secret Symbols of
the Rosicrucians"*
Pt 1, 1785

The Rose Cross from the title page of
"Summun Bonum Pt 1" by Robert Fludd, 1929

"Flower of the Cross, pure womb that blossoms
Overall blooming and burning,
Sacred Rose - Mary.

The open blossom is a mandala, pertaining to the heart centre, to love, to the paradise garden; the glossy red rose-hip is the emblem of rebirth, holding within its pod potential future generations of roses.

Nostradamus, the Provencal astrologer and soothsayer, in 1555 prophesied:

"A new sect of Philosophers shall rise,
Despising death, gold, honours and riches.
They shall be near the mountains of Germany;
They shall have abundance of others to support and follow them".

He was absolutely right. In the early part of the 17th century "a new sect of Philosophers" did arise in Germany, who shunned worldly satisfactions in favour of spiritual ones, and were said to have conquered death by the discovery of the elixir of life. They gathered supporters and eventually became known throughout the world, organisations claiming to be their descendants still existing today.

The first the uninitiated heard of the Rosicrucians was in 1614, when the original manifesto, *Fama Fraternitatis* was published, though it was possibly in private circulation as early as 1610. It suggested the Brotherhood had special and powerful knowledge.

In 1615 a second document, *Confessio Fraternitatis R.C.* appeared in Latin. It repeated the message of the *Fama*, promised to establish a reformed world, and was in effect a Memorandum and Articles of Association for the new Rosicrucian sect.

The documents supposedly revealed the existence of a secret fraternity founded by Christian Rosencreuz who had lived at the turn of the 14th/15th century. He travelled to the Middle East where he studied occult wisdom, and founded a Brotherhood that was to be devoted to spreading this acquired knowledge, and to healing the sick without charge. They were to remain strictly incognito. On his death at the age of 106, Christian Rosencreuz was buried in a secret grave, but the vault was to be rediscovered and opened after one hundred and eight years, which would be the signal for the Brethren to declare themselves and invite the learned elite of Europe to join their cause. It would herald the dawn of a new age. The documents invited anyone interested in the Brotherhood to make their interest known in writing or by word of mouth. Unfortunately no address was given, so presumably contact would need to be done magically, which was not considered beyond the capabilities of the professed magus.

In 1616 *The Chemical Wedding of Christian Rosencreuz* was published. In this the narrator, supposedly Rosencreuz himself, describes his experiences as a guest at the wedding of a king and queen who live in a wonderful castle. The guests are subjected to tests of their worth, and some of them are killed and restored to life by alchemical means. There are gates guarded by lions, magical fountains, and ships corresponding to the Zodiac. This document differed from the two previous manifestos since it dealt with personal renewal, but it is possible that at least the *Fama* and *The Chemical Wedding* were written by the same author, claimed to be Johan Valentin Andreae. Andreae was born at Würtemburg in 1586, the grandson of a distinguished Lutheran theologian, and was part of a group of idealistic Protestant philosophers at Tübingen University.

The manifestos told a romantic story, shrouded in titillating obscurity. The lost tomb was reported to have been discovered and opened. It was brilliantly lit from within, corresponding to the light of continual revelation; the floor and walls were decorated with strange esoteric symbols, and on the breast of Brother C.R.C. himself lay a small pamphlet that contained instructions to establish a Universal Brotherhood of peace and love, which would be a world college teaching magic and "ancient wisdom". This document was known as Liber T, and the inference is obvious in the punning title. The description, measurements and colours of the vault are strictly in accordance with the tenets of Cabala.

Andreae denied being the author of the manifestos, and said it was all a hoax, which nobody believed. In fact the initators of the Rosicrucian Brotherhood were spin doctors, and the manifestos were political propaganda, aimed at supporting the Protestant cause in Europe. The story of Christian Rosencreuz was not intended to be taken literally, it was an allegory of regeneration. Written in terms of mysticism and magic the manifestos were anti-Jesuit, condemned the Pope, Muslims, and "blasphemers against our Lord Jesus Christ", and promised political, religious and social reform. Their publication was a brilliant public relations exercise, and inevitably caused a huge uproar. The Rosicrucians had announced their presence, but claimed to be invisible, and that their temple was "not made with hands". Any attempt to contact them met with a fog of misinformation. The Brotherhood had the great advantage of not really existing - nobody ever admitted to being a Rosicrucian or having met one, but the word spread, everybody wanted to join, and belief in this unique group of initiates persisted.

On the death of Emperor Rudolph II in 1612, and the short interregnum of his elderly brother Matthias, the crown of Bohemia fell vacant. The most likely candidate was the fanatical Catholic Hapsburg Archduke Ferdinand of Styria, who became King in 1617, but Bohemia was primarily Protestant and determinedly anti-Hapsburg. The people rose in rebellion, and in 1619 they offered the Crown to Frederick V, the Elector Palatine. Frederick accepted, but it meant war with the Hapsburgs, Catholic against Protestant, which was to last for thirty years.

In 1613 Frederick had married Elizabeth, daughter of James I of England, and they lived in a grand castle at Heidelberg. The gardens were magnificent, full of speaking statues and mechanical fountains that played music, and bear a remarkable resemblance to those described in *The Chemical Wedding*. They were devised by a French Protestant, Salomon de Caus, who was expert in number and proportion, perspective, painting, mechanics and geometry, the required qualifications for a garden architect of that period.

Frederick expected his father-in-law to support him, but James was in a difficult position. He was the first Stuart monarch, the son of Mary, Queen of Scots, a Catholic woman executed for treason by the late enormously popular Protestant Virgin Queen Elizabeth I. Also, he was trying to marry his son Charles to a Catholic Spanish princess, so James sat on the fence. France was mainly Catholic but hated the Hapsburgs and might have joined Frederick, but hoped that if the Spanish marriage fell through Charles would marry a French princess - which in fact he did - and so abstained. Belgium, Holland and the Union of Protestant German Princes, thinking Frederick's chances poor, followed France. Frederick and Elizabeth, the "Winter King and Queen", were crowned in Prague cathedral in September 1619, the last ceremony ever to be held by the Bohemian church. They reigned for just ten months.

The Hapsburgs, under the Duke of Bavaria, defeated Frederick's little army at the Battle of the White Mountain in November 1620, and the Spanish armies decimated Bohemia and the Palatinate. Frederick and Elizabeth fled to exile in The Hague. Protestants were persecuted for heresy and witchcraft, and the Rosicrucian Brotherhood disappeared.

The appeal of their mystique, however, has lingered on, and during the 18th and 19th centuries several pseudo-Rosicrucian societies sprang up in England, Germany and France. These were mainly right wing and royalist. The Masons enthusiastically adopted the nomenclature for new grades, and the Societas Rosicruciana in Anglia (familiarly known as the Soc. Ros.), a higher degree of British Freemasonry, became the cradle of the Golden Dawn, the most famous 19th century British occult society, which numbered among its members the poet W. B. Yeats, Annie Horniman of tea and theatre fame, novelists M. R. James and Dennis Wheatley, actress Florence Farr, and Aleister Crowley who delighted in the title of the Wickedest Man in the World. There are still any number of modern sects, such as the Worldwide organisation AMORC (The Ancient and Mystical Order of the Rosae Crucis) based in the United States, who profess to be Rosicrucian.

´Eτ in Arcadia Ego´

One of the most persistent theories is that behind the conjecture, speculation, deduction, and fabrication that obscure the provable facts of the Rennes-le-Château mystery, is the existence of a hidden directing intelligence. It has been identified as being exercised by such diverse influences as aliens from outer space, survivors from Atlantis, occult secret Masters, the Freemasons, sinister political agitators, and commercial moguls. Evidence does seem to indicate a concern with politics and money, and for want of a better definition, the controlling power behind the mystery is identified as the Prieuré de Sion.

Gérard de Sède, in *Le Trésor Maudit*, offers no names and asks "...who could these instigators have been? Probably a Rosicrucian sect. The roses and crosses engraved on the porch (of St Mary Magdalene) are not the only sign". In analysing the decorations of Saunière's church, he mentions specifically the statue of St. Germaine, the shepherdess saint with her apron full of roses, and the Fleury mural of the Mount of Beatitudes where the foreground is strewn with roses. He also mentions the work of Jacques Duchaussoy who claims that the Rosicrucians show themselves publicly every one hundred and eight years, and each time open a tomb containing documents. De Sède points out that in 1783 Fr Bigou hid in the Rennes-le-Château church the documents entrusted to him by Marie Négri d'Ables, and that in 1891, one hundred and eight years later, Saunière found documents when engaged on the restoration of the altar. The parchments bear the word "Sion", and Marie Négri's alleged tombstone has "Et in Arcadia Ego" surmounted by "P.S." Pierre Plantard claims that "Et in Arcadia Ego" is his personal motto, and his stationery carried this inscription, surmounted by an encircled single golden fleur de lys.

The first written identification of the Prieuré appears to have been in *The Holy Blood and the Holy Grail*, Henry Lincoln's blockbuster bestseller based on the information provided to him and his co-authors, Richard Leigh and Michael Baigent, by Plantard and de Chérisey.

In 1982 *Rennes le Château, Capitale Sécrète de l'Histoire de France* by journalists Jean-Pierre Deloux and Jacques Brétigny, was published simultaneously in France, Belgium and Switzerland. This was a glossy magazine type book consisting mainly of coloured photographs, and concentrated very largely on the Prieuré and Plantard's claim to be of Merovingian descent. Deloux and Brétigny had formed part of the entourage accompanying Plantard to his meeting with Henry Lincoln in Paris in mid-April 1982, and the book was undoubtedly written either at the instigation, or with the approval of, the originators of the Prieuré. In it the authors state that "the considerable funds granted to Saunière testify to the importance of the mission with which he had been entrusted, the preservation of the genealogical documents..." and add "...the Prieuré de Sion watches over the treasures of Razès and the secrets of the Kings of the ancient race, in order to assure the continuation not only of a doctrine, but of a philosophy relating to traditional knowledge."

If Plantard and de Chérisey were the creators of the last version of the Prieuré de Sion, they had the perfect role model in the 17th century Rosicrucian Brotherhood. The alliance between political and esoteric knowledge is typical of the Rosicrucian manifestos. Plantard had obvious esoteric interests, as evidenced by his connections with the 1930's occult society Alpha Galates, and its magazine *Vaincre* which specialised in esoteric subjects.

There are parallels in the behaviour of the Rosicrucians, and the way the Prieuré conducted its affairs from the time the Dossier Secret was lodged at the Bibliothèque until Plantard resigned as Grand Master. Information was leaked to the public at carefully regulated intervals. The Prieuré remained secret just as the Rosicrucians were invisible, and was as inaccessible to the curious. Members were obliged to maintain anonymity, and when asked, to deny any involvement with their respective Orders. Even Henry Lincoln, supposedly admitted to Plantard's confidence, consistently met with blind alleys and false trails.

The Prieuré, like the Rosicrucians, preached Utopia, denying while propagating certain political precepts. Both organisations were Royalist, and supported pretenders to a throne. When they had achieved the desired end of rousing attention, and public attention looked like becoming too intrusive, they slid quietly from view. Once he had announced his resignation as Grand Master on 10 July 1984, Plantard could no longer be expected to be cognizant of the Prieuré's activities, so he escaped any further pressure from outside interests. He concluded his letter of resignation by wishing the brethren "victory in establishing a better society". Any attempts to obtain comments or information from members of the former Plantard cabal were met with stony silence. De Chérisey never answered letters, and could not be reached by telephone. Plantard himself disappeared and Lincoln received no further communications from him except the token Christmas card.

Both the Prieuré and the Rosicrucians were connected with secret documents and a concealed tomb, which formed an integral part of their legends. Andreae described *The Chemical Wedding* as a ludibrium, that is a fiction or jest, based on his two comedies *Esther* and *Hyacinth*. De Chérisey claims authorship of the parchments, signed his confession The Prankster, and admits that the decoded message is a concoction of puns, verbal glosses and "in" jokes.

Plantard was said to have been initiated into the Prieuré on 10 July 1943 on the recommendation of Abbé François Ducaud Bourgaet, a hero of the French Resistance, and was elected Grand Master on 17 January 1981. He formally resigned both as Grand Master and as a Member of the Order on health grounds, but hinted also at a falling out with "our English and American brothers" of whose manoeuvres he disapproved. He decried certain false allegations made about him in the press and published works, which led him to file a complaint at Nanterre on 16 December 1983, and he said that he wished to protect his independence and that of his family. He wrote to Lincoln stating that since March 1984 he had refused all meetings or interviews relating to the Prieuré de Sion, and behaved, in fact, very like the Royalty he claimed to be. Plantard was quite categorically disassociating himself from any facts the researchers may dig up about the Prieuré, and the inference is inevitably that the ludibrium, if that was what it was, had got out of hand.

Since that time there have been no more leakages of information - or even disinformation. There is, of course, always the possibility that Plantard's resignation was intended as a smoke-screen to protect the Prieuré in general, and himself in particular, from too intrusive investigation, and that, having discouraged further attention, the Prieuré continued its operations undisturbed. Philippe de Chérisey, described by Lincoln as "...an extraordinarily gifted novelist", died suddenly in July 1985, effectively cutting off one of the more fruitful sources of investigation.

In 1979 Plantard adopted the title of Pierre Plantard de Saint Clair, Comte de Sainte-Clair and Comte de Rhedae, thereby theoretically connecting his lineage with the ancient Sinclair family of Rosslyn Chapel and Freemason renown. Pretensions to noble birth are not uncommon - McGregor Mathers, for example, the founder of The Golden Dawn, arbitrarily adopted the fictitious title of Count of Glenstrae. De Sède maintained that Plantard had no claim whatsoever to royal blood, and that he was descended from a 16th century peasant who grew walnuts.

According to Pierre Jarnac, Pierre Athenasius Marie Plantard was born in Paris on 18 March 1920. His father, also named Pierre, was a wine merchant, and his mother, Raulo, died when he was less than three years old. In 1939 Plantard was studying Greco-Roman architecture at University, where he met and became friendly with a fellow student, Philippe de Chérisey, the son of a minor aristocrat from the Ardennes. Not much is known of Plantard's early life, apart from the fact that he worked as a verger at the church of St. Louis d'Antin in Paris. Although a man of wide interests, he lacked the intellectual attainments of de Chérisey. What he did possess was an expert knowledge of symbolism, and an intrinsic understanding of psychology. He seemed to know instinctively what had public appeal.

He claimed to have been active in the Resistance during the second world war, and to have been interned by the Gestapo at Fresnes from October 1943 until February 1944. Efforts to confirm this, however, failed to produce any conclusive evidence. In support of his alleged Resistance activities Plantard produced a letter which he said he had received from de Gaulle thanking him for his services, but according to Jean-Luc Chaumeil this was merely the Government circular sent to all Frenchmen after the war. Chaumeil also said that indeed Plantard had been in prison, but this was for a civil offence, and nothing to do with the Resistance.

Under the name of Pierre de France, Plantard became director and editor of a journal called *Vaincre*, copies of which still exist in the Bibliothèque. There were a number of distinguished contributors, and it contained articles dealing primarily with the "ancient wisdom" tradition, relating to subjects such as Atlantis, astrology, and mythic and esoteric themes.

Vaincre was listed as the "house mag" of an Order named Alpha Galates. Under the Nazi occupation, secret societies were illegal and subject to severe prosecution, and Alpha Galates therefore described itself as an Order of Chivalry, which was to be the instrument of national renewal, "...a reservoir for moral, intellectual and spiritual force throughout coming generations". This was vague enough to escape Nazi censure. The Order was not designated as Catholic, and appeared rather to be esoteric, pagan and theosophical.

As required by French law, Alpha Galates was said to have been registered in the French *Journal Officiel* on 27 December 1937, but no such entry is apparent. The French Ministry of Defence and the Prefecture of Police similarly denied all knowledge of it. The Director is listed as George Monti, known also as Marcus Vella. Monti was a native of Toulouse, born in 1880, educated by the Jesuits, became a Martinist, and was initiated into the Rose-Croix Catholique by its founder Josephin Péladan. Later he was introduced into the infamous Ordo Templi Orientis by Aleister Crowley, and was subsequently involved with several German lodges that assisted in bringing the Nazis to power. He had been a spy for the Germans in the first world war, and later for the Nazis. Believing in backing the odds both ways, Monti also joined the B'nai B'rith, a Jewish Masonic organisation, under the name of Count Israel Monti. He was thought also to have worked for British Intelligence, and was involved in initiating the plan to bring Rudolph Hess to England. He may have been a double, or even a triple agent, and not surprisingly he was assassinated, poisoned in Paris in 1936. It was through Alpha Galates that he became acquainted with Plantard.

Vaincre reported that Pierre Plantard became Grand Master of Alpha Galates in 1942. One of its primary objectives was described as "...the creation of a new western order", a "young European chivalry" whose keynote was to be "Solidarity... the first stage of the United States of the West". This was also one of the dominant themes of *Vaincre*.

Vaincre was pro-Vichy in its sympathies, and supported Pétain. It was also anti-Semitic, in one issue stating "..to restore our homeland to its rank...it is necessary to eradicate false dogmas...and the corrupt principles of the formerly democratic Jewish Masonry."   It should be remembered, however, that *Vaincre* was published during the Occupation, and if it was to survive had to show at least a token support of Nazi dogma. According to Plantard, the text contained coded messages and instructions which could only be deciphered by the Resistance.

Moreover, *Vaincre* was printed by Poirier Murat, Chevalier of the Légion d'honneur, holder of the Médaille Militaire, and an officer in the French Resistance, who would hardly have been involved with a genuinely Nazi-oriented publication. There were no more issues of *Vaincre* after 1943, and no evidence of any of Plantard's activities for another dozen years.

In 1956 the Prieuré de Sion was registered in the *Journal Officiel*, and copies of its Statutes deposited with the Sub Prefecture of St.Julien-en-Genevois near Annemasse on the Swiss border. These named Plantard as Secretary-General, and listed nine grades, all with chivalric titles, the head being the Nautonier. It was described as a Catholic Chivalric Order, and its imposing, if incomprehensible, sub-title was "Chevalerie d'Institutions et Règles Catholiques d'Union Indépendant et Tradionaliste" (Chivalry of Catholic Rules and Institutions of the Independent and Traditionalist Union), of which the initials are "CIRCUIT", the name of the organisation's magazine. The early issues are devoted mainly to news of housing associations, but perhaps employed coded information similar to that used by *Vaincre*. The policy was aimed towards the establishment of the national Committees of Public Safety which were instrumental in bringing Charles de Gaulle into power. Plantard maintained that de Gaulle had personally requested him to direct the French Committees of Public Safety, and when their task of installing the General was achieved, to preside over their dissolution.

Circuit supported the French Committees of Public Safety, and in one issue states that no solution to existing problems can be found "...except through new methods and new men...but do there still exist men capable of thinking only of France, as during the Occupation, when patriots and resistance fighters did not bother themselves about the political tendencies of their comrades in the fight". In another issue, Plantard writes "...the United States of Euro-Africa, which represents economically (1) an African and European community of exchange based on a common market, and (2) the circulation of wealth in order to serve the well-being of all, this being the sole stable foundation on which peace can be constructed".

Lincoln says he was given a copy of the Annemasse statutes, but was later told by Jean-Luc Chaumeil that they were spurious. Genuine or not, they conformed very closely to the statutes of Alpha Galates as published in *Vaincre*, and brought Plantard once again before the public eye.

In 1959 *Circuit* lists Pierre Plantard as Director, but now states that it is the official organ of the Federation of French Forces. An address is given in Aulnay-sous-Bois, which is ascribed by Anne Lea Hisler, Plantard's first wife, to the Secretariat-General of the Committees of Public Safety in metropolitan France. Like *Vaincre*, to which it often refers, *Circuit* published articles on chivalry and esoterica. Vines and viticulture also played a prominent part, and it is noticeable that the Dossier Secret uses the grafting of vines as an analogy for bloodlines.

In *The Messianic Legacy* Lincoln states that the Prieuré definitely does exist today, or did when he wrote the book in 1986, and that it continues to play its part in the machinations and intrigue of contemporary politics. In addition, it embodies the concept of chivalry, and is adept at manipulating archetypes. Plantard told him that the Prieuré was in possession of the treasure of the Temple of Jerusalem, looted in AD66, and that it would be returned to Israel "when the time is right". If this were true, the religious and political repercussions would be shattering. When Plantard met Lincoln in March 1970, however, he repeated that the Prieuré did hold the lost treasure of Jerusalem, but that the true treasure was spiritual, and that soon there would be changes in France which would bring about the restoration of the monarchy. The Prieuré claims to be the guardian of "le roi perdu", and the sacred bloodline, and that members are initiates of the secret wisdom tradition. Like the Rosicrucians they are invisible, which in no way lessens their appeal and influence.

Whether or not the Prieuré de Sion or its counterpart existed in the time of Bérenger Saunière, it is obvious that its 20th century incarnation as promulgated by Plantard and de Chérisey was modelled along Rosicrucian lines. It is possible to dismiss as coincidence the hints put forward by de Sède in *Le Trésor Maudit* - the decorations of the Rennes-le-Château church are nothing out of the ordinary, roses and crosses are universal emblems - but Orders of the Rosicrucian type continue to flourish and exercise a universal fascination. Perhaps it is the need of modern society to fill the gap left by the decay of religion and moral values. Mysteries provoke excitement, ritual provides colour and pageantry, chivalry instigates purpose and drive. Secret societies are a way of belonging, offer companionship, and bestow a sense of being special. The appeal of Utopia is eternal. If the pronouncements of organisations like the Rosicrucians and the Prieuré de Sion must be considered as fictitious, we might with benefit regard them as "poetic truth". Frances Yates in *The Rosicrucian Enlightenment* says "...this sense of standing on tiptoe in expectation of new knowledge is most characteristic of the Rosicrucian outlook".

Pierre Plantard died at Colombe in Paris on 3 February 2000, leaving a son and daughter, but there is no evidence of their involvement with the Prieuré de Sion. Perhaps he himself has the last word: "...it is useless for those who do not understand the symbolism of Rennes-le-Château to go there with pick, shovel and detector...one must know the secret to discover there something else..." In the "*Rennes Observer* No.28 his obituary reports that Plantard was born under Pisces, the fish, and notes that fish are notoriously slippery creatures. Just when you think you have one hooked, it can very easily eel-like slip through your fingers.

The Eternal Fountain

In the Prieuré de Sion, Plantard and de Chérisey had the perfect vehicle. The 18th and 19th centuries saw a revival of occultism and the establishment of a positive plethora of occult societies, but this was nothing new.

Modern society thinks it is living in a scientific age, but is it? Somewhere, deep down, the worm of superstition, the desire for "something else", persists. The idea of hidden knowledge, the way of the spirit, dates from before time was.

The "ancient wisdom" has two main sources: Cabala and Hermeticism. In the works of Raymond Lull, the 13th century Catalan mystic, there is an illustration of four men seated beside the fountain of Truth, while Intelligence, depicted as a lady on horseback, fords the adjacent stream of Wisdom. The four men represent Christian, Moslem, Jewish and pagan mysticism.

Cabala, the esoteric teaching of Judaism, traditionally stems from the Archmage Moses, who confounded the magicians of Egypt by turning his magic wand into a serpent, a feat still practised by the Arab entertainers in the main square at Fez. The somewhat lengthy time taken by God to dictate the Covenant to Moses is explained by his also receiving at the same time the mystic inner doctrine of Cabala. Moses had the best PR ever, Jehovah himself, but Cabala probably originated much earlier in Mesopotamia, and was brought to Canaan by the people of Abraham from the Fertile Crescent. The highest grade, Chariot mysticism or the Maaseh Merkabah, was taught only to a chosen few. The work of the Chariot was to glorify God.

The Hermetic tradition takes its name from Hermes Trismegistos, a mythical Egyptian sage who wrote down his philosophy on an emerald tablet. Hermes was the most versatile of the Greek pantheon, and acted mainly as the messenger of the gods. Trismegistos means thrice greatest. The *Corpus Hermeticum* was a collection of tracts dating from between the 1st century BCE and 2nd century CE, consisting mainly of dialogues between Hermes Trismegistos and the Egyptian gods Thoth, Ammon, Isis and Horus. Their teaching owed little to Egypt, and was based on the Orphic hymns, and the works of Aristotle and Plato. In medieval Europe the movement became known as Neo-Platonism.

To this amalgam might be added a spice of Gnosticism, which flourished from roughly the beginning of the Christian era. Gnostics were those who had gnosis (knowledge), not learned, but revealed by grace. Gnostics did not subscribe to any established religion, it was a new and revolutionary movement rebelling against the materialism of this world. They believed in Wisdom (Sophia) as the companion of God, and according to divine will, she brought forth the angels and powers by whom the World was made. Their belief might be summarised as the idea of a divine spark in man, deriving from God, fallen into this world, and needing to be redeemed by reawakening its divine counterpart, thereby achieving reintegration. Although Gnosticism as a religion did not survive beyond the second century CE, it had a considerable influence on the medieval Bogomils, Cathars and Neo-Platonists.

In the 15th century, the works of Plato and the Neo-Platonists were brought from Byzantium to Florence. Neo-Platonism was adopted with enthusiasm by the Medici Court, among whose most brilliant members were Marsilio Ficino and Giovanni Pico della Mirandola. In 1469 Ficino translated the *Corpus Hermeticum*, but in fear of the Inquisition concentrated on natural magic, and eschewed Cabala, which with its angelic hierarchy and conjurations by divine names might be considered heretical. It was Pico della Mirandola who, influenced by the *Sephir Yetzirah* and the Jewish Cabalists who had been driven out of Spain, amalgamated Cabala with the Hermetic tradition and created Christian Cabala.

A few years later Henry Cornelius Agrippa, born in Cologne in 1486, was carrying on the occult tradition of "ancient wisdom", and his *De occulta philosophia* combines Ficino's natural magic with Pico della Mirandola's Christian Cabala. Stigmatised in the 16th and 17th centuries as a black magician and the archetypal necromancer, his work is now regarded as the indispensable handbook of Renaissance magic. His magic in fact is very close to religion, and he was already inclining towards belief in an evangelical church: he invoked only good and holy angelic

influences, made sure that the star demons were made harmless
through their help, and accepted Jesus as the greatest wonder-
working Name. Agrippa travelled extensively, and was believed
to be in touch with various foreign groups as part of an occult
network. The witchcraft hysteria that swept Europe in the 16th
and 17th centuries started with an attack on Renaissance magic,
particularly on Pico della Mirandola and Agrippa, and witch-hunts
were used extensively against politico-religious movements which
the persecutors were determined to eliminate.

Agrippa's work was known and revered by Dr John Dee, the
greatest of the Elizabethan magi. Dee was an astute politician as
well as being an accomplished writer and brilliant magician. He
was a member of Sir Walter Raleigh's "School of Night", to which
the poet and playwright Christopher Marlowe also belonged.
Marlowe, as well as Dee, was an agent of Sir Francis Walsingham.
He was summoned to appear before the Star Chamber, accused
of blasphemy, sodomy and heresy, but before the confrontation
could take place, he was murdered at Deptford in an orchestrated
tavern brawl. He knew too much to be allowed to speak out in
public.

After the disappearance of the Rosicrucian Brotherhood and
the commencement of the Thirty-Years War, the stream of "ancient
wisdom" went underground, to surface again with the institution
of the Freemasonic lodges in the 18th century, and subsequently
the founding of the Martinists, and various Rosicrucian groups.
This movement reached its apogee in France after the Revolution
with pro-royalist organisations purporting to support "le roi
perdu". It was a climate perfectly suited to the idea of a 19th
century Prieuré de Sion, a chivalric religious-magical group
claiming provenance dating from the Templars, aimed at the
redemption and renewal of France. Its grafting onto the Rennes-
le-Château mystery was dramatically right. Saunière's story
provided mystery and excitement, midnight excursions to the
graveyard, a cast of important and glamorous people, secret
meetings, murder and mayhem. All it required to complete the

romance was an occult guiding intelligence. The Prieuré provided this, and added hidden treasure and a royal bloodline. Plantard and de Chérisey had the perfect set-up for a best-seller, which first de Sède and later the authors of *The Holy Blood and the Holy Grail* were quick to recognise.

ᚦe ᚦraumatic ᛦears

In 1720 a unique stranger appeared in the Paris salons. He called himself the Comte de Saint-Germain, and was believed to be the younger son of a Transylvanian prince. He dressed always in black, his jewellery limited to a prolific display of diamonds. He reputedly spoke every European language as well as Chinese, Arabic and Sanskrit, played the pianoforte and the violin, was an accomplished painter, and was suspected of being an alchemist. He said he was ageless, and had studied the ancient mysteries in the East. He supported Bonnie Prince Charlie's rebellion in 1745, and was imprisoned in England for a time as a spy. He was a Freemason, and had been initiated by Cagliostro using a Templar ritual.

How much of this is true is open to question. What is obvious is that he was a very clever showman, and created for himself a legend on a par with that of Appollonius of Tyana, the Greek magus, and the legendary Christian Rosencreuz. In the Age of Enlightenment, and particularly in ultra-rational France, it is extraordinary how successful he was, but it is a fact that human beings are very suggestible, and susceptible to glamour.

Most of the leading occultists of the 18th century were Freemasons, and Martines de Pasqually was no exception. He was born in the parish of Nôtre-Dame in Grenoble, and although a practising Catholic, was probably a Spanish Jew which may account for his occult interests. Following tradition, he visited the East and Egypt to acquire wisdom. In 1754 he founded the Society of Scottish Judges in Montpellier, based on Freemasonry, but the idea did not "take". In 1760 he reorganised the sect as the Order of the Elect Cohens to practise ceremonial magic based on the

Catholic mass and the teachings of Cornelius Agrippa. The object
was to spread "true Judaism", that is, Cabala. Initiates were
required to meditate, refrain from eating meat, and to practise
chastity and moderation. These tenets are familiar from Cathar
doctrine. The movement grew rapidly, and centres were
established at Foix (1760), Bordeaux (1761), Paris (1767), Lyon
(1768), with temples at Amboise, Tours, Blois and Poitiers. This
was Cathar country - the Count of Foix was one of the main
supporters of the Cathars during the Albigensian crusade. In
1774 Pasqually went to Port au Prince in the Caribbean and never
returned. In 1781 the Elect Cohens lapsed and were closed by
order of the last Grand Master, Sebastian de las Casas.

One of Pasqually's most ardent disciples was a young Army
Officer named Louis Claude de St Martin. He was initiated into
the Elect Cohens at Bordeaux somewhere between 3rd August
and 2nd October 1768, and in 1771 he left the Army to devote all
his time to studying occultism. He acted as Pasqually's secretary
and was largely responsible for collating and simplifying the
master's writings on Gnosticism, Cabala and Hermeticism. By
1774 he was living in Paris and preaching his own brand of
mysticism, which envisaged an ideal society governed by men
chosen by God, who would regard themselves as "divine
commissioners" to guide the people. Writing under the name of
"The Unknown Philosopher", his major influence was Jacob
Boehme, the 17th century German mystic, whom he regarded as
"the greatest light to appear on earth since the One who is the
Light itself". He was a strict Catholic, although his first book, "Of
Errors and Truth" was placed on the Index. St Martin died in
1803, but there is no public record of his death and burial. Nothing
more was heard of him until Papus resurrected his legend when
founding the Martinists.

The poet and novelist, Jacques Cazotte, may have been a
member of the Elect Cohens. He was an accomplished clairvoyant,
and at a dinner party in 1788 he prophesied the Revolution. This
perhaps demonstrates his political acumen rather than his magical

abilities, in view of the storming of the Bastille barely a year later. Cazotte was present at a Masonic lodge when Cagliostro, using numerology, predicted that Louis XVI and Marie Antoinette would end on the scaffold. When Cazotte asked Cagliostro who would succeed the King, Cagliostro gave only a number and said the man would end "pacing the circle of a melancholy island". The numerical value of the letters allegedly corresponded to the name of Napoleon Bonaparte.

With the coming of the Revolution, Catholicism was abolished. In 1792 the Legislative Assembly ordered that an altar to the Fatherland should be set up in every commune, engraved with the Declaration of the Rights of Man, and inscribed with the words "The citizen is born, lives and dies for the Fatherland".

A year later, the worship of Reason was established. Adrien Dansette, in his *Religious History of Modern France*, describes one such scene.

A temple, dedicated to Philosophy, was erected on a circular rock in the choir of Notre Dame in Paris. Half way up the rock burned "The Flame of Truth". On 10 November the members of the Commune gathered, and a number of girls marched up and down beside the Temple, saluting the "Flame". An actress from the Opera representing the goddess Reason, dressed in white, with a blue cloak and a red bonnet, entered from the Temple and sat down on a grass-covered throne, while the girls sang a hymn. Reason was then hoisted onto the shoulders of four stalwarts, and they all set off in procession for the Convention.

Similar rituals were performed in many other churches throughout France which had been converted into Temples of Reason. In 1794 Anaxagoras Chaumette, the main protagonist of the cult of Reason, went to the guillotine. Perhaps not surprisingly! The return to a kind of deist religion followed, which recognised the predominance of a Supreme Being, but when Robespierre was executed on 27 July 1794, the Supreme Being also died, to be followed by five years of atheistic anarchy.

In 1795 the Directory took control, and in 1796 the Theophilantropes began, which included basic religious tenets that everybody could believe, and was an attempt to find the lowest common denominator of all religions and sects. This was in many ways the forerunner of Theosophy which was established in France in 1875, and with which Theophilantropes shared a belief in mysterious Oriental Masters. The Theophilantropes prospered for a time, and attracted several prominent intellectuals and politicians, but its policy became too Leftwing, and the Government withdrew its support. Public interest waned, and in due course the Theophilantropes quietly folded.

In 1799 Napoleon seized power and re-established Catholicism. It was a signal for the return of the Magi, and the initiation of the French Occult Revival.

The Return of the Magi

By the late 18th and early 19th century, France was ready and waiting for a new revelation. It was a time of disillusion and uncertainty. The bloody horrors of the Revolution, the ineffectual rule of the Restoration and the Directory, and the waste of manpower and money spent on the Napoleonic wars in Europe, had resulted in moral decadence and political corruption, followed by unemployment, poverty, industrial unrest and social collapse. In times of national tribulation, there is inevitably a turning away from material values towards consolation of the spirit. There was a strong Catholic revival, but churches were derelict, priests dead or deported. This was fertile ground for the propagation of alternative religions. Freemasonry thrived, and alongside the established Roman church there grew up a number of organisations, and the emergence of occult writers and thinkers, that in various ways drew on the "ancient wisdom", adapting and re-presenting it in a way suitable for the contemporary scene.

In 1773 a slightly suspect Protestant theologian from Languedoc called Court de Gébelin published his multi-volume work, *Le Monde primitif*, detailing current trends in occultism. De Gébelin claimed he had been cured of various health problems by the maverick Austrian doctor Franz Mesmer, who practised animal magnetism, and attempted to harmonize the flow of fluids within the human body with the motions of the planets. De Gébelin claimed that Mesmer had completely rejuvenated his feet which had been icy cold for twenty-five years. The medical profession ostracised Mesmer as a fraud, but apparently he did have some real cures, specifically in cases of nervous origin.

De Gébelin's feet became a joke, but his book, although regarded by scholars as simplistic, was popular, and a copy was presented to Louis XVI. In 1776 he joined the Freemasons, and was later President of a Paris lodge. His one useful contribution to the occult scene was his promotion of Tarot cards which he believed were of ancient Egyptian origin. It was upon de Gébelin's work that Etteilla, whose pseudonym was the reversal of his real name Alliette, based his original and still popular version of Tarot. It was a trend that Eliphas Lévi was to perpetuate.

Lévi's revolutionary discovery about Tarot was that the twenty-two cards of the major arcana corresponded perfectly to the three Mother letters, seven double and twelve single letters of the Hebrew alphabet; the four suits of the minor arcana to the four elements and four worlds of creation; and the ten numbered cards of each suit to the ten sephiroth of the Tree of Life. Lévi was thereby able to correlate Tarot and Cabala for the first time. Dr Gérard Encausse, the founder of the resurrected Martinists, was a great admirer of Lévi, and his definitive book on Tarot was founded on Lévi's theories.

Eliphas Lévi's real name was Alphonse-Louis Constant, and he was born in Paris on 8 February 1810, the son of a shoemaker. He grew up in a poor but happy family, and was fortunate enough to gain a free place in the School of St. Louis en l'Ile. He became an ordinand at St Sulpice, and was made sub-deacon in 1832, but never made the final commitment. At the age of twenty-six he abandoned the priesthood to continue his occult studies, but remained a practising Catholic, and on occasion served as an auxiliary priest as Abbé Baucourt. His theology was somewhat unorthodox. Writing on Christian glory in *The Book of Splendours*, he says: "Catholic dogma...has been imposed without the acceptance of the free concourse of reason... If someone tells me, for example, that a virgin has become a mother while remaining a virgin, that a child has come out of her as a ray of sunlight that passes through a crystal without breaking it, I respect the image, but I cannot, unless I were a fool, believe that it is a question of a material and natural childbirth, for I know that such circumstances cannot be... If we read in the symbolic statement of Nicaea that the son of God was born of the father before the beginning of all time, and if we are simultaneously taught that he is eternal like the father, we must understand that this birth has nothing whatsoever to do with a normal, material one, since it is a question of a birth that is not even a beginning..."

Lévi wrote prolifically, and in 1841 was imprisoned at St. Pelagie, Paris, for publishing subversive literature. In 1846 he married 16-year-old Noémi Cadicot. Having presented him with three children, Noémi left him in 1853, unable any longer to tolerate his preoccupation with magic, and in 1865 she obtained her divorce. Lévi became a Freemason in 1861, and in March that year was initiated into the Rose of Perfect Silence Lodge.

He was deeply shocked by the defeat of France in the Franco Prussian war and the fall of the Second Empire, for he regarded his country as the saviour of civilisation. During the Siege of Paris he lived alone in the rue de Sèvres, and suffered great privation which seriously undermined his health. He died on 31 May 1875 and was buried in the cemetery at Ivry. The funeral oration was given by his friend Henri Deyrolle, and concluded: "...rest in peace and may the sincere grief of your friends be proof of the void which you have left among them. Adieu! adieu! and perhaps au revoir!"

Lévi believed the purpose of magic was not to conjure spirits, but to enable the magician to direct his own will to the greatest effect, in order to become a more fully realised human being.

However, he was not above indulging in practical magical evocations, and claimed to have contacted the spirit of Apollonius of Tyana. He considered that the reign of the Son had achieved its purpose, and that the reign of the Holy Spirit was about to begin. He prophesied that in 1879 "a universal empire will be founded and will secure peace to the world". On another occasion, he declared that "Enoch will appear in the year 2000 of the Christian world, then the Messianism of which he will be the precursor, will flourish on the earth for a thousand years." Although perhaps a little way-out in his prognostications, there is no doubt that Lévi's influence on his contemporary thinkers was profound.

The young genius, Arthur Rimbaud, was first attracted to occultism through Lévi's work, which he regarded as a protest against established authority, something he well understood, being possessed of a conventional but tyrannical mother. He was born in 1854 at Charleville, and was seventeen when his first book of poems was published. Shortly afterwards he met Charles Brétigny, a customs official with a strong interest in occultism, and went to live with him in Paris. Based on his studies of magic, mysticism and Cabala, Rimbaud developed a philosophy of life, the object of which was to become an "illumine" by achieving oneness with the absolute through self annihilation, in which he regarded himself as successful. His purpose then was to communicate this vision through his poetry, which required a new language wherein words could represent the quality of the things they expressed. This language Rimbaud found in alchemy, inner-plane correspondences, and the "barbarbous names of power".

Alchemy, of which Gérard Encausse's friend Albert Poisson was a leading practitioner, was the "in" preoccupation with Parisian occultists of the period, but authors were drawing on all branches of the esoteric sciences for inspiration. Gérard de Nerval was another poet whose work is full of magical imagery. Although he was acquainted with the artists associated with the symbolist circle, and collaborated with Dumas père in playwriting, he belonged more to the romantic than the symbolist movement. At the age of twenty-eight he fell in love with actress Jenny Colon, who was not at all interested. When she married someone else, de Nerval had his first breakdown, and recovered only to find that she had died. In the authentic tradition of the magus, he travelled to Germany and the Near East in search of knowledge, in the company of Théophile Gautier. His life was plagued with intermittent periods of harmless madness, and one of his pleasures was to walk naked through the Palais Royale gardens leading a lobster by a pink ribbon. Finally he committed suicide by hanging himself on the railings in a little street near the Châtelet, using an apron string which he believed was the Queen of Sheba's garter. In spite, or because of his eccentricities, de Nerval's work raises the authentic shiver that is the mark of a true poet.

The priest and the pretender

Among the serious thinkers and writers of this time there were also many eccentrics. One of the more spectacular of these was Pierre Michel Eugene Vintras, a contemporary of Eliphas Lévi's. He was born in 1807 at Bayeux, Normandy. His parents were poor, and he consequently received little education, but he was intelligent and hardworking, and by his own efforts rose to be the manager of a small cardboard-box factory at Tilly-sur-Seule. In 1839 he met a dubious lawyer named Ferdinand Geoffroi, and through him became an adherent of the Pretender Karl William Naundorff, who claimed he was Louis XVII, son of Louis XVI, having survived the Revolution. Vintras believed the restoration of the monarchy would bring about a golden age, and he firmly supported Naundorff's candidature all his life.

Vintras had been brought up in a devout family, and early on began to receive visions of the Archangel Michael. Later he saw the Virgin and St. Joseph, who instructed him to gather together a band of disciples, and preach a new gospel to be known as "The Work of Mercy". He would thereby save the world from disaster and institute a new Kingdom of God. Accordingly, he set up an oratory at the cardboard-box factory, where he kept blood-stained Hosts which he said were sent to him by people who wished to save them from profanation by the evil-minded. A number of physicians certified that the stains were human blood. The Hosts were certainly stained with matter which could not be identified, and it has been suggested by modern analytical chemists that they were perhaps contaminated with some sort of fungus that defied classification, which being organic prevented their being condemned as fraudulent.

Vintras soon collected a considerable following, but in 1841 the Bishop of Bayeux condemned his practises as contrary to church dogma, followed by an official reprimand from Pope Gregory XVI. The Government was also worried about the amount of support Naundorff was receiving through the movement. A year later Geoffroi was accused of defrauding two maiden ladies of 3000 francs, and in spite of the representations of the victims, Vintras was sentenced to five years' imprisonment. In 1848 his sect was declared heretical, and he was excommunicated. He fled to Belgium and then to London, where he set up a new centre at 33 Marylebone Road, and continued to preach his gospel, and to wage a campaign against black magic. In 1863 he returned to France, and died at Lyon on 7 December 1875.

The Advent of the Holy Spirit

In 1884 Madame Blavatsky, the founder of the Theosophical Society, burst upon the Parisian scene, with the intention of conducting a recruiting campaign. A branch of the Society already existed, founded and run by Lady Caithness, Duchesse de Pomar, a wealthy woman who believed she was the reincarnation of Mary Queen of Scots. The promotion went quite well and enough new members joined to make regular meetings feasible, but Theosophy never attracted the sort of wide-spread popularity in France that it had attained in America or Britain.

At a meeting of the Isis Lodge in 1888, Colonel Olcott, Mme Blavatsky's right-hand man, announced that "M. Encausse, who had been initiated the previous October, had been elected to the General Council of the Theosophical Society".

The ubiquitous Gérard Encausse, who later became universally known by his pen-name Papus, had rather more than one finger in most of the magical pies of the period. He was born at Coruña, Spain, on 13 July 1865. His father was French, his mother Spanish. He enrolled in the Faculty of Medicine, Paris, in 1884, and took his doctor's degree in 1894. The unusually long period it took him to become qualified was due to the amount of time he spent on occult studies, writing and travelling around Europe, and at the date of his admission to the Theosophical Society he was still a medical student.

In 1895 he is listed among the members of the Golden Dawn's Ahathoor Lodge which Annie Horniman had consecrated in Paris the previous year in order to celebrate the rites of Isis. Ellic Howe, the historian of The Golden Dawn, says that a number of Golden Dawn members were Martinists, Encausse's own brotherhood, their ideas and aims being compatible.

Encausse was a Freemason, and a member of the Cabalistic Order of the Rosy Cross, which was headed by Marquis Stanislas de Guaita and Josephin Péladan. Initiatory succession was through Péladan, Abbé Lacuria, and Eliphas Lévi, who had been initiated into the English Rosicrucians in London in 1853 by Edward Bulwer Lytton. The "English Rosicrucians" presumably refers to the Society of Rosicrucia in Anglia, a higher Masonic degree to which Lytton, and also Wynn Westcott, the creator of the Golden Dawn manifesto, both belonged. Among Papus' friends were Debussy, Wilde, Yeats, Gide and Proust. One of their favourite meeting places was Edmond Bailly's bookshop in the rue d'Antin.

In 1891 Encausse helped to found Jules Doinel's neo-Cathar church at Carcassonne, which was consecrated by an Eastern bishop of obscure denomination in the living room of the Paris apartment belonging to Theosophist Lady Caithness, wife of Sir

James Sinclair. The church was "Gnostic catholic", and Doinel proclaimed himself Gnostic Bishop of Mirapoix. Papus also became a bishop, and took over when Doinel retired in 1895. The church was later run by Fabre des Essarts, a poet of the Symbolist movement, who called himself the Patriarch Synesius. There was said to be a Cathar pope still living at Arques, near Rennes-les-Bains, up to 1940.

It was in 1888 that Papus met a professed alchemist, St Yves d'Alveydre, who claimed to be Grand Master of the Martinists, but there is no evidence that his organisation had any direct descent from the original Elect Cohens. Four years after Pasqually disappeared to the Caribbean, one of his disciples, Jean Baptiste Willermoz, tried to establish the Order of the Holy City at Lyon with the intention of perpetuating Pasqually's teachings, but it aroused little interest, and the idea was soon abandoned.

One small point of interest is the coincidence that Bacon de la Chevalerie, the Deputy of the Elect Cohens, wrote to Brother Marquis de Chefdebien on 5 August 1807, deploring the lack of activity in carrying out the orders of the Grand Master. Chefdebien was founder of the Philadèlphes Masonic lodge, and it was with his grandson that Saunière's brother Alfred took service as tutor. It is notable that money listed in Saunière's accounts as coming from Alfred probably did, in fact, come from Chefdebien. Alfred, as well as Bérenger Saunière, could have been associated with the Martinists who, rightly or wrongly, claimed descent from the Elect Cohens.

D'Alveydre, whose real name was Joseph-Alexandre Saint-Yves, had written a number of books mixing politics and occultism, in which he proposed an ideal society ruled by an intellectual elite. In *Le Monde invisible*, Jules Bois describes meeting with d'Alveydre at his house in Paris. "He was in the habit of sitting against the light to give a more profound impression... He had beautiful grey hair, a sly smile, hands loaded with rings, and was dressed in a frock coat. He told me, with the appearance of serious conviction, that he had written 400 pages in three days and that he communicated by telepathy with the Grand Lama of Tibet..." D'Alveydre also claimed to be in constant touch with his dead wife, and a place for her continued to be laid at his table for all meals.

Papus had already set up a study group called Groupe Indépendant d'Etudes Esotériques, and this soon became integrated with d'Alveydre's neo-Martinists. The new Order attracted considerable attention, and lodges multiplied. In 1899 Papus went to St Petersburg to found a Russian Martinist lodge. Through his friend Philippe de Lyon he was introduced to the Tsar and Tsarina, and became acquainted with Rasputin. He visited Russia again in 1900 and 1906. Many people, including the Russian royal family, believed that it was his power alone that held at bay the disaster threatening their country, and that with his death the protecting shield was broken.

Papus was able successfully to combine his occult and medical work, the former giving him a special expertise in diagnosis. In 1913 the Hermanubis Lodge issued a proclamation that twice a week, on Wednesday and Sunday, Martinists were invited to meditate on the supreme force, Love, and intercede to the Master Christ for the relief and cure of the sick.

At the outbreak of World War One, Papus joined the Army Medical Corps and served at a hospital on the Western Front, where he contracted tuberculosis, of which he died on 25 October 1916. He is buried in the cemetery of Père Lachaise in Paris, and his well kept grave names him as Grand Master of the Martinists, which office he had been granted in perpetuity.

Through his occult connections, after Eliphas Lévi's death Papus was able to acquire a number of Lévi's manuscripts as well as his ceremonial sword and some of his robes, which are still in the possession of the modern Martinists at their headquarters in Paris. He was instrumental in getting *The Book of Splendours* published posthumously, and included in it a lengthy appendix in appreciation and explanation of Lévi's beliefs, many of which are a reasonable gloss of Martinist teaching.

There is also an observable parallel between Martinism and Catharism, according to what little we know of Cathar doctrine. They have common elements. Both use St John's Gospel as their bible, and preach the Risen and Healing Christ rather than the earthly Jesus of the synoptic gospels. J. B. Phillips, the translator of the *New Testament into Modern English* puts the date of St John between 90 and 110 CE, and most bible scholars agree that the author was not the apostle, John bar-Zebedee, and remains unknown. St John's Gospel deals almost entirely with the great themes of life, light, love and truth, which are reflected in the theology of both Cathar and Martinist.

Ᏽhe Ᏸᴀᴛᴛʟe oꜰ ᴛhe Roses

The secret societies of that period formed a close, practically incestuous network. They shared a considerable number of members, and claimed in common a desire to improve the life both of the individual and of mankind as a whole, and the coming of a new Kingdom.

The Cabalistic Order of the Rosy Cross was one of the leading occult societies of the time. Marquis Stanislas de Guaita was born on 6 April 1861 in Lorraine, and was educated by the Jesuits. He was a poet, with three volumes of verse to his credit, and in Paris he soon became immersed in the life of the Latin Quarter. It was after reading the works of Eliphas Lévi that de Guaita became interested in occultism, and then in 1893 he met Josephin Péladan in a cafe in Montmartre.

Péladan was an eccentric ex-bank clerk who loved dressing up, and would appear in public clothed in anything from a monk's robe to medieval doublet and hose. He called himself the Sar Merodack Péladan, Sar meaning King in Assyrian, and Merodack being a gloss on the name of Marduck, a Chaldean god associated with the planet Jupiter. He was a prolific writer, and featured in one of his own occult erotic stories as Merodack the magician, a followed of Marquis de Sade.

Having read Péladin's novel, *Le Vice Supreme*, de Guaita contacted him asking for a meeting, which after some coy skirmishing was granted, and the two became friends. In 1888 they jointly founded the Cabalistic Order of the Rosy Cross, whose threefold aims were to study occultism, enter into spiritual communion with the Divine through meditation, and to spread the word among the uninitiated.

Péladan was a devout Catholic, and soon became disenchanted with the Rosy Cross, some of whose activities, which included spiritualism, Freemasonry and Buddhism, he regarded as pagan. Accordingly he resigned, and initiated his own Order of the Catholic Rose Cross the Temple and the Grail, with the declared intention of once again reuniting Catholicism with occultism. But it was to be more than just an occult society. He envisaged a group from which would emanate a new set of religious, moral and aesthetic values, for which purpose he set up a series of annual salons that promoted the pictorial arts, theatre and music.

De Guaita took strong exception to this rival organisation. He also objected to Péladan's extreme antipathy to all things German, being himself a great devotee of German literature, to Péladan's devotion to astrology, in which he did not believe, and to what he considered to be Péladan's amorous excesses. "Your soul is perpetually haunted and obsessed by ridiculous sentimental cravings" he protested "can you not live for one week without your spirit being preoccupied with these futilities?" Receiving no reaction to this, on 13 August 1891 he wrote saying "...we can have nothing to do with the acts of wilful madness which you have been perpetrating... furthermore, your "Letter to Papus" and your Declaration of "Exodus" contain errors of fact which it is necessary for us to deny..." Péladan accused de Guaita of creating a storm in a teacup, and asked for a meeting to discuss the problem. De Guaita wrote again in somewhat stronger terms, stating that conversation would solve nothing.

Péladan ignored all this rodomontade, his salons were successful, and his Order continued to prosper. In 1893 de Guaita publicly denounced Péladan as having "shamelessly usurped the title and emblem of the Rose Cross, to drag its revered name and symbol through every contradiction and ridicule..." and declared Péladan to be a schismatic and apostate Rosicrucian. Papus signed this denunciation as Delegate General of the Cabalistic Order of the Rosy Cross, but later recanted, and in 1900 wrote in an article for *Les Sciences Maudites* saying "...Josephin Péladan, that admirable artist to whom the future will render justice at the final reckoning...took the head of a movement to spiritualise aestheticism, whose fruits are only now beginning to be apparent, and which will have profound repercussions on contemporary art".

De Guaita was not entirely paranoid in his obsession with defamation of himself and his Society. He was accused of being involved in killing Abbé Boullan, who featured in J-K Huysmans' occult novel *La-Bas* as Dr Johannes, a white magician, although he was believed by many to be very definitely "black". A minor art critic called Philippe Auquier, and a great admirer of Boullan, hinted in Boullan's obituary of 7 January 1893 that de Guaita and his Rosicrucians might have had something to do with Boullan's death. Huysmans himself and his friend Jules Bois were more explicit, and publicly accused de Guaita of murdering Boullan. Bois was the editor of *L'Echo du Merveilleux*.

De Guaita responded in his usual rather hysterical declamatory fashion. He wrote "For several days now the press has been spreading certain pieces of gossip about me which in fact reflect less on me than on the malicious or naive people who have launched the rumours that dog me so relentlessly." He goes on to complain that it had been said his Rosicrucian College was dedicated to Satanism, and that he himself was accused of "the most odious practices of sorcery", that he used spells mixed with subtle poisons and toxic vapours to kill anyone who displeased him, and that he kept prisoner in his cupboard a familiar spirit who emerged only at his command. "Is this enough!" he demands, "No. All these fine details are nothing but a preamble, the main contention being that the ex-Abbé Boullan, the Lyon thaumaturge whose recent death caused something of a stir, only succumbed because of my efforts combined with those of my black colleagues, the brothers of the Rosy Cross".

He denied that Boullan died of anything but a weak heart and diseased liver, and challenged Huysmans and Jules Bois to a duel on account of the "evil lies" that they had spread about him. Wishing to avoid any scandal, both Huysmans and Bois apologised through their Seconds, but a few months later Bois repeated his accusations, and no conciliation being possible, he and de Guaita fought with pistols. Bois was later challenged to a duel by Papus who was a skilled swordsman, in which Bois was slightly wounded.

Joseph-Antoine Boullan was born on 18 January 1824, and was certainly one of the more colourful figures of the occult revival. He was a genuine priest, at one time the Principal of the House of the Missionaries of the Precious Blood in Alsace. In 1856 he went to Paris where he became the spiritual director of a young nun named Adele Chevalier, who was given to receiving remarkable visions. In 1839 Boullan and Sister Chevalier founded their own community, known as the Society for the Reparation of Souls, at Bellevue near Paris. Soon rumours began to circulate that they were dispensing fraudulent medicines, that they were lovers, and had sacrificed a child born of the liaison in a black mass. In 1861 they were accused of fraud and Boullan went to prison for three years. Five years later he was in trouble with the Holy Office in Rome, but on confessing was rehabilitated. Back in Paris he was soon again attracting attention, accused of holding heretical views and improperly exorcising evil spirits, and in 1875 he was placed under a solemn interdict by the Archbishop of Paris. Boullan retaliated by leaving the church.

About this time he met Eugene Vintras, the prophet of the famous blood-stained Hosts, and in the face of some opposition, shortly afterwards took over as head of the Sect when Vintras died. Undaunted, he next settled in Lyon with a small group which included his housekeeper, Julie Thibault, otherwise known as the Apostolic Woman. Julie was an unlikely prophetess, being described as "a little middle-aged woman in a bonnet and a cheap black dress, clutching an umbrella and a prayer book, with a tin crucifix hanging from her neck and a pair of pince-nez on the end of her nose." She appears, however, to have been a lady of some determination, having for many years walked 25,000 miles all over Europe visiting shrines of the Virgin Mary, carrying only her umbrella and a bundle of clothes, and living on nothing but bread, milk and honey.

The aim of the new group was to spread the doctrine of love, and activities were centred around secret rituals involving sexual intercourse, both with other initiates and with celestial spirits It was into this coterie that de Guaita came, humbly kneeling at the feet of the Apostolic Woman, but whether he was sincere or merely gathering information to be used later against Boullan is not certain. Inevitably he rushed into denunciation. With another initiate, Oswald Wirth, who had deliberately penetrated Boullan's group as a spy, he set up an initiatory tribunal to judge Boullan, and declared him guilty. They jointly wrote to Boullan stating that "true Initiates will tolerate no longer your profanation of the Cabala...and your mixing of the dung of your profligate imagination with the exalted doctrines of the Masters of Wisdom... You are condemned...the sentence remains suspended over your head until the day when, for lack of any more merciful means, its application will become inevitable." Not surprisingly, Boullan considered this letter a declaration of war, and it played a significant part in the accusations later made against de Guaita regarding Boullan's death.

Five years later de Guaita, suffering from a blood disease, died of a drugs overdose. Péladan died in 1918. Huysmans, prompted in part by his knowledge of Boullan's behaviour, abandoned occultism and converted to Catholicism, becoming an oblate attached to a Benedictine monastery.

Followers of Vintras who refused to recognised Boullan, regrouped under Edouard Souleillon at Champigny-sur-Seine, and they also had two chapels in Paris. They claimed to be perpetuating the true faith, and awaited the coming of a new age of the Holy Spirit. Pierre Geyraud, writing in *Les Religions nouvelles de Paris* in 1939, said that he had attended a Vintras ceremony, which indicates that the sect had survived at least until the outbreak of World War Two. This, which may or may not have been the traditional Vintrasian "Sacrifice of Glory", took place in a room in a private flat. The altar was a chest of drawers, covered by a red cloth, on which were placed a champagne glass, a small plate containing Hosts - though presumably not the celebrated blood-stained ones - and a lighted candle. Above hung a portrait of Vintras and a cloth embroidered with the Tetragrammaton. The celebrant was barefooted, and dressed in a long red chasuble covered by a white cloth cross, hanging below his belly to signify the "crucifixion of the phallus". His wife acted as assistant, also barefooted, dressed in a white tunic and green cape. The congregation consisted of Geyraud and two other worshippers.

The celebrant recited prayers and invoked the Archangel Michael, his wife giving the responses. The champagne glass was filled with white wine, and another ordinary glass with red. The celebrant pointed at Geyraud and muttered a long exorcism. He then took a Host, broke it into two pieces, and burnt the edge of each piece in the candle flame, saying "Here is the communion of bread and fire". He offered a piece to Geyraud who, to his consternation, politely refused it. The celebrant and his wife then each drank the wine - he the white, she the red, and there followed more prayers and an invocation of the Holy Spirit. This closed the ceremony.

Geyraud gives a glimpse of one other Rosicrucian group which he mentions as listed in Paul Sedir's 1910 *Histoire des Rose Croix*, called the F.T.L. and reputed to have been founded in 1898. Like the original Rosicrucians, there is no location or contact address. All Geyraud's effort to find out about F.T.L. met blind alleys, but he says he did meet one man who worked in films, but who refused to provide any information. "None the less", he says, "I have been able to find out that its present head is M.C...., a friend of Barlet who was Grand Master of the Cabalistic Order of the Rosy Cross that has a branch at Bordeaux called the Saint-Graal; and that its founder was ... Sedir himself".

It is tempting to imagine that the man in films was Jean Cocteau, prominent writer, actor, film-maker and occultist, and who is listed in the Dossier Secret as the penultimate Grand Master of the Prieuré de Sion. Two other famous writers precede him, Victor Hugo and Charles Nodier.

Hugo, in fact, was a spiritualist rather than an occultist, brought to the practice by grief at the death of his daughter in 1843, which led him to endeavour to communicate with the dead. His work does, however, show that he was familiar with Cabala and the theories of Swedenborg, and his poetry reveals him as a prophet, believing himself to be endowed with a special mission to be a channel for the divine light. His occult knowledge was undoubtedly obtained from his friend and contemporary writer Charles Nodier, and he probably knew Eliphas Lévi through the Rosicrucians.

Victor Marie Hugo was the most prolific of all French writers. He was born in 1802 in Besançon, and according to himself he was of distinguished aristocratic descent. His first play was written at the age of fourteen, and was followed by an almost endless stream of drama, poetry, and novels. When only seventeen he founded a publishing house in association with Nodier, whose work he admired, and they issued their own magazine of which Nodier was editor. In 1822 Hugo was married in St Sulpice, Paris. 1825 saw the two friends, with their wives, on a prolonged visit to Switzerland, but later that year they travelled back to Paris together to attend the coronation of Charles X.

Hugo was a staunch Royalist, in favour of the restoration of the Bourbons, but his loyalty was to the Orléanist King of the French,

Louis-Philippe, who was a personal friend, rather than to the legitimate line. With Louis Napoleon's coup of 1851, Hugo fled into exile in Brussels before moving with his family to St Helier, Jersey, where in a little house overlooking the sea he held his first séance, with his son Charles acting as medium. He believed he was successful in communicating with his daughter, and this was followed by conversations with several illustrious writers, including Shakespeare, Molière, Dante and Aeschylus. Shakespeare was his most frequent contact, and Hugo had the temerity to ask him if he was still writing on the astral plane. Shakespeare replied that the question was invalid. "Heaven would be incomplete if I were able to create anything" he said, "a masterpiece would usurp God". Nonetheless, he apparently relented, and dictated some poetry to Hugo in French, which he said was superior to the English language. From then on, Shakespeare apparently always communicated in French. Aeschylus and Molière also dictated verses, and conversations between Hugo and these illustrious ghosts were always conducted in the familiar "tu". After a while Hugo became nervous and abandoned the séances.

With the fall of the Second Empire, Hugo returned to Paris in 1870, and was made a Senator in 1876. When he died in 1885 he was given a national funeral.

Charles Nodier was a not particularly good novelist, essayist and short-story writer, but nonetheless he was a popular one. He was immensely erudite, wrote in the tradition of E.T.A. Hoffmann, and earned the right to be buried in Père Lachaise cemetery among the famous. He was already considered something of a literary celebrity when in 1824 he was appointed Chief Librarian of the Arsénal Library, a treasury of manuscripts dating from the earliest times, reputedly owning the alchemical works of Nicholas Flamel, and actually containing the library of Cardinal Richelieu which included many important magical, cabalist and hermetic books. There was also a vast collection of papers from the Vatican, plundered by Napoleon in 1810, and the collections of various monasteries destroyed during the Revolution.

To all this material Nodier had unlimited access. It was his job to sort and catalogue it, and among his assistants were Eliphas Lévi and Jean Baptiste Pitois, whose *History and Practice of Magic* became the seminal 19th century magical textbook.

Among Nodier's later writing is his non-fiction multi-volume appraisal of *Ancient French Sites*, which includes previously disregarded information on the Merovingians, and sections on the Templars and the strange episode of the "cutting of the elm" at Gisor. In 1815 he published anonymously the *History of Secret Societies in the Army*, which may or may not be fiction, but which implies that such societies were involved in the downfall of Napoleon. As a contemporary of Lévi, Nodier could not help but be involved with Parisian occult societies, and he admitted to being a member of the Philadèlphes Masonic Lodge.

It has been suggested by some academics that Nodier was the author - at least in part - of *The Saragossa Manuscript*, generally attributed to a mad Polish Count named Jan Potocki. It tells the story of a soldier during the Napoleonic war in Spain who takes refuge in a haunted inn, and the adventures that befall him there, which take the form of a series of exotic and erotic episodes that open out within each other like a magician's box of tricks. It is a bitter satire on the mores and manners of the post-Napoleonic era, and also the story of a man's search for his own identity. The book is unfinished, and provides no easy answers - it is for the reader to reach a solution. The original manuscript is in French, and was apparently published in St Petersburg in 1805 when Potocki was attached to the Court of Tsar Alexander I, but it was not published in Paris until 1813. It is totally different from anything else Potocki wrote, both in style and content, which has thrown doubt on his authorship.

Jan Potocki was an eccentric member of the Polish aristocracy: a Freemason, soldier, scientist, author, occultist and spy, a serious ethnologist and historian, and a pioneer of archaeology. He was an enthusiastic traveller and took part in the first voyage by balloon. Gossip said he committed incest with his two daughters.

In 1815, for no apparent reason, he shot himself with a consecrated bullet fashioned from a silver strawberry taken from the lid of a jam pot, which suggests that he believed himself to be supernaturally possessed. There is really no reason to attribute the work to Nodier, except that it fits his particular style of fantastic eroticism and political affiliations, and like his novels is a fascinating story untidily told, and taps a wide area of occult knowledge, including Tarot and Cabala.

Nodier was one of those flamboyant characters who are born to be catalysts, rather than creators in their own right. He was gregarious, and liked to be the centre of attention, but he obviously had charisma, because his salons at the Arsénal attracted many of the most important poets, artists and writers of the time including, in addition to his particular friend Victor Hugo; Balzac, Delacroix, Dumas père, Lamartine, Musset, Théophile Gautier and Gérard de Nerval.

His influence on the artistic elite of the later 19th century was enormous, and peaked around the 1890's when Claude Debussy was the alleged Grand Master of the Prieuré de Sion, and Saunière initiated the work that was to transform Rennes-leChâteau from an impoverished rural village into a glamorous artistic and political centre.

Claude Achille Debussy was born in 1862 in St.Germain-en-Laye, Paris, and was educated at the Conservatoire. His music was unconventional, following no laws of harmony or form. He was a member of the symbolist circle, and set to music poems of Victor Hugo, and Stephen Mallarmé's *L'Après-Midi d'un Faune*. Through Mallarmé he would have met Maurice Maeterlinck, Emile Hoffet, W. B. Yeats, André Gide, Marcel Proust, and Emma Calvé. Emma was acquainted with de Guaita and Péladan, and Jules Bois was her lover. W. B. Yeats was a member of the Golden Dawn. The ubiquitous Gérard Encausse, Papus, was involved with all of them through the occult network.

Yeats was something of an Irish Nationalist, and was in the habit of recommending any patriotic sympathisers to McGregor

Mathers, founder and magus of the Golden Dawn's Parisian lodge. Mathers claimed to be a specialist in military matters, and that he had a plan dedicated to the regeneration of Europe which he was anxious to put into force immediately as part of his occult mission. According to Yeats, Mathers saw himself as a kind of Napoleon, with Scotland a principality and Egypt restored. Occultists were obsessed with Egypt and Egyptian magic, and the Golden Dawn revived the cult of Isis, for which Jules Bois had written a ritual.

Mathers and his wife Moina moved their occult activities from London to Paris in 1892, but the accommodation they found at first was unsuitable for meetings, and in 1894 they went to Number 1 Avenue Duquesne, where Annie Horniman dedicated the new temple to Ahathoor. Both Mathers and Moina were Roman Catholics, although Moina was Jewish by birth, and here they associated with minor French and Spanish nobility whose religion was strongly Catholic, whose politics were extreme Right, and whose loyalties were essentially Royalist. Mathers no doubt had to keep his connection with the Freemasons very quiet indeed, for it was certainly from the Masonic Higher Grade of the Rose Cross that the Golden Dawn had evolved. In 1910 Mathers returned briefly to London, but by 1912 he was back in Paris, where he died of Spanish influenza in 1918. If Saunière did indeed visit Paris, he could well have been involved with the Golden Dawn through Jules Bois, Papus and Jules Doinel.

The last Grand Master listed by the Dossier Secret is Jean Cocteau, the *enfant terrible* of the avant-garde Paris salons, practical joker, suspected collaborationist with the Nazis, homosexual, drug addict... What did this extraordinary young man have that would make him eligible? The answer is: talent. He was all things to all men. He had unlimited creative abilities, a brilliant mind, and an extraordinary sensitivity. He was involved with Royalist Catholic circles, and had contacts with Péladan and the Rose Croix. His friends included Picasso, Proust, Gide; Debussy for whom he designed the opera *Pélleas et Mèlisande*; author Maurice Barres, who wrote *La Colline Inspirée* which some people believe is an allegory of Rennes-le-Château and Bérenger Saunière; and Victor Hugo's grandson who introduced him to spiritualism and hermeticism. In 1958 he was invited by De Gaulle's brother to make a public address on the general subject of France, which he greatly enjoyed. In 1949 he was made a Chevalier of the Légion of d'honour. Cocteau himself insisted he had only one claim to fame - that he was a poet.

It is easy to mock the curious cults of the 18th and 19th century as misguided at best, dotty or even criminal at worst, but they could all claim in one form or another to be part of the continuing stream of the "ancient wisdom" tradition. Their aim was to better the cause of humanity. They saw France as the centre of a new world order which was to be the catalyst for the ideas and ideals of a coming golden age that would miraculously change society and bring about a new era. Their tragedy was that they could not agree how this was to happen. For the Royalists there was only one way - the Restoration of the Throne of France. In practical terms of the period, this meant the return of the Bourbons.

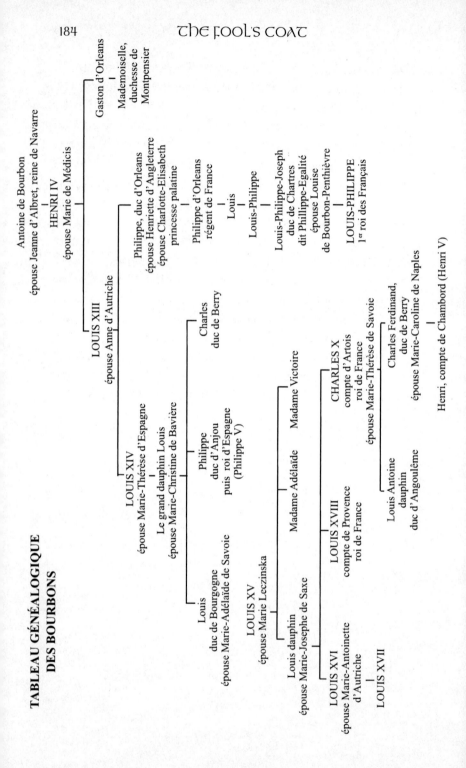

TABLEAU GÉNÉALOGIQUE
DES BOURBONS

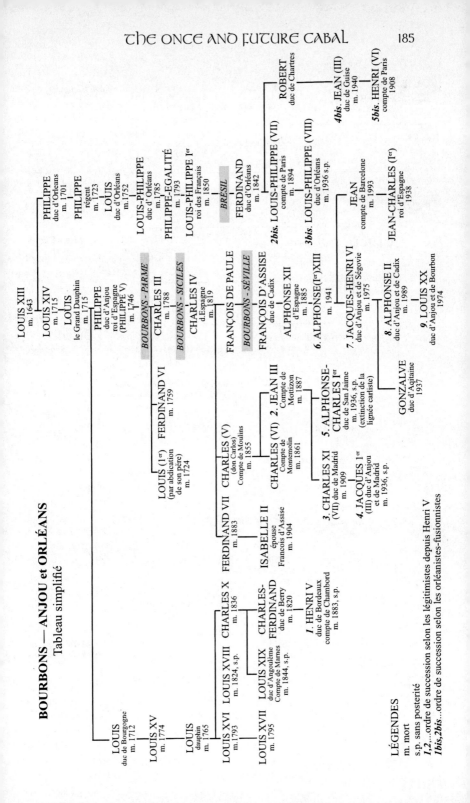

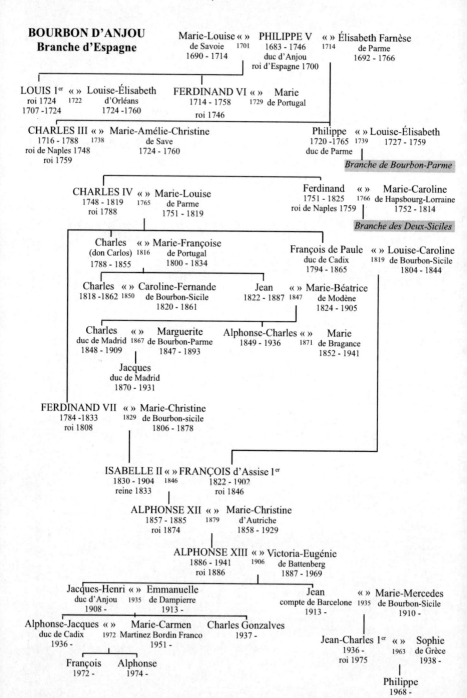

**BOURBON D'ANJOU
Branche d'Espagne**

Marie-Louise « » PHILIPPE V « » Élisabeth Farnèse
de Savoie   1701   1683 - 1746   1714   de Parme
1690 - 1714   duc d'Anjou   1692 - 1766
      roi d'Espagne 1700

LOUIS 1er « » Louise-Élisabeth   FERDINAND VI « »   Marie
roi 1724   1722   d'Orléans   1714 - 1758   1729 de Portugal
1707 -1724   1724 -1760   roi 1746

CHARLES III « » Marie-Amélie-Christine   Philippe   « » Louise-Élisabeth
1716 - 1788   1738   de Save   1720 -1765 1739 1727 - 1759
roi de Naples 1748   1724 - 1760   duc de Parme
roi 1759   *Branche de Bourbon-Parme*

CHARLES IV « » Marie-Louise   Ferdinand   « »   Marie-Caroline
1748 - 1819   1765   de Parme   1751 - 1825   1766 de Hapsbourg-Lorraine
roi 1788   1751 - 1819   roi de Naples 1759   1752 - 1814
            Branche des Deux-Siciles

Charles « » Marie-Françoise   François de Paule « » Louise-Caroline
(don Carlos)   1816   de Portugal   duc de Cadix   1819 de Bourbon-Sicile
1788 - 1855   1800 - 1834   1794 - 1865   1804 - 1844

Charles « » Caroline-Fernande   Jean   « » Marie-Béatrice
1818 -1862 1850   de Bourbon-Sicile   1822 - 1887 1847   de Modène
    1820 - 1861   1824 - 1905

Charles   « »   Marguerite   Alphonse-Charles « »   Marie
duc de Madrid 1867 de Bourbon-Parme   1849 - 1936   1871 de Bragance
1848 - 1909   1847 - 1893   1852 - 1941

Jacques
duc de Madrid
1870 - 1931

FERDINAND VII « » Marie-Christine
1784 -1833   1829 de Bourbon-sicile
roi 1808   1806 - 1878

ISABELLE II « » FRANÇOIS d'Assise 1er
1830 - 1904   1846   1822 - 1902
reine 1833   roi 1846

ALPHONSE XII « » Marie-Christine
1857 - 1885   1879 d'Autriche
roi 1874   1858 - 1929

ALPHONSE XIII « » Victoria-Eugénie
1886 - 1941   1906 de Battenberg
roi 1886   1887 - 1969

Jacques-Henri « » Emmanuelle   Jean   « » Marie-Mercedes
duc d'Anjou 1935 de Dampierre   compte de Barcelone 1935 de Bourbon-Sicile
1908 -   1913 -   1913 -   1910 -

Alphonse-Jacques « »   Marie-Carmen   Charles Gonzalves
duc de Cadix 1972 Martinez Bordin Franco 1937 -   Jean-Charles 1er « »   Sophie
1936 -   1951 -   1936 -   1963 de Grèce
            roi 1975   1938 -

François   Alphonse
1972 -   1974 -   Philippe
            1968 -

Chapter Four

'A kingdom for a stage, princes to act
and monarchs to behold
Henry V, Prologue

THE BROKEN LILY
The Secret Conspiracy

What conclusion can be drawn from this ragbag of history, myth, magic and gossip? There have, throughout history, been dedicated or ambitious people who have banded together into discreet groups with the purpose of following a common interest. They have shared a faith, either an established religion, or an unorthodox interest in "ancient wisdom", and in natural or ritual magic, all of which serve to bind them into a brotherhood. They have kept their organisations secret, due to fear of betrayal, persecution, or ridicule. Although money is needed to underpin the infrastructure of such organisations, it is not a primary objective.

In general, avowed aims are both personal and political: to become the channel for divine grace, and the establishment of Utopia. In other words, promoting the idea of self-renewal as a means of uniting disparate minds, with the object of achieving power and exerting political pressure.

Such organisations include Templars, the Companie du Saint Sacrement, 17th century Rosicrucians, Freemasons, Martinists, the Golden Dawn, 19th century neo-Rosicrucian secret societies, Opus Dei, the Nazis and in particular the SS, and sundry ancient and modern chivalric Orders such as AMORC, Papal Knights and the Order of the Garter. To this list may be added Alpha Galates, the semi-political occult group with which Plantard was associated; and if it existed other than in their literary promulgations, Plantard and de Chérisey's 20th century Prieuré de Sion.

There is evidence that there was, or could have been, such a group behind Saunière's bizarre activities at Rennes-le-Château. Money they had to have, but both he and Marie Denarnaud insisted that it was not, and never had been, their money. It was given in trust for a specific object. De Sède hints that there was such a group, which he calls "Rosicrucian" without giving it a specific title, and subsequent writers name as the Prieuré de Sion. The evidence is circumstantial, but convincing.

This shadowy organisation operating in Southern France at the end of the 19th century obviously had nothing in common with the original Order of Nôtre Dame de Sion in 12th century Jerusalem. Nor was it the forerunner of the Prieuré de Sion, featured by Plantard and de Chérisey in the 1980s. Officially it does not have a name, but for convenience might be called Prieuré Two, with Nôtre Dame de Sion as Prieuré One, and Plantard's cabal as Prieuré Three. Prieuré Two was a group of rich or titled people of right-wing and Royalist sympathies, who together with a number of local priests were working through the agency of the church to re-establish the French monarchy. Their "seed" money came from the Comtesse de Chambord, widow of the last legitimate Bourbon heir, in the form of 3000 Fr. as a gift to Saunière towards his church restoration fund. Money continued to flow from donors with Royalist sympathies, and possibly from the Hapsburgs through Archduke Johann Salvator via Fr Henri Boudet. The Hapsburgs had a finger in most of the European royalist pies, and would have welcomed a return of the monarchy and the re-establishment of the Roman Catholic church in France.

Saunière lived well, but it is true that he also worked hard to raise money for his church, which he wanted above all to make attractive as a pilgrimage centre, a spiritual place of refreshment to complement the physical benefits of the healing waters of Rennes-les-Bains. The cost of the refurbishment of St Mary

Magdalene was provided mainly through Boudet, who had access to funds to disburse for building purposes, such as the grant he made to the diocese of Carcassonne towards the repair of the Abbey of Prouille.

Saunière was Royalist by birth, upbringing and inclination, as evidenced by his first rash denunciation of the Republicans from his pulpit at the time of the 1885 elections. His father and brother were involved with the local aristocracy, and St Mary Magdalene had long been under the patronage of the Hautpoul family. But doubtless the bait to involve himself in political intrigue was money to refurbish and decorate his church. It came in instalments, and ceased after the outbreak of the 1914 War, presumably because the dream of a Bourbon Restoration was destroyed for ever by the exigencies of world wide hostilities and the destruction of the Hapsburg empire, by which time the conspirators were scattered or dead. Saunière, however, never gave up his plans to attract pilgrims to Rennes-le-Château, and at the time of his death was discussing various grandiose but hypothetical building projects, such as a baptismal pool and a ziggurat type pulpit from which to preach.

Many of the accounts for the refurbishment of St Mary Magdalene survived. Saunière was adamant in his assertions to the Ecclesiastical Court of Enquiry that he raised this money himself, and therefore they should not complain because he chose to spend it on his own church. Rather, they should be grateful. The money for the domaine - Bethania, Tour Magdala, the gardens, furniture and appointments - as well as the considerable sums spent on food and drink, came out of the invisible funding that originated from his backers, the source of which Saunière would not reveal under any pressure. If this money came from a group involved in subversive political activities, his refusal is understandable. Whatever Saunière's personal morality or professional ambivalence, his loyalty to his invisible masters was absolute; nothing could induce him to betray them, though whether this was through expedience, conviction or fear is a question left unanswered.

It has been suggested that Saunière himself was in some way involved in the affair at Coustassa. If Father Gélis, with the indiscretion of old age, spoke out of turn, then his murder could well have been a matter of necessity to prevent further leakages of vital information. If Gélis was aware of the Rennes-le-Château conspiracy, then Saunière, although not necessarily involved personally, would have known who his murderers were, and perhaps this was the knowledge imparted on his deathbed that sent his Confessor into shock.

Saunière's explanation to the Bishop for building such a beautiful house and estate was that he intended it as a retirement home for aged priests. This is a very specious argument, and certainly no aged and indigent clergy ever used it. Retired priests would have little use for a fortified tower like Magdala, which Saunière commandeered as a "library". If he was in possession of letters or treasonable documents and holding illicit funds on behalf of Prieuré Two, then a strong room would have been essential. It was necessary to have an elegant place where visiting V.I.P.s could meet in pleasant and, more importantly, private surroundings, and Bethania and the gardens provided just such a retreat. Saunière did not live in Bethania, he continued to occupy the Presbytery with the Denarnaud family. As the land was in Marie's name, she technically owned all the buildings on it, but she herself only lived there after Saunière's death, when the whole flimsy structure of Prieuré Two had collapsed.

Bethania is a villa, rather than a mansion. It is charming, but not particularly large. Built parallel with the Presbytery, and sharing an interior courtyard with it, Bethania is a double-fronted house with three reasonably sized rooms on each of the ground and first floors, and has in addition attics in the steep roof, and a cellar opening onto the courtyard. A lot of the space is taken up by long corridors and a wide, elegant staircase, on the walls of which are displayed original prints of the heroes of the Vendéan wars.

Jean-Luc Robin, who was responsible for the domaine during the period that it was in the possession of the American consortium, was enough a Royalist to fly the Fleur de Lys at half-mast for the death of Henri d'Orléans, Comte de Paris, the Bourbon Pretender to the throne of France, on 19 June 1999.

In his Preface to Henri Boudet's book *La Vraie Langue Celtique* Plantard states categorically that Boudet was the main protagonist in the Rennes-le-Château affair, that Saunière merely acted as his agent; and there is evidence in Boudet's accounts that he paid money to Marie Denarnaud, presumably on Saunière's behalf. In "le Carré" terms, Saunière was apparently "the man in the field" with Boudet as his Control. His wanderings around the countryside, ostensibly collecting rock specimens, or selling donated antiques, were excellent cover for secret meetings and the dissemination of information. His journeys further afield, covered by Marie who kept up the fiction at home that he was not absent, have never been explained, but could well have been on behalf of Prieuré Two's Royalist activities.

Both Saunière and Boudet would have known Jules Doinel, who was a prominent member of the local Society of Arts and Sciences, and Librarian at Carcassonne. In 1890 Doinel, with Gérard Encausse, created the neo-Cathar church at Mirepoix. Encausse was the founder and Grand Master of the Martinists who had a branch at Lyon. Saunière was known to have dealt with shops in Lyon, spent time there, and may have belonged to the Lyon Martinist lodge. This is more likely than the suggestion sometimes made by contemporary writers that he was a Freemason, since the Martinists were right-wing and monarchist, dedicated to the foundation of a new World under the aegis of a religious leader, whereas the French Freemasons were left-wing and Republican. A Martinist lodge would have been the ideal place of recruitment for the kind of organisation envisaged as being behind the Rennes-le-Château Royalist conspiracy, if indeed the Martinists were not actively engaged in it.

The aristocratic, rich and famous were known to come to Rennes-le-Château, and Saunière maintained that it was these visitors who in gratitude filled his alms boxes with gold. The celebrated diva, Emma Calvé, who was a native of Languedoc, was not only wealthy but passionately patriotic. The inference is that Bethania was used by Prieuré Two as a headquarters and meeting place. Invoices still exist for quantities of food and drink that would indicate large numbers of visitors needing to be accommodated: From Joseph Camredon, Baker at Couiza 276 Frs; Michel Sabatier, Wine Merchant, Carcassonne 230 Frs; Defretin-Severin, Grocer, Lille 186 Frs.; Etienne Armbruster, Castlenaudary for foie-gras 36 Fr.; to name but a few. The Prieuré would have paid these bills for which Saunière kept no official accounting. In 21st century terms the amounts are incredibly high.

His visits to Paris, which Marie Denarnaud insisted did actually happen, could well have been to visit his Royalist paymasters. Doinel knew Josephin Péladan, founder of the Order of the Catholic Rosy Cross, the Temple and the Grail, whose manifesto was "the accomplishment of works of mercy, with a view to preparing for the reign of the Holy Spirit." Calvé and Papus were both members. For Royalists it was not blasphemous to equate the restoration of the monarchy with the coming of the divine kingdom. McGregor Mathers, founder of the Golden Dawn, said that at the meeting of an occult society in Paris, he met the "Pretender to the Throne of France". This was probably the Comte de Paris, King Louis Philippe's grandson, but it may have been Naundorff, or any of the other Pretenders.

Le ʀᴏɪ ᴘᴇʀᴅu

In these modern times, when Royal persons are habitually referred to by their forenames, and their intimate doings decorate the front pages of the more sensational newspapers, it is difficult to appreciate the passionate adherence of the Royalists to the Throne, and their determination to restore France as a monarchy.

Despite any personal shortcomings, the King was regarded as divinely appointed to care for his people, their oriflamme to which all right-minded patriots must rally. The Royal Throne was seen enhaloed in a rosy glow of nostalgia, the focal point of faith, wisdom and hope; a symbol of all that men could desire; a promise of the best, in the best of all possible worlds, in this life, and the hope of heaven to come. Adherents were willing to pour out their gold and their life's blood - and did most abundantly - in pursuit of this impossible grail.

Even the most ardent supporters could not regard the Bourbons as great rulers, but Louis XVI and his beautiful, extravagant Queen had died as martyrs to the bloodthirsty monster of the Revolution, and their little son, the Dauphin, was lost.

The conception of "le roi perdu" is an archetype deeply rooted in national consciousness: history, literature and legend are littered with such characters. The idea of the King who does not die, but waits somewhere for the summons to come and lead his oppressed people to victory, is the eternal fairy-story with a happy ending. It was inevitable that the belief should proliferate that the little Dauphin, who on the execution of his father was regarded by the Royalists as Louis XVII, had not died in prison, but would come back to restore the glory of the Bourbon dynasty.

By 1799 the red tide of the Terror had receded, and First Consul Napoleon, waiting in the wings, had not yet succeeded in establishing his Empire. The time had come for the resurrection of Louis XVII, and a number of claimants came forward.

Fuelled by wishful thinking, and supported by the madder element of the occult underground, Pretenders arose thick and fast. According to the Duchess d'Angoulème, Louis XVI's daughter and the only member of the immediate family to survive the Revolution, there were twenty-eight contenders. Most of these have passed into oblivion, but of the remainder, six have some credibility.

The first was a beautiful boy called Jean Marie Hervagult, who was possibly an illegitimate son of the Duke of Valentinois.

Another, known only as Bruneau, was much less aristocratic, and was something of a con-man. The next was the Baron de Richemont, origin unknown, who claimed to be Duke of Normandy, and who was strikingly like the Bourbons. The most fantastic was Eleazer Williams, also known as Onwarenhiiaki, the Indian Iroquois Chief. The most interesting possibly was an Englishman named Augustus Meves, whose mother was a lady-in-waiting to Marie Antoinette, and who claimed she had been entrusted with the true Dauphin, the child who died in prison being a substitute. The most credible was Karl William Naundorff, who bore a remarkable resemblance to the late Louis XVI, and may have been the illegitimate son of the King's youngest brother the Comte d'Artois who later became Charles X, and who was famous in his youth as a tireless philanderer.

The extraordinary thing is that the Duchess d'Angouème refused to see any of the Pretenders. It was of course to her advantage that her only brother should remain dead. As a woman she could not herself inherit the crown, because France adhered to the old Salic law, but her husband was the heir apparent, and even after his death she insisted upon retaining the title of La Dauphine. On the other hand she was childless, and it is conceivable she might have preferred that her brother or his heirs should ascend the throne, rather than her nephew the Comte de Chambord, whose mother she disliked. She had inherited her parents' private fortune, but by the time of the Restoration much of it had been dissipated to settle the debts incurred by the Royal Dukes while in exile. Even if any one of the Pretenders had succeeded in getting her to share the remnant with him, which many cynics considered to be the main objective, he would have been disappointed in the yield.

Marie Thérèse Charlotte was born in 1778, and was seven years older than her younger brother Louis Charles. Marie Antoinette's first son Louis Joseph Xavier had died in 1789 at the age of eight. Her teens had been spent in prison in the Temple, and after her release in December 1795, she went to Vienna where the Emperor regarded her as a pawn in the political

European game. Forced into marriage with her mentally unstable cousin, and manipulated by two unscrupulous Uncles, she became bitter and withdrawn, rudely repelling with every sign of impatience any attempt at friendliness.

She had been an enchanting child, and one of the theories to account for the remarkable change in her character is that she knew her brother was alive, and was weighed down by guilt. A more romantic - but apocryphal - explanation is that there had been a substitution, and that the girl released from the Temple was not Marie Thérèse Charlotte.

What then had become of the real Princess? With the rise of the romantic novel in Germany in the mid-nineteenth century, the legend grew that Marie Thérèse Charlotte was the mysterious Countess who lived in a little castle called Schloss Eishausen near Hildburghausen. Two strangers arrived there in 1810, and no-one, even the authorities, knew who they were. They appeared not to be married, but the locals called them "The Count and Countess", and it was believed that they were French emigrés. The lady was apparently of very high rank, and it was rumoured she was in some respects a captive, and that at night she was locked in. On the rare occasions that she went out walking she was heavily veiled. The "Count" received considerable sums of money from an Amsterdam bank, and was liberal in his gifts to charity. The couple lived in luxury, and the "Countess's" dresses were sent from Paris. She died in 1837, her identity still secret, though it was said some of her possessions were marked with a lily, and among them was a sketch portrait of a lady resembling Marie Antoinette. The "Count" died in 1845, and some so-called cousins claimed he was Leonardus Cornelius van der Valck, and took possession of his estate. His papers were believed to reveal that he had had very intimate relations with various royal personages, but all the documents disappeared. Was he a lover or a gaoler of the mysterious lady? There is no documentary evidence to support the theory that the "Countess" was Marie Thérèse Charlotte except in works of fiction.

Although gaining considerable public support, none of the Pretenders succeeded in persuading either the Royal Family or the Government of their authenticity. The only one who adhered to his claims in spite of every ridicule and discouragement was Naundorff, whose children and grandchildren continued to be regarded by some of the Legitimists as the true heirs to the throne.

Aꜰᴛᴇʀ ᴛһᴇ Fᴀʟʟ

Napoleon I was a dictator waiting to happen. With the execution of Robespierre and one hundred and fifteen of his adherents on 28 July 1794, the Revolution collapsed. The constitution of the notorious Committee of Public Safety, which had for the past three years been the virtual dictator of government policy, was changed in a way that deprived it of power, and authority transferred to the members of the Convention. The dreaded Commune, which had been the creator and instrument of the Reign of Terror, disappeared for ever.

The country was exhausted. Riots against rising food prices were a daily occurrence. Paris was in turmoil, and on 29 May 1795 an angry mob invaded the Convention. Contrary to tradition, the Convention tried to defend itself, and one member was killed, his head triumphantly paraded on a pike. The National Guard moved in and dispersed the rioters at bayonet point. Two days later the Army, which included a young Corsican officer named Napoleon Bonaparte, entered Paris and the crisis was over. The six deputies who had shown leniency towards the insurgents were summarily convicted. Three committed suicide, and the corpse of one of these was guillotined with the three surviving sympathisers.

There was a strong movement throughout the country to restore the child-king Louis XVII to the throne. Louis XVI's exiled brothers were identified in the minds of many citizens with the idea of foreign invasion and émigrés' revenge. Establishing Louis XVI's young son as a constitutional monarch would have proved a sensible solution, as by reconciling the nation to the government it would have ensured the members of the Convention continuing in power. The death of the boy, which was announced on 8 June 1795, effectively put an end to this plan.

Louis XVI's eldest surviving brother, the Comte de Provence, had assumed the title of Louis XVIII. From his Court in Exile at Verona he issued a proclamation declaring merciless punishment on the regicides, and the total restoration of the "ancien regime", with the former parliament restored to its old powers, and the higher orders to their privileged positions. Catholicism was again to be the established State religion. This manifesto, which totally disregarded any concession to the new movements in France, was totally implausible and could only have been imposed by force.

The ultra Royalist, ultra Catholic West had never ceased fighting for the Restoration of the Bourbons. It was mainly guerrilla warfare, small bands of pious peasants commanded and financed by noblemen who had escaped the Revolution, supported to a small degree by British money and arms. When Charette, the main Royalist leader, surrendered to "force majeure" and signed a peace treaty in February 1795, the Vendéan Royalists disbanded. The long promised British troops arrived at Quiberon in June, but it was too late. The small remnants of the Royalist army had been left isolated in Brittany, and crushed by the Republican troops under Marshal Hoche, they were massacred.

On 26 October the Convention was dissolved to be replaced by a more moderate group, the Directory. A new era had begun with the emergence of the *nouveau riche*. With the abolition of financial controls, expenditure and inflation ran riot. The value of the assignat fell from 100 francs to 15 sous, and in any case there was nothing to buy. Food was requisitioned from the countryside to feed the towns, which led to the furious dissatisfaction of both parties. Robbery and pillage were the norm.

Partial elections in April 1797 resulted in the return of only eleven former members of the Convention, the remainder being constitutional monarchists. The Royalists were reviving. If the

Legitimists had been willing to make concessions, combined forces with the Constitutionalists, and together produced a competent leader, the Restoration would have been accomplished.

Among the new Government leaders, there was no statesman of any stature capable to taking on the responsibility of restoring order and prosperity. This left a convenient gap asking to be filled by a man of Napoleon's talents: a sense of realism, executive capacity and ruthless strength of will.

The Corsican peasant beloved of history, a rough soldier with a genius for military strategy, is far from the truth. Napoleon was born in Ajaccio, Corsica, in 1769, the second son of Carlo Buonaparte and Letizia Ramolino. His father was a lawyer, and both his parents were resistance workers against the occupying Genoese government of Corsica. Napoleon was educated in France, entered the military academy at Brienne, and graduated from the École Militaire, Paris, as Second Lieutenant in the artillery. He changed his name to Bonaparte, to make it more French.

In 1792 Austria and Prussia had declared war on the Revolutionary Government, and after the execution of Louis XVI the Allies combined to establish a European Coalition which included Holland, Germany, Italy, Britain and Spain, involving France in fighting simultaneously on three separate fronts.

Napoleon was a professional soldier and quickly gained promotion. In 1793 he was in charge of the barrage at the siege of Toulon, which brought him to the attention of the Convention and resulted in his becoming a Brigadier General. In 1794 he was appointed artillery commander of the Army in Italy, and a year later he was in command of the Army of the Interior.

He continued to gain favour under the Directory, and was given command of the Army of Italy in 1796, where his unbroken line of victories over the armies of Austria and Piedmont gained him both the respect of the military authorities and the loyalty of his troops, who nicknamed him "the little corporal".

By 1798 only Britain remained to be conquered, and inevitably Napoleon was put in charge. Britain, however, was a great sea power, and without sea supremacy invasion was considered impractical. Napoleon decided on a different method of attack, and hatched a plan to invade Egypt as ground from which to launch an offensive against Britain's interests in India. His Army of the Orient defeated the Egyptians, but his fleet lost to Admiral Nelson at the Battle of the Nile in Abu Qir Bay, and his army was blockaded in Egypt.

Napoleon was not a man to remain idle. His aims were twofold: he wanted an Empire, and to found a dynasty. While in Egypt he entered into a plot to overthrow the Directory, which led to the Coup of 9 November 1799. Supported by the Army, he assumed the role of First Consul and effectively became dictator.

His priority was to defend France against the Coalition forces. He reorganized the Army, and by 1802 had succeeded in ending the Revolutionary Wars and returning France to economic stability. By popular consent he was appointed Consul for life. He initially endeavoured to preserve the Revolution's gains: equality before the law, religious toleration, and the abolition of privileges.

Catholicism was re-established; the appointment of Bishops and clergy salaries were made the responsibilities of the State. Protestants were given freedom of worship. Napoleon himself had nothing more than a romantic attachment to Christianity, but he appreciated the value of the Church's support, especially in primarily Catholic areas such as Brittany. The Royalists plotted to kidnap him, but failed.

In 1804 he was proclaimed Emperor, and crowned in the Cathedral of Nôtre Dame de Paris. By 1807 he controlled an Empire stretching from the Elbe in the North, across Italy, and from the Pyrenees to the Dalmatian coast. By 1812 the French Empire and its satellite states included Spain, Italy, the Confederation of the Rhine, Switzerland, Holland, Belgium and Poland. He was King of Italy, and had made his brothers Kings of the conquered territories: Jerome of Westphalia, Joseph of Naples and briefly of Spain, Louis of Holland.

A new pope, Pius VII, had been elected in 1800. A simple and pious monk, he was willing to make concessions to regain France for the Catholic Church. He accepted Napoleon's assumption of the role of Emperor, thereby giving him the necessary seal of approval. It was a title consciously chosen to avoid the traps implicit in the words "royalty" and "republicanism", but it had a special meaning for Napoleon who was plagued with territorial ambitions. He was determined that the Empire should be a reality, and did not care how he achieved it. His reputation as a brilliant General rested primarily on weight of numbers, and his complete disregard of casualties. For him soldiers were disposable.

Conscious as he was of his somewhat ambiguous position, Napoleon was concerned to ensure a good future supply of suitable Government officials. He established boarding schools (Lycées) for the sons of the elite, which adopted military uniforms and imposed military discipline: there were also specialist schools for law and medicine. The education of the poorer classes was left in the hands of the clergy, which meant that the barest literacy was imparted to the smallest number of students. Art and literature under the Empire was minimal: writing fell mostly into the category of propaganda and journalism. Decorative taste was luxurious and heavy, adding Egyptian and Etruscan motives to a prevalent classical revival.

In 1796 Napoleon had married Josephine de Beauharnais, the widow of Vicomte Alexandre de Beauharnais who was guillotined during the Terror. She was beautiful, the mother of two children, and the toast of the salons of the Directoire. However, she failed to produce the heir that would ensure the Bonaparte dynasty. In 1809 he divorced her, and contracted a dynastic marriage with Marie Louise, daughter of the Austrian Emperor. They had one son, François Charles Joseph, born in 1811, who sadly lived only to reach the age of twenty-one.

Duc de Berri
(*The Return of Louis XVIII,* by
Gilbert Stengerm" 1908)

Louis XVIII

The Comte de Chambord
(after a drawing)

The Comte d'Artois

The Duc and Duchesse Angoulème

As time went on Napoleon, and consequently the Government, became increasingly tyrannical. The more able ministers were replaced by yes-men of inferior calibre and untried loyalty, many with royalist sympathies. The Court itself was a hotbed of intrigue and favouritism. The Press was put under State authority and censored accordingly. There was unemployment and industrial unrest. To avoid the newly imposed Customs duties, smuggling became a way of life, and corruption was rife.

Jealous of Russia's power, and suspicious of the Tsar, Napoleon invaded Russia in 1812, but although he succeeded in capturing Moscow, the position was untenable and that winter his army was forced into a long and bitter retreat. The following spring Prussia, Austria and Sweden joined the Allies who invaded France. In March 1814 Paris fell, and Napoleon, forty four years old, abdicated in favour of his son. The succession was rejected by the French Senate. Napoleon tried unsuccessfully to poison himself. He went into exile to Elba, which he regarded as his "kingdom", and where his first task was to revive the island's ailing economy.

On May 3 1814 Louis XVIII entered Paris to restore the Bourbon Monarchy. When the courier, carrying the news to him of Napoleon's abdication, announced "Sire, you are King of France", Louis replied "Have I ever ceased to be?"

Under the 1814 Treaty of Paris Napoleon had been promised that his wife and son should be allowed to join him, and that he would receive a state pension. When the French government failed to honour either of these undertakings, and encouraged by rumours that the reign of Louis XVIII left much to be desired, Napoleon left Elba and landed in the South of France with 1500 men. Gathering strength en route he entered Paris in triumph in March 1815. Louis fled to Holland.

For the next hundred days Napoleon again reigned as Emperor. He raised a Grand Army and set out to disperse the scattered forces of the Allies. On 16 June 1815 he faced Wellington's Anglo-Dutch Army at Waterloo and suffered a devastating defeat.

Again he abdicated in favour of his son, and surrendered to the British to avoid reprisals by the Bourbons. He was exiled to St Helena, where he lived in considerable comfort, and where he died, probably of cancer, in 1821.

On 18 July Louis XVIII returned to Paris for the Second Restoration. He was met at St Denis by the Prime Minister, the Duc de Talleyrand, whom the King's advisers had urged him to accept. Louis, however, had no intention of being a Constitutional monarch. He believed utterly in his indefeasible, hereditary, divine right. He was no longer young; he was immensely fat and suffered from gout which made walking difficult; but he had an innate dignity which his physical appearance would otherwise have negated. He was like an old idol, hedged about with a spurious sanctity. He had learned nothing during his years of exile, and like his younger brother, considered it would be preferable to be a wood-cutter to being the King of England.

There was no chance, however, that the Bourbons could reign once more as absolute monarchs. The political ideas that Louis XVIII, on the insistence of his advisers, embodied in the Charter of 1814 included recognition of the principles of liberty and equality, and the assurance that opinions and votes expressed before the Restoration would be consigned to oblivion. The Civil Code and existing laws were to remain in force, and Napoleon's administrative and social structure retained. To reconcile two such opposing viewpoints was to create a situation which was of necessity untenable.

The next point at issue was an equally thorny one. During the Revolution much property, belonging both to émigrés and to the Church, had been confiscated and had passed into other hands. Legal recognition of the new owners was inevitable, but those who had been deprived did not take kindly to such a ruling when the King was enjoying his own again.

Religion also proved a problem. Napoleon had re-established the Catholic Church. The 1814 charter proclaimed religious toleration. Catholicism, which had declined during the eighteenth

century, was having a vigorous revival in the nineteenth. The
twofold question arose: would the militant Catholics tolerate
enemies? Alternatively, with anticlericalism deeply embedded in
the newly educated classes, would they recognise Catholicism as
the official State religion?

Politically there was also an ambiguity. It was to be a
constitutional but not a parliamentary monarchy. The King held
executive power and had the initiative in legislation. Parliament
was composed of two chambers and was to discuss and vote on
laws and taxes, and the Chamber of Deputies had the right of
impeachment of King's ministers before the upper chamber. There
was also a house of peers, similar to the House of Lords in Britain,
which was to be an assembly of the highest dignitaries, lay,
ecclesiastical and military, drawn from the old regime and the
Empire, and nominated by the King, which was decorative rather
than useful. The strongest parliamentary party was the Right, the
Ultra Royalists, supported by the secret society of the Chevaliers
de la Foi, who looked for leadership to the Comte d'Artois, in
his youth a leading member of the Counter-Revolutionary
movement. The moderate Royalists supported the King and
formed the political Centre. The Left, only now gradually emerging
from the trauma of Napoleon's Hundred Days, took refuge under
the banner of Independents.

The leader of the Ultra-Royalist party in the Chamber of
Deputies was Villele, a minor noble from Toulouse, whose power
was enhanced by being a friend of Mme de Cayla, the King's
favourite. In view of his health she was unlikely to have been
Louis' mistress, but she was his regular chess-partner. In 1822
Villele became the President of the Council, and being a financial
wizard, his great contribution was to create a budgetary system
and financial control that put the country on a sound financial
footing. Peaceful international relations were established and
trade increased. In general, under Louis XVIII France had an
efficient and honest government that during his lifetime achieved
moderation and a reasonable degree of stability.

In September 1824 Louis XVIII died. He was childless, and the next in line was his younger brother the Comte d'Artois who succeeded to the throne as Charles X. Louis XVIII's health had precluded his undergoing the rigorous ceremony of coronation, and Napoleon had crowned himself, but in May 1825 Charles X was crowned at Reims with the full elaborate religious ritual of the *ancien regime,* an act which immediately gave rise to suspicion that he intended to bring back the old forms and privileges of absolute monarchy.

Like his brother, the new King was a widower, but in other respects a quite different sort of man. At sixty-seven years of age he was still remarkably active, and a great huntsman. Tall, elegant, and possessed of graciousness and charm, he had in his youth been an energetic womaniser, but now in his more mature years he had turned again to religion. Politically, he was unsatisfactory as a constitutional monarch; he was rigidly Right wing, and disliked the provisions of the Government Charter which he was now expected to support. Moreover, he lacked Louis XVIII's balance and sound judgement.

Nonetheless, the new reign began reasonably auspiciously. Villele was not much liked, but he was recognised as a man of considerable ability. Charles' first attempt to gain popularity was to abolish censorship and grant a limited amnesty to political prisoners, but the Ultras' plan to transfer the control of education to the church, and amend the Civil Code regarding the rights of inheritance, met with strong opposition both from the Government Left and from the Press. Some part of the programme was nonetheless forced through, and compensation was voted to dispossessed émigrés, expenditure that was bitterly resented by many of the bourgeoisie who thought the money involved could have been better spent.

There was a strong lobby by the anti-clericalists who feared the rise to power of the Jesuits, particularly as they were largely in charge of education. This group included deists and free-thinkers, Liberals and Bonapartists, but also some moderate

Catholics and Royalists. In 1826 the Comte de Montlosier, an ardent Royalist, published a book denouncing "the odious and forbidden society of Jesus" and "the existence of a religious and political system tending to the overthrow of religion, society and the throne", which fanned the flames of fanaticism and further split the Royalist party. There was a rumour that the King had himself become a Jesuit.

France's foreign policy also came in for criticism as being lukewarm, and tension was increased by the Government's failure to support the cause of Greek independence with which public opinion was widely sympathetic. The situation worsened in April 1827 when Charles organised a review of the Paris National Guard at which some men in the ranks shouted "Down with the Ministry and the Jesuits". Charles countered by issuing three ordinances: the first dissolving the Chamber and ordering new elections; the second by creating seventy-six new peers; and the third by abolishing once again the newly re-imposed censorship.

The election resulted in the Opposition gaining a majority of more than sixty, and Villele, probably one of the most able of France's Finance Ministers but an indifferent statesman, resigned in January 1828. It was a bitter blow to Charles, but he made the best of it. The new Ministry included a number of the moderate Right Centre, and was prepared to attempt reconciliation between the opposing parties. Freedom of the Press was confirmed, and the intake of pupils to the seminaries was limited.

In 1829 Charles, just returned from a successful tour of Eastern France, considered his universal popularity to be firmly established, and promptly dissolved the Ministry whose moderation was anathema to him. The choice of his new Ministers appeared to be either completely tactless, or deliberately provocative. He could not have chosen men more unsuitable or more disliked, both at home and abroad. His action was regarded by many as a prelude to a coup d'état. In January 1830 a new newspaper, *Le National*, published an article praising the "Glorious English Revolution of 1688", and suggested that an unsatisfactory monarch could with benefit be replaced by another member of the same family who had broader views. That this referred to the Duc d'Orléans was obvious to all. In his opening speech to the March 1830 session of the Chamber, Charles hinted that if necessary opposition would be met with force. The Chamber promptly passed a vote of no confidence. The country again prepared for another election, and the Opposition returned fifty-three extra members.

Charles refused to accept the situation. In July four ordinances were issued, suppressing the freedom of the Press, dissolving the Chamber, modifying the electoral law which meant in effect that the electorate was limited mostly to landowners, and fixing a date yet again for new elections. Official Government resistance to the ordinances was passive, but Paris was in the throes of a recession and ready to explode into revolution.

It seems incredible that neither the King nor his Ministers foresaw the people's reaction. They apparently imagined that Paris would just accept the decree by default. Charles went off to hunt at Rambouillet, leaving his Deputy Minister of War to deal with the situation. No preparations had been made, no plans organised for defence, no arrests envisaged of the Opposition leaders. The garrisons were depleted by the Army's expedition to Algeria, and no troops were available. When the tricolore was anonymously hoisted over Nôtre Dame, revolutionary fever ran high. Barricades were erected. Workmen and shop-keepers, led by veterans of the Revolution and Napoleon's Armies, stormed through the streets demanding the deposition of the Bourbons. On 29 July 1830 two regiments defected to the insurgents.

Charles remained obstinately optimistic, pursuing his normal course of Court etiquette at St Cloud, ignoring the tumult, and refusing to make any concessions. Finally, he did agree to revoke the ordinances and appoint new Ministers, but it was too late. The Moderates had decided to replace him with Louis Philippe, Duc d'Orléans. Charles could only have overcome the decision by force, which he did not have, and there was no course open to him but to abdicate, naming his little grandson, the Comte de Chambord, as his heir.

Charles' eldest son, the Duc d'Angoulème, was insane, and his second son, the Duc de Berri, had been assassinated five years earlier. However, the Duchesse de Berri had given birth to a posthumous son, and it was on this "miracle child" that the hopes of the ardent and pious Royalists were centred.

On 31 July Charles took his family to Rambouillet. There was no food, and they had to sell the silver plate in order to buy provisions. Three days later the Commissaires came to inform Charles that he had been deposed, and to collect the crown jewels. Charles refused and withdrew his abdication. The Duchesse de Berri wanted to parade through Paris with her small son, believing this would change everything and the people would accept him as King, but Charles refused to countenance such madness.

Drums were beaten, and a rabble of some twenty thousand strong marched on Rambouillet. They looted the palace, found the crown jewels, and took them back to Paris. Not one piece was missing. The royal family had gone.

On the Feast of the Assumption of the Blessed Virgin, Charles X said goodbye to his Guards and went into exile for the third time. He wore a shabby coat and no decorations. An officer handed the Fleur-de-lys to him, and as the men passed by, many of them weeping, they touched the white silk of the flag. Charles told them to dry their tears, because one day, he said, his grandson would have need of them. Next morning the royal family embarked at Cherbourg. The Comte de Chambord, wearing a light blue coat and white trousers, climbed the gangway behind his grandfather, followed by his sister Louise, and the Duc and Duchesse d'Angoulème. At 2.30 the ship sailed, taking Charles X and his family away from France for ever. Those left behind were mad with grief, and later the same night one manservant shot himself. Charles X died six years later at Goritzia near Trieste. Only the young Comte de Chambord remained to challenge Louis-Philippe.

Louis-Philippe - The Expedient King

On 30 July 1830 Louis-Philippe entered Paris, and was met by a group of deputies who offered him the post of Lieutenant- General. It was only one step from the throne itself, and barely a week later the Chamber offered him the position of Constitutional Monarch. Pressing the Tricolore flag to his heart, Louis-Philippe accepted on condition that he should be styled "King of the French", but underneath this display of political correctness he desired wealth and power. The Orléans branch, being directly descended from Philippe, second son of Louis XIII, had always considered they had a right to the throne. Charles had left the care of his grandson's affairs in Louis-Philippe's hands, and the Legitimists never forgave Louis-Philippe for what they considered to be his consummate act of betrayal.

He was fifty-six years old, a gossiping, fussy, undignified man, lacking in grace or romantic appeal. The son of the left-wing Duc d'Orléans, Philip Egalité, and educated in sentimental philanthropy by the Duc's mistress, Mme de Genlis, Louis-Philippe's politics were ambivalent. For twenty years he had lived as an impoverished émigré in England, wandering around the neutral countries of Europe, and imbibing the principles of democracy in the United States. As a young man he had served as an officer in the Revolutionary army.

In 1809 he had married Marie-Amélie, daughter of Francois I of Sicily, who was a good wife, a devoted mother, and an ideal queen. She duly presented her husband with five handsome sons and three daughters.

On Louis-Philippe's accession the eldest boy, Ferdinand Duc de Chartres, became Duc d'Orléans. He was a beautiful, restless, and violently republican young man, who constantly clashed with his father. As heir-apparent, it was important that he should make a dynastic marriage. The French Ambassador in Russia was asked to investigate an alliance with the Grand Duchess, but nothing came of it. The Archduchess Thérèse, a daughter of

Archduke Charles, was also suggested but this too failed. The snobbish nobility of Europe were not anxious to ally themselves with the Orléans, who were inevitably still tainted with Philip Égalité's treachery in voting for his cousin, Louis XVI's death, and by what was regarded by many as Louis-Philippe's usurpation of the French throne. Finally the Princess Hélène of Mecklenburg Schwerin accepted. She was young, amiable, clever and well educated, but - a Protestant. In spite of his mother's objections, in 1837, at the age of twenty-seven, Ferdinand married her in a civil ceremony, and they took up residence in the former apartments of the Duc and Duchesse de Berri. Two sons were duly born - Louis-Philippe in 1838, and Robert in 1840 - thus securing the succession.

Of Louis Philippe's other sons, the Duc de Nemours was good-looking, with dreamy eyes and blonde wavy hair, but very shy. The Duc d'Aumale was still at College. He was very wealthy, having inherited money from his godfather the Prince de Condé, whose murder in 1831, when he was planning to join Charles X in England, had been hushed up. The most popular of the boys was the Prince de Joinville, a great charmer, gifted, a writer, careless in his dress, who swore like an old sea-dog.   The youngest, the Duc de Montpensier, known as Ton Ton, was a small boy, full of life and vivacity, and his father's favourite. The three girls all made good marriages: Louise was a beauty, who married Leopold of Saxe-Coburg: Marie Christine was not pretty, but she was witty, artistic, mischievous, and a devout republican - she married Alexandre of Würtemburg; Clementine the youngest was ravishing, and captivated Charles X when she visited the Tuileries and danced with the young Comte de Chambord. She married Auguste of Saxe Coburg, and her son became King Ferdinand of Bulgaria. All the boys achieved some distinction in their respective fields, but were damned for ever by a 19th century "Wit" who labelled them "a family of brilliant second lieutenants."

Within ten years Louis-Philippe had established himself firmly on the throne, and the dynasty appeared secure.   His tastes and manners were simple, and he knew how to play to the gallery by adopting the dress and behaviour of the bourgeoisie. Committed to being a Citizen-King he mixed freely with the people; dressed in the conventional frock-coat, wearing a top-hat, and carrying an umbrella, he walked daily through the streets of Paris. At first the Parisians were enchanted by such a novelty, but later they were to find him drab and boring, and longed for a bit more pomp and splendour.

The first changes made in the Charter by the new regime were directed towards granting greater liberty to the individual. The qualifications regarding age and property for electors were revised, the National Guard was reorganised, and the term of compulsory military service reduced by one year. The tricolore again flew as the national flag of France, the close alliance between Church and Throne was mitigated, and education underwent drastic reform, although it was not compulsory, and illiteracy remained widespread.

There was, however, still considerable unrest. The Ultra Royalists continually plotted against the Orléans regime, and between 1835 and 1846, six attempts were made on the King's life. On Shrove Tuesday, 1831, a few Royalists gathered at the Church of St German l'Auxerrois for a memorial service commemorating the eleventh anniversary of the murder of the Duc de Berri. As a young officer came forward to pin a picture of the Comte de Chambord on the catafalque, a mob invaded, looted and totally destroyed the church. Next day they broke into and pillaged the Archbishop's Palace near Nôtre Dame. The Royalist's cause was further weakened by the 1832 Legitimist rising in Vendée which was a disastrous failure, and by the spread of liberal Catholicism which opposed the old religious regime supporting the divine right of Kings.

The Bonapartists were also active, but their hopes of a Napoleonic restoration were dashed in 1832 by the death of the Emperor's son and heir, l'Aiglon of romantic legend, at Schönbrunn in Austria. It was said that thousands of old soldiers in Paris wept. Louis-Philippe regarded the Bonapartists as comparatively harmless, and in 1833 he exploited the legend by sending Joinville to bring Napoleon I's body back to Paris with great ceremony, for reburial in Les Invalides.

The greatest threat continued to be the strong Left, and the fatal weakness of the Government was that it failed to accede to public demand to reform the electoral procedure to include the workers, or to deal with the widespread acute social problems that beset them. Since the end of the Revolution and the development of industry, the cities had become hopelessly overcrowded. No consideration was given to health, sanitation or poverty. Cholera and tuberculosis spread in the crowded and unsanitary living conditions; low wages and the exploitation of female and child labour encouraged disease, drunkenness and immorality. The workers had expected the new regime to be a panacea for all their ills, whereas all it had done was to increase unemployment and hardship.

In November 1831 the silk-workers of Lyon rose in revolt and demanded that a meeting should be held between employers and workers to negotiate a fixed scale of minimum wages. This was the first occasion on which an organised industrial dispute in France had employed collective bargaining. The meeting was duly held and an agreement reached. Unfortunately most employers refused to abide by the agreement, and the revolt escalated into violence that had to be put down by force.

The result was to encourage the workers to seek more effective ways of enforcing their demands. Propaganda led to the wide distribution of Republican leaflets, and many malcontents were drawn into Left-wing secret societies such as the Société des Droits de l'Homme . Strikes and disturbances were carefully organised which the authorities drastically repressed, even those which had no immediate political implications. Casimir Perier, the Government's most talented and honest politician during the first part of Louis-Philippe's reign, summed up the position as follows:

"The Legitimists are hostile, and the clergy are Legitimist. The Bonapartists are for war. I am for peace. The Republican claims are impossible, and their aim is to make me fall out with the middle classes. In these conditions I cannot govern the country".

Perier sadly died in May 1832, a victim to the current cholera epidemic.

For three years the Press had enjoyed freedom from censorship, but by April 1834 the Government came to the end of its patience, and curtailed the liberties of the Press in the interests of law and order. Fresh strikes broke out in Lyon involving days of bitter fighting, and there was a simultaneous rising in Eastern Paris, organised by the Société des Droits de l'Homme, which was savagely crushed. The Press was put under strict control, and insults to the King or Ministers were now to be regarded as threats to the security of the State. Judicial procedures were modified to ensure quick judgements.

A period of comparative peace now reigned. Louis-Philippe missed Perier's firm hand, but in fact he had never had the intention of being a King who reigned but did not govern. The problem was that if he appointed weak Ministers, they could not control the rebellious populace: if he chose strong Ministers they pursued their own policies notwithstanding. Accordingly he played "general post" and there was a continuous coming and going of Government officials.

In 1840 Francois Guizot was appointed Minister of Foreign Affairs. He was a highly intelligent man, an austere Huguenot, well-educated, an able financier, and regarded by many as the greatest statesman of the 19th century. It was said that under his administration France was like a commercial company whose sole purpose was to make dividends for the shareholders. He regarded power as the prerogative of the upper classes, political equality as a dangerous illusion, and universal suffrage as an instrument of destruction. Contrary to expectation, he was to become Louis-Philippe's chief adviser for the remainder of his reign.

The main preoccupation of the new Cabinet was with European politics. Louis-Philippe, building on his knowledge acquired during his travels in exile, considered himself an expert in foreign affairs, and in fact he was not unsuccessful. France was at peace, he had been instrumental in organising the conciliation of European adversaries, and he had maintained France's own prestige. Unlike Napoleon, Louis-Philippe had little interest in overseas dominions. Apart from the long drawn-out conquest of Algeria, which he had inherited from Charles X, and which was bloodily concluded in 1848, he preferred negotiation to war. He always felt that he was regarded by other Royals as an outsider. According to Victor Hugo, Louis-Philippe believed that both he and France were hated by the rulers of Europe: "I tell you frankly," he said, "they hate me because I am an Orléans, and they hate me for myself".

He achieved a precarious peace with Britain, and Queen Victoria and Prince Albert visited Paris on 2 September 1843. Her sole comment appears to have been that the French Court was a muddle and lacked dignity. Twelve years later she was staying with Napoleon III and the Empress Eugénie at St. Cloud. In 1844 Louis-Philippe returned Victoria's visit, accompanied by the Duc de Monpensier, whom the Queen created a Knight of the Garter.

In 1846 disaster struck. The basic cause of the economic problem was the widespread bad weather, which destroyed the wheat and potato harvests throughout Northern France. By May 1847 the price of bread had more than doubled. There was less money for essential purchases, and none for luxuries. There was acute depression in the textile trades, leading to unemployment and in some places to a cut in wages. The iron, coal and mining industries were hard hit. Construction work on the new railways ceased. Prices and profits collapsed, aggravated by the financial crisis caused by previous over-speculation in railway shares and lack of capital investment. Gold reserves at the Bank of France dropped dangerously low. In spite of the Government taking swift action to import wheat, and the good harvest of 1847, there was no amelioration of the misery or resentment.

1846 also brought about a break with England over the Spanish succession, which was used as a pawn in the renewed nineteenth century quarrel between Britain and France. The Infanta Isabella II was a Queen in her own right, and both she and her sister were up for bids in the marriage market. Queen Victoria put forward Leopold of Saxe Coburg as a prospective bridegroom for Isabella. Louis-Philippe suggested his son Montpensier, which infuriated Victoria. Isabella's cousin, the Duke of Cadiz then bribed Louis-Philippe with eight million francs to support his own suit. The idea met with some opposition from Isabella. She disliked Cadiz, who was known as "Paquita", but ultimately she gave in and married him. Montpensier married her sister, the Infanta Luisa. Victoria was outraged and broke off relations with Louis-Philippe. Guizot regarded the coup as a major triumph for French diplomacy, because it was assumed that Cadiz could not give Isabella a child, and that therefore an Orléans prince would ultimately inherit the Spanish throne. It was a misapprehension, because Isabella in due course gave birth to a son.

Louis-Philippe, with extraordinary insensitivity, gave a sumptuous fête in honour of Isabella, regardless of the fact that his subjects were starving. He appeared blind to public opinion. The monarchists, republicans, anarchists, communists and socialists, all hating each other, were united against the King. He was growing old, his life-style had become luxurious, and the people were tired of him. Then two major scandals broke out.

In May 1847 M. Teste, the President of the highest Court of Appeal, and an ex-Minister, was accused of accepting a bribe of 94,000 francs from General Cubières, another ex-Minister, in return for granting him a salt-mine concession. Teste was arrested, and at the trial it was revealed that he was guilty of this, and other fraudulent practices. When proof was produced in the form of his own signature on incriminating documents, he confessed. He was condemned to three years' imprisonment, and the General was downgraded and fined.

An even more shocking event was the murder of the Duchesse de Choiseul-Praslin a few weeks later. In 1814 the Duc, then nineteen years old, had married a sixteen-year-old Corsican, Mlle Sebastiani, and they had nine children. She was wealthy, and although she knew that her husband was often unfaithful to her he was careful not to give proof, lest her father should disinherit her. In 1841 he introduced into the household a woman of twenty eight, Mme Deluzy-Desportes, as governess to his younger children, and she became his mistress. The Duchesse was mad with jealousy and demanded that the governess be dismissed. On 18 August the Duchesse was found dead in her bedroom, a tuft of her husband's hair clutched in her hand. He was arrested, tried, and found guilty. On 21 August he took poison, thus cheating the guillotine.

There was inevitably a cry of "corruption". Guizot himself was not above using bribery to maintain his majority in the Chamber. In spite of growing criticism and the revival of the demand for parliamentary reform, no action was taken. Crowds gathered to demonstrate against Guizot's ministry. Barricades were erected in working-class districts, and red flags hoisted. Despite entreaties by the Queen and the Princes, Louis-Philippe had previously refused to dismiss Guizot, but the imminent danger now led him at last to relent. Guizot was banished. Louis-Philippe sent for Thiers, the chief Opposition leader, to form a new Government, promising that he should choose his own Ministers. He hoped thereby to demonstrate that he was open to change, but it was too late. The next day Thiers returned and tendered his resignation.

On the evening of 23rd February, troops guarding the Ministry of Foreign Affairs opened fire on the demonstrators crowded in front of the building, leaving eighty dead or wounded. Paris erupted. Cobbles were torn up for use as weapons, and gunsmiths pillaged. An armed mob descended on the Tuileries. Urged by Montpensier, Louis-Philippe abdicated, naming his grandson, the

Comte de Paris, as his heir. The boy's father, Louis Philippe's eldest son Ferdinand, had been killed in 1842 by being thrown from a carriage when the horses bolted. The King informed the Duchesse d'Orléans that he was leaving, but that she had every right to stay and guard her son's interests.

At Dreux, where the royal family had stopped for the night, the Sous Prefect, M. Marechal, arrived to tell the King that France had declared a Republic. The Duchesse d'Orléans and her son had gone to the Chamber of Deputies, but had been mobbed. Louis-Philippe and Marie-Amélie, disguised as Mr and Mrs Smith, were smuggled aboard the ferry at Honfleur on 2 March 1848, and the King went once more into exile. He died on 26 August two years later. His son, the Duc de Nemours, notified Queen Victoria who decreed Court mourning. Louis-Philippe was seventy-seven years old. He had been a royal prince, a Jacobin, a vagabond, a soldier, a teacher of mathematics, a King, and finally a fugitive.

It was very possible that the Chamber would have accepted the Comte de Paris, with the Queen as Regent during his minority, but the incursion of the mob into the inner sanctum of Government, their derision and discourtesy to the Duchesse and her son, made it clear that no compromise was possible. The Orléans monarchy had been at best a demonstration of expediency, not of conviction.

Yet Louis-Philippe's reign was not without its successes. The years between 1830 and 1848 witnessed great material advances that changed the way of life and added much to its amenities. It was a period of great cultural achievement. It did much for higher education, and witnessed the publication of some of the greatest works by French writers, including Lamartine, Vigny, Musset, Gautier, Stendahl, Dumas, Merimée and George Sand. The Duchesse d'Orléans was an admirer and patron of Victor Hugo, who never forgot the debt he owed to the house of Orléans. Many new artists attained eminence: the great cartoonist, Daumier, created a fantastic gallery of Orléans officials, and the painter Corot, sculptor David d'Angers, and architect Viollet le-Duc were gaining recognition. Industry was reacting to new technology. Roads were built that enabled farmers to transport their produce more rapidly, and facilitated the establishment of a regular postal service. The railways were developing, and 1844-1846 brought French railway mania, involving collaboration between the State and private enterprise. The Paris-St Germain line opened in 1837. In 1840 the first steamer crossed the Atlantic. Invention of the daguerreotype, precursor of the camera, brought family portraits within the reach of the most modest purse.

The Orléans monarchy fell because it failed to bridge the gap between itself and public opinion. The King did not represent either a principle or a national glory, and not one hand was raised to save him. It had been an "administrative monarchy", and served its purpose. Now there was no longer any need for it, it ceased to be useful, and ended.

Second Republic, Second Empire

The proclamation of the Second Republic at the Hotel de Ville, Paris, on 24 February 1848 caused both alarm and rejoicing throughout Europe. It had happened almost by accident, caused by the inherent weakness of the French government. Since 1789 no regime had possessed the conditions necessary for stability. In 1848, political opinion was sharply divided. On one side were the Royalists: the propertied classes, which included the Legitimists and clerics for whom an Orléanist king was worse than no king at all - and also the Orléanists themselves, including the "new rich" and officials who considered themselves liberal, were inclined towards anti-clericalism, and were not dissatisfied with Louis-Philippe. Opposed to both groups was the Left comprising the new educated classes and professionals with Republican sympathies, the rural masses who were regarded as "peasants", and the potential revolutionaries. Accordingly, Paris was a seething cauldron of dangerously conflicting ideologies.

The hopes of the Royalists were destroyed in July by the invasion of the Hotel de Ville by the National Guard, shouting "A bas la Chambre". A provisional left-wing Government was set up, which included one Albert, a token worker. Their first act was to proclaim the right of universal suffrage; their second was to free slaves throughout French territories, which immediately caused a state of economic crisis in the colonies.

The problem with universal suffrage was that the majority of the new electorate were illiterate peasants, who blindly followed the lead of the clergy and local landowners. In rural communities the Church was far stronger than the State. This was not at all what the Chamber had intended. Elections were scheduled for Easter Sunday, in the hope of keeping the faithful away from the polls, but mass was celebrated early, and the villagers marched to vote in processions headed by their priests. The result was that the Constituent Assembly was mainly conservative and traditionalist; half the deputies were Royalist, with the Orléanists twice as strong as the Legitimists. There was a mere sprinkling of extreme Republicans, and fewer Socialists.

In Paris the left-wing clubs embarked on a furious press campaign, but their attempt in May to overthrow the Assembly by a mob demonstration was easily dispersed by the National Guard, and landed their leaders in prison. A month later another revolt erupted. Living conditions were getting worse, and semi-starvation was the common lot of the increasing number of unemployed. In June a decree was passed drafting all unmarried workers in the so-called National Workshops into the Army, sending the remainder to the provinces, under penalty of losing their "dole". Paris, as usual, erupted. Barricades were once again erected; the Army, reinforced by contingents from the National Guard and volunteers from the provinces, moved in. After six days of bitter street fighting the rebellion was quelled. Many were killed. and thousands of prisoners were deported as forced immigrants to Algeria. The extraordinary thing about the uprising was that no leaders were identified.

The Assembly, under the protection of the Army, set about attempting to reconstitute itself. In December an election was held to appoint the First President of the Second French Republic, to be chosen by the whole nation. Among the candidates was Louis Napoleon Bonaparte, nephew of the great Emperor - or perhaps as scandal decreed, his illegitimate son by his step-daughter Hortense de Beauharnais. Hortense was married to Napoleon I's younger brother Louis, who became King of Holland. Charles Louis Napoleon, Hortense's second child, was born in 1808.

In the by-elections to the Constituent Assembly in June and September, a number of departments had chosen Louis Napoleon to be their deputy. Aided by a brilliant publicity campaign and clever propaganda, in December he was elected Prince President by an overwhelming majority.

The Man of December

Napoleon I had deliberately created a heroic public image. He presented himself as the saviour of France, a man of destiny who would save the people from the Jacobins and the Terror, and heal the internal strife that was tearing the country to pieces; as the protector of religion; the champion of liberalism and freedom from oppression; the efficient administrator to ensure financial security and economic prosperity; the soldier who created an Empire and restored France to international prestige and power. It was a romantic legend that his defeat at Waterloo in 1815 had tarnished a little, but the nostalgia lingered on. The Orléanists regarded it as a harmless bed-time story and Louis-Philippe had not hesitated to exploit it for his own ends.

Louis Napoleon's two abortive attempts against the French throne, at Strasbourg in 1836 and Boulogne in 1840, had been ludicrous fiascos, and relegated him to comparative obscurity. He spent six years in comfortable imprisonment in the fortress of Ham, where amenities included the services of a mistress. In February 1846 he walked out disguised as a builder's labourer, and escaped to England where he enrolled as a special constable.

He had little of the first Napoleon's charisma. His appearance was unattractive, his manners awkward, shy and irresolute, and he spoke French with a strong German accent. But he had two big advantages: his name and his determined belief in his ascendant star.

France was disenchanted with the Republic, which had brought nothing but disorder, instability, and increased taxation, ending in a profound disillusionment which the new Prince President subtly promoted. The remedy, he hinted, could only be found by giving him a free hand to restore the Empire. On 2 December 1852, he assumed the Imperial title with the name of Napoleon III, a *coup d'état* that was generally welcomed. Financiers and industrialists hoped that his accession would guarantee a strong government and promote economic recovery. Workers believed he would protect their interests, and Catholics looked forward to a new alliance between Altar and Throne, disregarding the fact that the new Emperor was in fact an agnostic. Everyone believed the Empire stood for order and social security, a misapprehension which Louis Napoleon did much to encourage. Only a small minority whispered that the Constitution was suppressed by "the man of December", the one person who had sworn to uphold it.

The Constitution of 1852 was in fact a replica of Napoleon I's of 1800, the only amendments being that the Legislative Body was to be elected by universal suffrage, and slavery was abolished. The Emperor appointed all officers, was Commander in Chief of all forces and had the right of declaring war and making treaties. Senators, deputies, magistrates and state officials were required to take an oath of allegiance, and the police were given extensive powers to control possible malcontents or subversive activities. The Paris Clubs, hotbeds of socialism, were suppressed; the National Guard disbanded except in Paris; and the Press was subjected to strict scrutiny, whereby after three warnings publication could be suspended. State education was rigidly controlled, even to the extent where school-teachers were required to shave off their moustaches, "in order to remove the last vestiges of anarchy from their costumes as well as their morals".

It was necessary for the new Emperor to marry and perpetuate the dynasty. Having failed to attract one or two of the minor available royal princesses, Louis Napoleon's fancy fell on the beautiful red-haired Spanish Countess, Eugénie de Montijo. She was twenty-six years old, a notorious virgin, and in January 1853 he married her. As reported by the British Ambassador, "he could get her in no other way". She was religious in a Spanish fashion, and sexually unresponsive, so that her husband consoled himself with the Countess de Beauregard among others. A son, the Prince Imperial, was born in 1856, nearly costing the Empress her life, and after that, marital relations ceased. There were also family difficulties. Her mother was regarded by many of the more pompous aristocracy as a mere adventuress who collected debts and lovers.

In spite of bad harvests and cholera epidemics the economic state of the country improved, stimulated by a programme of public works, which included Les Halles, the great central metal and glass market, and rebuilding the Garnier Opera House. The Bois de Boulogne, a rather dull royal forest, was refurbished as a landscaped park, and presented to Paris for the citizens' recreation. The most useful contribution was Haussmann's great underground channel, the Cloaca Maxima, which drained the city streets and prevented flooding. Unfortunately it did not take sewage, and sanitation was still very primitive.

France's prestige stood higher than at any time since the First Empire. Cordial relations were established with Great Britain, and when Queen Victoria paid a state visit in 1855 she was impressed by Louis Napoleon's belief that all he had done, and was doing, was in fulfilment of his destiny.

The Emperor himself made decisions on foreign policy, partly because he did not trust his ministers, and partly because of his ineradicable belief in his own "star". He needed successes abroad to compensate for the loss of liberty at home. He involved France in the Crimean War on the excuse of protecting Roman Catholic interests in the Near East, and the Peace Congress held at Paris in 1856 acclaimed his triumph, though it is difficult to see what was achieved.

In January 1858 an Italian revolutionary, Orsini, attempted to assassinate Louis Napoleon and Eugénie as they arrived at the Opera, which killed eight people and injured many more. Orsini was executed, but the Emperor, ever the opportunist, promptly cast him as a romantic patriot, and by reviving the legend of Napoleon I as the great liberator of Italy, was indirectly able to proclaim his own allegiance to the ideal of Italian liberation.

In July the Emperor secretly met Cavour, the Sardinian Foreign Minister, at Plombières, and gave his verbal agreement to support a war against Austria, which then largely dominated Northern Italy. After a year of considerable skirmishing by the various powers involved, and in the face of opposition from his ministers, the clergy, the peasantry and most of the middle-classes, in April 1859 war was declared. In accordance with Napoleonic tradition, Louis Napoleon was expected to be a military genius, and perhaps he thought he was. At any rate, the departing troops were cheered in the streets of Paris, and there were scenes of enthusiasm at the Gare de Lyon, from where the Emperor left for the front.

The Austrians had advanced into Piedmontese territory, but were defeated at Magenta, which saved Milan, and then at Solferino. The Allies were preparing to invade Venetia, but internal revolutions in some of the smaller Italian states, and the increased opposition of the French clergy, called a halt. Prussia was mobilising, and the Austrians were entrenched in the famous fortresses of the Quadrilateral. Louis Napoleon promptly opened negotiations with Emperor Francis Joseph, and an armistice was signed at Villafranca, under the terms of which Lombardy was ceded to France for transfer to the Kingdom of Sardinia; Austria kept Venetia, and the Italian states which had taken part in the revolution were restored to their former rulers.

Louis Napoleon now began to think that perhaps, as he had said at the beginning of his reign, "the Empire should mean peace". France was against further hostilities, and the Emperor had thoroughly stirred up Europe and shattered the status quo. For ten years France had been involved in war. In 1860 he announced that efforts would now be concentrated on developing national wealth, and improving living conditions for the agricultural population and general workers by Government loans. A free-trade treaty was negotiated with Britain, reducing tariffs and abolishing the prohibition of imports, which immediately raised fanatical objections from French industrialists, but it did not harm French prosperity. Britain abolished Customs charges on all French imports except wine and spirits, and foreign competition brought down the price of iron which in turn stimulated the growth of railways and the introduction of machinery, both of which were beneficial to the economy.

In 1861-62 came the disastrous Mexican venture, when France attempted to establish a new Latin Catholic Empire in Mexico that it was hoped would develop sufficiently to counterbalance the power of the United States. The scheme was intended to compensate Catholics for the humiliation suffered by the Pope during the war of Italian liberation, and at the same time to promote French financial interests in the New World. The French had no idea of the kind of resistance they were to meet. For five years they sought to maintain on the throne the puppet Emperor, the Hapsburg Archduke Maximilian, during which time 6000 men were killed or died of disease. The United States threatened intervention, and Louis Napoleon, unable to face war with the U.S.A., withdrew his forces. Maximilian was murdered by the Mexicans, and the embryonic Empire collapsed.

France had achieved a position of prestige and influence in Europe, but in the age of Cavour and Bismarck, Louis Napoleon was out of his class. The Emperor never forgot that he only held his position by the will of the people. Unlike Napoleon I, he had no army behind him, and there was no one great political party to support him. Louis Napoleon, already unwell, was no longer able to battle against the inevitable.

Seeking to appease public opinion, he sought to introduce further Liberal reforms. The 1863 elections had produced a Third Party, mainly consisting of moderate Orléanists, who favoured limiting the Emperor's personal power and establishing a parliament. In 1867 Louis Napoleon introduced some reforms, but retained the Ministers who were opposed to concessions, which did nothing to inspire confidence. Nonetheless, the Legislative Body were successful in frustrating the Emperor's policy on two important issues: it rejected on the grounds of economy a Government proposal to strengthen the Army by the creation of a trained reserve; and required a guarantee that France would never abandoned Rome.

As a result of the 1869 elections, 116 deputies backed the Third Party's demand for a parliamentary government. In November Louis Napoleon appealed to the Legislative Body "to help him establish liberty in France", and in January 1870 he asked Emile Ollivier, formerly a Republican deputy, to head a Ministry which would be responsible both to Parliament and the Emperor. In the 1870 plebiscite the country voted overwhelmingly in favour of the new policies, which in effect was not only a vote of confidence in the government, but in the Emperor himself.

The speculation inevitably arises as to whether, carried by this unexpected wave of enthusiasm, the Second Empire might have survived had it not been for the machinations of Bismarck. Louis Napoleon himself was sad and tired, weakened by illness, and had lost belief in his guiding star. Many of his old and ablest supporters were dead. The Liberal reforms that he had unwillingly instituted created their own problems. The Press were no longer muzzled by the warning system or the need for prior authorisation. Prosecution of newspaper men merely produced martyrs. When a remote cousin of the Emperor's, Prince Pierre Bonaparte, shot a young Republican journalist, Victor Noir, in a fit of ungovernable temper, the sensation it created was mind-blowing. Noir was buried in Père Lachaise cemetery, and his full-length portrait in bronze, lying recumbent on his grave, has incredibly become a cult attraction, due mainly to the rather too pronounced anatomical detail.

On 3 July 1870 Paris learned that a Hohenzollern prince had been accepted as a candidate for the vacant Spanish throne. France was outraged by what it regarded as Prussian aggression, even to the extent of threatening to declare war, and Spain promptly cancelled its acceptance. The Emperor, however, wanted more than a mere withdrawal of the candidate. He wanted a personal denial from the Prussian King, and a telegram was accordingly sent to the French Ambassador in Berlin instructing him to demand such a guarantee. The decision to do so had been taken, not by parliament or by any head of government, but by a small irresponsible group at the Court of Saint-Cloud headed by the Empress, who believed that only a diplomatic victory would bolster an Empire crumbling under the assault of liberalism. Victory over Bismarck was the essential objective.

The King of Prussia refused, since to accede to such a demand would have implied dishonesty on his part. He considered the Spanish Government's assurance should be sufficient. Bismarck saw this as an opportunity not to be missed. He gave a short statement to the Press which read like a brusque rebuff to the Ambassador from William I. Everyone in France - the Empress, Ollivier, the Legislative Body, the newspapers, and the people on the streets, cried out in fury. Next day the Imperial Council, attended by the Empress, but not by the Emperor who was too unwell, met and voted for immediate mobilization. The decision was communicated to the Legislative Body by Ollivier, and although it was resisted by some members of the Centre and the Left who felt they could not support a policy "that would shed torrents of blood to avenge a few rude words", Ollivier was carried away by his own eloquence, and said that he accepted responsibility for the war with a light heart. On 19 July France declared war on Prussia.

The Army was under the supreme command of the Emperor, who was now so ill that he could only sit his horse in extreme agony. Current foreign policy had resulted in France having no allies, and apart from Louis Napoleon himself, she did not consider she needed any. In fact, the French Army was below strength and ill-equipped, and mobilization was hopelessly muddled. The Prussians, superior in numbers and guns, better disciplined and commanded, and for the first time in warfare using railways for transport, immediately took the offensive, and by the first week in August had won victories at Wissembourg, Froschwiller and Forbach. Alsace and Lorraine fell. Bazaine, who had cut his teeth in the Mexican campaign and was known for his personal courage, replaced Louis Napoleon as Commander-in-Chief, but considered final responsibility remained with the Emperor, and would take no positive action without him. He withdrew with a large part of the Army to Metz, where he was isolated by the victory of the Prussians at Gravelotte. Meanwhile, the Emperor and Marshal McMahon were endeavouring to recruit a new army at Chalons.

Back in Paris Eugénie, acting as Regent, summoned the Legislative Body which demanded the dismissal of the Ministers it regarded as responsible for the French Army's defeat, and the appointment of a new government nominated by the Assembly. Eugénie refused. She chose General Cousin de Montauban, Comte de Palikao, to replace Ollivier as head of a Bonapartist ministry selected by herself. A victory in battle was essential if the Empire was to survive, and Palikao ordered McMahon to march to the relief of Bazaine, for political rather than military reasons. It was a hopeless task. Bazaine did nothing, and was later to be charged unreasonably with treachery, since his policy of inaction was inevitable as he was awaiting the Emperor's personal orders which it was impossible to get to him. The relieving Army was trapped by Prussian artillery at Sedan, and on 1 September, to save further slaughter, the Emperor surrendered with 84,000 men,

2,700 officers and 39 generals. The Emperor and McMahon were both taken prisoner.

Paris was devastated. The Empress and the Prince Imperial fled to England. A year later the Emperor followed, a sick and broken man, and the Second Empire collapsed.

The Third Republic

The Legislative Body, anticipating a revolutionary coup from the Left, instituted a provisional Government of National Defence, headed by General Trochu, the military governor of Paris. The new Minister of the Interior was Gambetta.

Gambetta was born at Cahors, of humble parents. His father was an Italian immigrant, and his mother a Frenchwoman from Gascony. He was trained in law, and in 1869 at the age of thirty-one, had been elected as a Radical to the Legislative Body as the member for Belleville. He was a "rough diamond", with charm, ability and remarkable oratorical powers, and was regarded by many of his contemporaries as a second Danton.

By the end of the month Paris was surrounded by the Prussian Army which had occupied all France north and east of Orléans. On 7 October Gambetta crossed the German lines by balloon and went to Tours to assume the role of Minister of War. Paris was well defended and well provisioned, and general optimism decreed that it could hold out against the besieging Prussians until Gambetta arranged for a relieving force from the provinces, but this was a complete misapprehension. The troops inside the city were poorly trained and ill-disciplined, and the Prussian observation posts were so well placed that they were able to detect any military manoeuvres almost before they happened. The few attempts made to break out, undertaken more as a sop to the increasingly hostile Republican party's demands for action than in the hope of achieving anything useful, were doomed to failure from the outset. By Christmas it was obvious to everyone that surrender was inevitable. The New Year brought heavy bombardment from the Prussian guns, and on 28 January 1871

Paris capitulated. Ten days earlier the King of Prussia had assumed the title of Emperor of Germany, and a kind of coronation ceremony was held at the Royal Palace of Versailles, a gratuitous insult that the French bitterly resented.

The terms of the Treaty of Frankfurt dictated by Germany were unbelievably harsh. The indemnity demanded was so enormous that it was improbable that France would ever be able to pay it in full. Five hundred million francs was to be paid within thirty days after the re-establishment of a French Government. Another four and a half billion francs was payable by instalments by 1874, and an interest of 5% per annum was payable on this outstanding balance. Payment was to be in metal, gold or silver, or in Prussian, Belgian or Dutch bank notes. With a fixed rate of exchange of 3.75 Fr. francs to the Prussian thaler, the inflated amounts due to be paid were even greater. Only after payment of the first five hundred million would evacuation of the occupying forces begin.

In addition, France had to cede Alsace and a large part of Lorraine to Prussia. They were industrial areas, one of the main sources of iron ore, and the centre of the French textile industry, but the blow to French economy was nothing compared with the consternation of the local inhabitants, who regarded themselves as French and had no desire to be reclassified as Germans. For the next fifty years they nourished dreams of revenge on Germany, the hated enemy.

Bismarck was shrewd enough to realise that the National Defence Government was a makeshift affair, and that any treaty concluded with them might well be repudiated by their successors. In order to be sure of negotiating with a properly constituted body, he permitted elections to take place within two weeks of the surrender of Paris. The problem was that this left no time for candidates to canvass the electorate, or for political parties to organise their campaigns. The main issue was continuing the war or concluding the peace, and the country was almost unanimous in its desire for peace. Local dignitaries, mainly drawn from wealthy establishment families, presented themselves as candidates standing for conciliation and public order, and were elected in almost every case. It also so happened that the majority were Royalists, although they were split between Legitimists and Orléanists. As men of wealth and property they were averse to any change in the social hierarchy.

Adolphe Thiers, who had been Louis Philippe's leader of the loyal opposition in the 1840's, was asked to form the new government, with the title of Chief of the Executive Power. His Ministers represented a fairly wide range of political opinions, with the exception of the extreme Left. Thiers understood that the first priority was the re-establishment of order, if any part of the huge sum of the indemnity was to be raised; social revolution was bound to create economic disruption, and must be avoided at all costs. Paris had always been regarded as a centre of political disruption and social discontent, and in an effort to avoid any untoward confrontation the Assembly moved to Versailles, 22 kilometres away from potential revolutionary activity.

Throughout the war, and particularly during the time of the siege, many Parisians had fallen on hard times. Businesses failed, causing unemployment and financial hardship. Possessions were pawned, rent fell into arrears, and shopkeepers could only continue to operate on a system of promissory notes, allowing them both to give and receive credit. In March 1871 the Assembly made a move against these practices, ordering that rent owing had to be paid, goods pawned must be redeemed or sold within a limited time, and promissory notes must be met in cash as soon as they became due. The citizens of Paris, who had just suffered six months of shocking stress and severe privation, were now faced with ruin. The position was aggravated by the return of the refugees who had fled from the city to avoid the Prussians and now returned intending to take up their old life, except that the old life no longer existed. Paris felt it was being unfairly victimised, and for once rich and poor were united in their resentment against the Government.

Thiers was determined that Paris should not once again become the centre of revolution, and as a preventive measure sent in troops to recover the 417 cannons belonging to the National Guard. The cannons were stored in the arsenal at the top of Montmartre hill, and due to the difficult terrain and a lack of horses it was impossible to move them. The bewildered troops were surrounded by an angry mob, and two of their generals were murdered. It was a virtual declaration of war. All troops and Government officials were ordered by Thiers to withdraw.

The Massacre of Paris

The vacuum thereby created was quickly filled by the Central Committee of the National Guard, who took over the city and organized elections. Paris was declared a Commune, an independent political enclave responsible to no-one but itself. Their hope was that the pattern would be repeated in other areas of France, and so form a federal state. Their manifesto, pasted up on the placards of Paris, called for recognition of the Republic, "the only government compatible with the rights of the people", the guarantee of freedom of the individual and of conscience, and the right to work. It also condemned the old order of "clerics, militarism, officialdom, exploitation, monopolies and privileges to which the proletariat owes its servitude, and the country its ills and disasters".

This vision of an ideal communist paradise was not only impractical, it was not even what the majority of Parisians wanted, and although they disliked the Government they did not consider the Commune a viable alternative. There was even dissent among the Commune's own leaders, who spent much time in arguing and little in doing. No move was made against the Government at Versailles, who undisturbed went into action.

Thiers reached agreement with Bismarck that the French Army could be increased beyond the limit proscribed by the armistice, and that these extra troops should be trained for civil warfare. Since 1848 there had been a shift away from the type of men recruited as Army officers. They were no longer fervent revolutionaries, and with loyal men in command Thiers felt justified in moving against the Communards.

The Government had more men, better trained, with superior equipment. By the beginning of May they had entered Paris, and there followed a week of street fighting and horrific bloodshed. Prisoners were shot as a matter of course. The Commune forces were largely disorganized, ill-disciplined, and inexperienced. Barricades were erected in the working-class districts, heroically but ineffectively defended to the death by both men and women. Buildings were set on fire in an effort to stop the attackers' advance. The flames had little effect, but the press heightened the tension by dramatic references to the "blazing city". Many important buildings, including the Hotel de Ville, were destroyed. More than seventy hostages were taken by the Communards as bargaining counters, but proved useless as Thiers would not negotiate, and were shot.

In the aftermath, Government troops swept through Paris shooting anyone without question who looked grubby enough to be a Communard, including one innocent lady chimney-sweep. It is estimated that 25,000 died and were buried in mass graves, and a further 50,000 were brought to trial. About half of these were freed for lack of evidence, the rest were executed, imprisoned, or transported and died in appalling conditions.

Paris soon returned to normal, at least on the surface. The debris was cleared away, bodies disposed of, buildings repaired, and businesses restarted. But there remained a deep psychological scar. Not only Paris, but all France was affected. One was for the Commune or against it, there was no middle way; and the traumatic effect of defeat by the Prussians had lasting and tragic results that culminated in the wholesale slaughter of the First World War.

ꜰhe Ðukes' Repuꝑlic

Adolph Thiers was at this time 74 years of age, and he had been very much a fringe politician for nearly thirty years. Now he had the position and power he had long coveted. There was little opposition, and as both Head of State and a member of the National Assembly, he had a double voice. He was also lavish with hospitality as a means of winning support, and it was said by some of the lesser favoured that his court was grander than that of Napoleon III. He maintained good relations with Bismarck and ensured that no excuse was given for further penalties to be imposed. In addition, he set to work to raise the money for the indemnity by issuing two public loans which incredibly were oversubscribed, and the last German soldiers left France in September 1873, earlier than anyone had anticipated.

With the destruction of the Commune, and a temporary lull in revolutionary activity, the scene appeared to be set for the Restoration of the Bourbons. The Monarchists had achieved a large majority in the 1871 elections, and it was assumed that Thiers was acting simply as a caretaker. The Legitimists, the stronger of the two royalist parties, were adamant that the next king should be the Comte de Chambord, Charles X's grandson, but Chambord was fifty, and childless. The Orléanists, who favoured Louis Philippe's grandson, the Comte de Paris, realised that alone they would never succeed, and so were prepared to make a deal and accept Chambord on condition that he named the Comte de Paris as his heir. In the course of time they would thus ultimately achieve what they wanted, a constitutional Orléanist Monarch.

It was Chambord himself who was the problem. He had spent forty years in exile, surrounded by inflexible supporters of the divine right of Kings. He regarded it as his sacred duty to cleanse France of the ills imposed upon her by the Revolution and Empire, and his terms for restoration of the monarchy left small room for negotiation. His manifesto stated that he was prepared to accept a Parliamentary government and universal suffrage. The sticking point was over the flag, and on this he was not prepared to compromise. France, he said "will recall me and I shall come to her intact - with devotion, my principles and my flag...I received it as a sacred trust from the old King, my grandfather...it has always been, for me, inseparable from the memory of my absent fatherland. It floated over my cradle: may it overshadow my grave...In the glorious folds of this unsullied standard I shall bring you order and liberty".

For the ordinary people of France, the white flag of the Bourbons, with its golden lilies, was a reminder of the bad old days when liberty was the sole prerogative of the crown. The soldiers of the Revolution, the purveyors of liberty, equality, and fraternity, had raised the tricolore; Napoleon I's victorious armies had marched under it. The national standard of France was more than an empty symbol, it was a matter on both sides of the principles for which they stood.

Thiers, being a realist, recognised that this was a deadlock. The by-elections of July 1871 had been won largely by Republicans, including the re-election of Gambetta. The Orléanists were becoming increasing suspicious of Chambord, and as their primary objective was a parliamentary type of government rather than an absolute monarch, they were beginning to lean towards an alliance with the more conservative Left. In November 1872 Thiers openly declared that he was in favour of a Republic. "It exists", he said, "it is the legally elected government of the country; to replace it would be a revolution of the most dangerous kind". Many of the Orléanists supported him. The remainder, and all the Legitimists, were outraged. Thiers, the Monarchist, who had been appointed as President of the Republic on the understanding that the government was provisional, had betrayed them.

They were determined to be revenged. Thiers was denounced as an opportunist at best, a traitor at worst, and derided as someone who mistakenly considered himself indispensable. Under their new leader, the Duc de Broglie, and supported by some Bonapartists, the Monarchists convinced the Assembly that Thiers was too ambitious; he was defeated and resigned.

Marshal McMahon, Duc de Magenda, was appointed the new President, with the Duc de Broglie as Prime Minister. McMahon, the descendant of an Irish gentleman who had served with the French Army in the eighteenth century, was a retiring sort of man - he accepted the Presidency only after being persuaded by his wife that it was his duty to his country to do so. He was by conviction an Orléanist, but he had been a leading general in Napoleon III's Italian campaign of 1859, and had led the Government troops against the Paris Commune. This diversity of loyalties now stood him in good stead.

The death of Napoleon III in 1873 left the Bonapartists free to play political games in the Assembly; and with a number of the Orléanists having followed Theirs' option to support the moderate Republicans, the true Monarchists felt increasingly isolated, and were becoming anxious. Time was running out.

The Duc de Broglie was faced with finding an answer to the problem of Chambord and the flag. Several deputations were sent to Frohsdorf, the castle where Chambord lived in exile, to discuss a compromise, and finally news came that Chambord had agreed to accept the tricolore if that was what the people wanted. The National Assembly as the people's representative was to decide. The Monarchists were relieved and overjoyed, and plans for the Restoration, including the commissioning of a new Royal coach, were immediately put in hand. Unfortunately the celebrations were premature, based on a mutual misunderstanding. Chambord had agreed that the National Assembly should decide as he was under the impression that they had a large Legitimist majority who would support his insistence on the "lily banner". The National Assembly, however, had interpreted his words as meaning that he would accept the tricolore because that was what they wanted. Full stop. Nothing was further from his mind or intention.

It was clear that the Restoration could not now take place. The Legitimists would accept nobody but Chambord, and as he had not, and would not renounce his claim to the throne, de Broglie could not approach anyone else. The only hope of the Monarchists was to wait until Chambord died, and so cleared the way for the Comte de Paris, and in order to prolong the situation, in November 1875 McMahon's Presidency was extended by seven years, in the hope that time would solve the problem.

The tide had again begun to turn. The Monarchists, who had been elected as representatives of law and order, had begun to be regarded as reactionaries and warmongers. As a result of the unification of Italy in 1860, the territory controlled by the Pope had been largely reduced, and what remained had only been tenable due to the support of French troops. When these troops were withdrawn to fight in the Franco-Prussian war the Italian Army moved in, and in protest the Pope locked himself up in the Vatican. French Catholics - and Catholic and Monarchist were virtually synonymous terms - were in favour of sending troops to liberate the Pope, but the bourgeoisie and working-classes were against it.

There was a religious revival taking place in France, and many people believed that the humiliation of their recent defeat was an expression of God's displeasure at the atheistic behaviour of the Revolutionaries, and the subsequent lapse of morals. Only a public exhibition of repentance would bring redemption. There were pilgrimages, a renewed cult of the Virgin Mary, and money was freely donated to build Sacred Coeur on the hill of Montmartre as a church of perpetual intercession. Since the Monarchists, and especially the Legitimists, believed that only a divinely appointed King could redeem the realm, they fell into the trap of becoming identified with the more fanatical aspects of the religious revival.

They were unlucky in their choice of leaders. McMahon was a sincere and honest man, but he lacked charisma, and compromise was unknown to him. Also, he was not a member of the National Assembly, so lacked the opportunities to press his opinions that had been available to Thiers. The burden of decision therefore rested on de Broglie, who had the misfortune to be personally unpopular. He was hardworking, intelligent, courageous, and a good speaker, although somewhat hampered by bad diction, which was satirised by his detractors as "gargling". He was not actually a snob, but as the head of an ancient family he was regarded as unapproachable and haughty. His opponents considered him arrogant, and it is true that he was out of touch with ordinary people who believed he had little to offer by way of helping to solve their future problems.

The political situation was further scrambled by the arrival on the scene of the Prince Imperial, Napoleon III's son, a romantic and appealing young man who presented himself as an attractive alternative to the rigid Bourbon regime. The Bonapartist party hailed him with pleasure, and as a consequence gained considerably in popularity.

De Broglie's immediate concern was to ensure that the Monarchists kept their majority in any elections, and to institute a form of government that would be flexible enough to allow for the Restoration when it became feasible. What to call such a government provided a difficulty - the term "Republic" was if possible to be avoided as the Monarchists wished to avoid any suggestion that the Republic was permanent. On other hand, the Republicans were determined that it should be, and be seen to be, permanent.

The matter was finally resolved when Wallon, a Republican Deputy, proposed that the Constitution of 1875 should contain the words "The President of the Republic is elected by the plurality of votes cast by the Senate and the Chamber of Deputies united as a National Assembly". A number of moderate Right-wing Deputies, believing there was no point in opposing what was already a fact, voted with the Republicans, and the Third Republic was officially constituted by one vote - 353 for and 352 against. Regardless of this result, the majority of Deputies in the 1875 National Assembly were still in favour of the restoration of either the monarchy or the empire. The fact remains that the Republicans were defeated on all other issues, and power remained in the hands of the Right, who firmly believed that the country should be run by men of breeding, wealth and worldly experience, and not by the common people who were regarded as being only interested in promoting themselves at the expense of their betters.

Two other institutions were therefore organised to counterbalance the mainly Left-wing Chamber of Deputies: the Senate and the President, both of which were Right-wing. Out of the 300 members of the Senate, 75 were to be life members, which would ensure a permanent core of loyal Monarchists. The remaining members would be elected, but not by general suffrage. Instead, special colleges would be set up in each Department consisting of one member from each village, town or city in the area, and these would elect the Senators. This ensured that voting remained largely in the hands of the conservative countryside. The President would be elected by the combined Chamber of Deputies and the Senate, and as the Senate would be mainly Monarchist, it would ensure that the President was sympathetic to the Monarchist cause. Even election of the members of the Chamber of Deputies was weighted in favour of the Right: instead, as previously, each elector being presented with a list of as many candidates as there were Deputies in his Department, elections were now to take place in single member constituencies. It was hoped, by limiting choice in this way, to increase the probability of a local dignitary being elected, and local dignitaries were on the whole conservative.

It was a clever idea, but things did not go quite as planned. The elections for the Senate misfired, and instead of having 75 Monarchist life members de Broglie found himself with 57 Republicans and 18 Bonapartists. By January 1876 the balance had been readjusted to give a Right majority again, but it was straws blowing in the wind. The elections of February and March for the Chamber of Deputies were a triumph for the Republicans who had a two-thirds majority. Of the other third, about half were Bonapartists, and most of the remainder Orléanists. There were only 30 Legitimists out of 533 members.

In theory, the remedy rested with McMahon, who as President could if he wished replace all the Government ministers, and over-rule the Chamber of Deputies through the Senate. Gambetta, as leader of the Chamber, claimed that only elected representatives of the people had the right to decide Government policy. The showdown came on 16 May 1877 when led once again by de Broglie, McMahon dismissed the Republican ministers and replaced them with Monarchists. The Chamber refused to support him, and without the support of a majority in the Chamber, the government could not operate. In accordance with the Constitution of 1875, McMahon exercised his right as President to dissolve the Chamber.

In an attempt to enlist total Presidential support, the official candidates for re-election were given considerable free publicity through government publications, and much against his inclinations McMahon, who hated public appearances, himself toured the country on an electoral campaign.

Although there were considerable internal conflicts between those who wanted to keep things as they were, and the supporters of radical changes, the Republicans presented a united front, and fought the campaign on the issue of parliamentary government rights. The contention was that ministers had to receive support from the majority of the Chamber, because only the Chamber represented the true will of the people. The result was decisive, and the government failed to get the vote of confidence it needed. The Chamber lost only ten per cent of their seats, and the Republicans maintained their majority.

Gambetta's assessment of the situation was that, of the options open to him, the only practical course of action was for McMahon to resign. In fact, what he did was dismiss de Broglie and appoint Ministers whom he considered to be acceptable to the new Chamber of Deputies. They were moderate men with Republican sympathies who advocated change, but slow change. Then in the indirect election of the Senate in 1879, the Republicans triumphed. This was the last straw for McMahon, and somewhat relieved, he resigned. With a Republican majority in both Chamber and Senate, the new President was Jules Grévy, their own candidate.

The Republic of the Republics

Grévy was a popular choice, because he believed implicitly in a system of government consisting of properly elected representatives. One of his first acts as President was to assure the Deputies that he would never act as his predecessor had and dissolve the Chamber, because that would be to negate the will of the people who had elected them. His moderate views were shared by the majority of the Chamber elected in 1877, and again in 1881, but there was still a section of the Left who advocated radical reform, and a certain number of the Right who supported restoration of the monarchy in some form. In the 1885 elections, the Right redoubled its number of seats.

The most prominent, and able politician of the time was undoubtedly Gambetta, whose pronounced radical views prevented Grévy from employing him until 1881, when he at last asked Gambetta to form a ministry. Contrary to expectations, Gambetta failed to gain the support of the Chamber, and he resigned after only three months. His death the following year at the age of 42 was a loss which France did not then appreciate, but would undoubtedly have come to recognise in the years of crisis that followed.

One of the most remarkable results of the new Republic was the speed with which ministries came and went. Grévy had assured the Chamber that there would be no elections for four years, which meant that the real power rested with the Deputies who could decide matters of policy against the wishes of the Minister concerned, so that it was not unusual for a ministry to last only a month or so. Those that lasted longest were the ones that did nothing.

Jules Ferry was probably the third most important contributor to the new Republic. He was born at St Die in the Vosges, and had trained as a lawyer. As a young man, he landed the most unpopular jobs: in 1870 he was responsible for organising food rationing in Paris, and he was involved with suppressing the attempted insurrection of 22 January. As Minister for Instruction Ferry was active in reforming education which had until then been primarily in the hands of the Catholic Church. Ferry realised that education played an important role in the political thinking of future citizens. His aim was to remove clerical influence from the state-run organizations, as well as to ensure that the teachers were properly trained, which many of the monks and nuns who had hitherto had the monopoly of teaching, were not. In 1881-82 primary education was made compulsory for all, mostly in state schools, so that large numbers of children grew up having virtually no contact with religion. This meant the Church was increasingly antagonistic to the Republic and aligned its interests with the Right, which greatly strengthened its desire for a change of regime.

The Chamber would, by rights, liked to have abolished the Senate altogether, which it regarded as a body that existed only to frustrate the will of the people. Since this was too drastic an action, action was taken to weaken the Senate's power; the electoral procedure was modified, and life membership abolished. Numbers of votes for the country areas, where population was scarce, were diminished, and those for large urban centres were increased. The appointment of mayors and councillors was to be by election, and the recruitment of civil servants organised by competitive examination rather than by patronage. Freedom of the press was confirmed, trades unions legalized, and divorce permitted.

Ferry had Colonial ambitions, and during his second term as Prime Minister in 1883-1885, he encouraged France to expand her interests in Algeria, Tunisia and Egypt, in order to acquire new sources of raw materials and develop overseas markets. In this intention he was encouraged by Bismarck who hoped thereby to distract France's attention from attempting to recover Alsace and Lorraine, and perhaps to embroil her in conflict with the interests of Great Britain and Italy.

The results of the 1885 elections was a sharp shock to the Republicans, who had envisaged this as an exercise in support of the current regime, and a celebration of the Republic's "coming of age". The Right did remarkably well and destroyed the Government's anticipated majority, forcing them to woo the Moderates or minority parties to support their policies.

In January 1886 a new star dawned on the political horizon. George Boulanger, at 48 the youngest of the Army's generals, was appointed Minister of War. He was blond, good looking, charming, and attractive to both men and women. He was also ambitious. By the 14th July military parade, hero-worship had reached the heights now only accorded to pop stars and footballers. In the following Spring Boulanger's reputation was enhanced by his involvement with an under-cover agent in Alsace-Lorraine. The organiser of a local French network had been arrested by the Germans, and Boulanger promptly started making ominous threats. Bismarck abused him as a warmonger, but officially released the agent. "Here was the man who could lead France against Germany", people said, "the new Napoleon who could wreak vengeance on her enemy; cure her hurts and humiliation". There were others more cautious, who knew that France was still too weak to consider starting a war with Germany. The only way to avoid confrontation was to dissolve the whole ministry and put Boulanger out of office, which was what the government did.

Boulanger was appointed to a Command in the far South. News leaked out that he was travelling by train, and huge crowds of fans invaded the station and lay down on the rails to prevent him from leaving. The authorities had to smuggle him away onto a second train waiting at another platform. They hoped the crisis was over, but they were wrong.

While Boulanger was comparatively forgotten, ruralising in his remote southern Command, Paris was shaken by a scandal that almost killed the Republic. Daniel Wilson, the President's son-in-law, and a Deputy of some distinction, was accused of using family connections to sell political honours. He lived at the Presidential palace, and used the President's free postal service for his own private business. He was undoubtedly guilty, and there was nothing for it but for his father-in-law, Jules Grévy, to resign. Only Grévy refused to do so, and the Government had to resign en masse in order to force his hand. When all the leading politicians had refused to form a new ministry, Grévy was left with no option. Even then, he dragged out his resignation until the beginning of December in order, the cynics said, to draw an extra month's salary. He was known to be very mean, and perhaps he was anxious not to lose the money as well as his reputation and his job. The Monarchists at least were delighted with the story, confirming as it did their contention that the government was corrupt.

The obvious replacement for Grévy would have been Ferry, but the Chamber did not want a strong President. The choice fell on Sadi Carnot, the son and grandson of Republican supporters, and by repute a brilliant engineer. Otherwise he had no noticeable qualifications for the position of President, and the best that could be said of him was that he was well-meaning and thoroughly mediocre. It is said he was elected in accordance with Clémenceau's instruction to his followers to "vote for the stupidest".

There was another possibility. Boulanger had not lost credibility during his exile, and his attitude to Germany over the Alsace-Lorraine affair recommended him to the Right, who thought he might be a suitable leader for their party. The death of Chambord in 1883, and of the Prince Imperial in 1879 had left them without a suitable figurehead. They had the Comte de Paris, but he lacked glamour, and his milk-and-water republicanism was a deterrent. Boulanger was a star, and although in theory a

Radical, he was an opportunist of no special principles, who might be prepared to bow to expediency.

Boulanger was certainly willing to listen to overtures, perhaps because the Right had access to money for a major electoral campaign, but perhaps too because he was disillusioned with the Republicans. The plan was simple but very clever. He was to stand for every possible election as it occurred, and then resign as soon as he had won so as to be free for the next vacancy. His manifesto would be anti-parliamentarian, demanding that the Chamber be replaced by an Assembly that would be empowered to draw up a new Constitution providing a strong leadership from the top. Naturally the leadership would be provided by Boulanger.

He won six out of seven in the 1888 by-elections, and the publicity built up excitement to fever pitch. The finale came in January 1889 with the first seat to become vacant in Paris. Boulanger won by an amazing majority, capturing most of the Radical Republican votes as well as all the Right. Amidst noisy celebrations, an imminent coup was expected along the lines of Louis Napoleon's institution of the Second Empire. Nothing else happened.

The Government could not believe its good fortune. As the days passed they waited, bags packed ready to flee, but still there was no move from Boulanger. Gradually they crept out of hiding. A rumour was circulated that Boulanger was to be arrested for an attempt against the State - he had already been dismissed from the Army on a charge of indiscipline during the by-elections. In April came the news that he had fled to Belgium, and the crisis was all over. In the 1889 general election his supporters won 40 seats, but Boulanger never returned.

Why did he fail? The answer must lie somewhere within his own personality. Certainly he was ambitious, but he lacked application. Nothing was really important to him except enjoying life, and by the time of the Paris by-election he was much in love with his current mistress and preferred her to the Presidency. He was certainly not willing to risk imprisonment, and perhaps death, for the dead-sea fruit of political power. After two very happy years, his mistress died, and Boulanger was so devastated by grief that he shot himself on her grave. His death, as his life, was high drama, but achieved nothing.

Betrayal and after

In the 1890's two major scandals rocked the Third Republic so badly that for a time it seemed unlikely it could ever recover.

The first concerned the Panama Canal scheme. Ferdinand de Lesseps was a canal addict. He had successfully master-minded the building of the Suez canal, and confidently expected to repeat his achievement in Panama, but he failed to take into account the vastly different conditions prevailing there. Suez ran across flat desert, but Panama was a mountainous country necessitating the construction of complicated locks or deep cuts, both of which were very costly. In addition, the climate was unhealthy, and it was difficult to recruit enough experienced workers to replace the hundreds who died of various indigenous fevers.

The initial capital was subscribed by public investment, but de Lesseps badly miscalculated, the project was under funded, and money soon ran out. It was proposed to raise additional funds by lottery loans, a system rather resembling the modern "Ernie" bonds, whereby the investor never lost his principal, and stood to win substantial prizes. The scheme had worked well in Suez, but required government permission, and the government sat on the application for three years before consenting. As an interim measure further shares were issued, but the public had lost interest. By the time the lottery scheme was approved the Panama Canal Company was bankrupt and in the hands of receivers.

The reason for the collapse was ignorance and mismanagement rather than criminal intent, but to the small investors who had lost their savings this was no comfort. In 1892 the Press launched a campaign claiming that the key Republican ministers dealing with the Panama scheme had been bribed by international Jewish financiers in a bid to seize political power - a similar allegation used to even greater effect by Hitler in the l920's and 30's. There was no evidence of malpractice, and everybody lied so much that it was impossible to determine exactly what had happened, but it is possible that there were some dubious transactions involving payments for favours received or withheld. De Lesseps, his fellow directors, and some politicians were put on trial. De Lesseps was found guilty of fraud and imprisoned, but was quickly released on appeal. Only one politician admitted guilt and was sentenced to five years in gaol. The rest were acquitted through lack of evidence.

There were inevitably allegations of corruption, and a number of leading politicians, including the leading Radical, George Clémenceau, quietly disappeared, but the government as a whole denied responsibility and refused to resign. The Right, demoralised by the *affaire-Boulanger*, and lacking adequate leadership, failed to take up the challenge, and in the 1893 elections, which were poorly attended, many of those suspected of being involved in the Panama scandal were returned to office. There was a belated bonus for the Monarchists however, since the defrauded public came to believe that the Panama scandal merely confirmed what they had always thought, and that parliamentary democracy was a snare and a delusion, organised by the influential few for their own benefit. Faith in politicians and the present political set-up was at its lowest, and it was widely held that only a change of regime would restore law and order.

The so-called Dreyfus Affair further inflamed dissension between Left and Right, and was to divide the country more dramatically than anything since the 1789 Revolution. It started as a simple, somewhat ludicrous spy-story, and ended with betrayal and tragedy. Up until that time there had been no formal military intelligence organisation in France. Spies were freelance operators who bought and sold their scraps of information where and when they could, but by 1890 there existed within the War Office a small unit known as the Statistical Section, consisting of four officers and a clerk, who dealt with military secrets. Security was nonexistent. Secret documents were widely circulated, no trace was kept, and leakages were inevitable.

The Statistical Section employed as an agent a French servant working in the German Embassy in Paris, whose job it was to collect the contents of waste-paper baskets. In 1894 Major Henry, one of the Section officers, discovered among the rubbish a hand-written letter offering a list of highly desirable secret documents to the Germans. The letter was unsigned, but from its contents it was obvious that the writer belonged to the War Office, moved around various sections, and was an expert in artillery.

Members of the Army staff were investigated, and a likely culprit was found in Captain Alfred Dreyfus, who fitted the conditions, whose handwriting matched the original letter, and whom Major Henry considered to be a likely type for a spy. Dreyfus was generally unpopular, being both overzealous and arrogant; he was standoffish, not "one of the lads"; and above all, because Major Henry was anti-Semitic, Dreyfus was a Jew. In spite of his protestations of innocence, Dreyfus was court-martialled and found guilty. He was deported to Devil's Island, a former leper colony off the coast of South America, where he was kept in solitary confinement. The War Office hoped he would soon die of fever or go mad, and so rid them of an embarrassment. Government, Press and public were delighted that the traitor had been caught and dealt with so expeditiously.

The matter did not end there. The Dreyfus family were convinced of Alfred's innocence, and were determined to prove it. Major Picquart, newly appointed to the Statistical Section, agreed to investigate. He had little expectation of success, but he was by nature a scrupulously honest man. He found that the prosecution possessed a so-called top-secret file that was said to contain definite proof of Dreyfus' guilt, but which no-one had seen, and when Picquart finally acquired and examined it, it was found to contain only the flimsiest circumstantial evidence.

Meanwhile, the German Embassy continued to receive military intelligence. In 1896 the waste-paper baskets yielded another letter, apparently a draft, addressed to Major Esterhazy at the War Office, which implicated him as an informer. Moreover, Esterhazy's handwriting was discovered to be identical with that of the letter that had condemned Dreyfus. Picquart reported his suspicions to the Minister for War, whose only reaction was to suggest moving Esterhazy to a foreign posting where he could do no more damage. Nothing was done about Dreyfus.

Major Henry then made a fatal move. He felt that it was quite unsuitable that there should be any doubt about Dreyfus' guilt, so he forged evidence that appeared irrefutable, using bits of documents salvaged from the waste-paper baskets, which he cut and pasted together. He also set about discrediting Picquart. In both these operations he was aided by Esterhazy, who was happy to tell any lies that ensured his own protection.

The matter fell into abeyance until the following year, when the Press picked up on the story and demanded a retrial, naming Esterhazy as the spy. The Minister for War reluctantly agreed that Esterhazy could be court-martialled on condition that he was found "not guilty". Picquart was dismissed from the Service for indiscipline.

The story exploded into a major scandal. On 13 January 1898 Emile Zola's famous letter, "J'Accuse", which accused the government and the army of a gigantic cover-up, was published on the front page of a national newspaper and sold several hundred thousand copies. Zola and his publisher were sentenced to imprisonment, which Zola avoided by fleeing to England. But his objective had been achieved. The enormous publicity made the public aware of government corruption, and the dangers inherent in undue military influence. Major Henry committed suicide.

France was split in two: among those who believed that Dreyfus had been shamefully wronged were active Republicans, socialists, pacifists, and the predominantly anti-clerical. The anti-Dreyfusards were anti-Semites, fervent nationalists in favour of a strong France based on military superiority, hostile to democracy, and pro-Catholic. In simpler terms, it was the extreme Left who supported Dreyfus, and the extreme Right, including the Monarchists, who condemned him. In fairness, it must be said that Dreyfus' innocence was never finally established, and the doubt remained that he could have been in collusion with Esterhazy. In 1899 Dreyfus was granted a retrial, and again declared guilty, but with extenuating circumstances that allowed for a reduction in the sentence. The President hastily granted him pardon on health grounds, and at the same time craftily extended an amnesty to all who had been involved in the affair. It was not until 1906 that Dreyfus was legally declared innocent.

Politically the Dreyfus Affair was instrumental in turning many Moderates back towards the Right. They wanted a change of regime, though they were not clear about what it should be. Had the Monarchists struck then, they could well have succeeded in establishing the Restoration.

On the other side, the extreme Republicans were dissatisfied with matters as they were, and demanded action rather than vague promises. The 1890's saw a rise in anarchism, which sought to overthrow the regime by individual acts of violence against leading members of the establishment, and in 1894 President Sadi Carnot was assassinated by an anarchist. The movement never gained popular support, however, and was quickly suppressed through tough punitive action by the military and police.

In the elections of 1893 the Socialists secured sufficient votes to increase their holdings of seats to over a hundred, and by 1903 they had succeeded in acquiring some minor ministerial posts, but when France declared war on Germany in 1914, the government was not much different from the one that was in power at the start of the Franco-Prussian war, 43 years earlier.

Revenge had been the one aim of almost every Frenchman since the humiliating Treaty of Frankfurt. The Franco-Prussian war had left the country isolated, the people traumatised, the Army crushed. Much as the more militant crusaders would have liked to take immediate provocative action, it was imperative to prevent Germany from making a pre-emptive strike. It had cost France an enormous effort in energy, money, diplomacy, and dedication to ensure that the timing was right. Above all, it had taken patience, but now at last France was ready.

Her first move had been to make friends. Bismarck had done his best to stir up trouble between France and her European neighbours, but when he fell from power in 1890, and the Kaiser made it clear that Germany's interests were with Austria-Hungary rather than Russia, the way was clear for France in 1894 to enter into a Franco-Russian alliance. Both countries were apprehensive about Germany's intentions, and the alliance provided a bulwark on both national borders which would effectively split the German forces in any military action. In 1904 came the Anglo-French Entente. Britain and France had never been very friendly, but Britain was increasingly suspicious of Germany's sea power and colonial ambitions, both of which threatened British overseas markets, so that it was advantageous for her to support Germany's enemies.

On 28 June 1914 Archduke Francis Ferdinand, heir to the Austrian-Hungarian throne, was assassinated by a mad anarchist at Sarajevo. It provided just the excuse that the Kaiser needed, and Austrian troops were moved in. With Russia committed to support Serbia, France to support Russia, and Britain tied to the Anglo-French Entente, Europe mobilised. On 3 August Germany declared war and invaded Belgium; patriotic fever mounted, and volunteers queued at the recruiting offices. The next day Britain declared war on Germany. The First World War had begun, and the map of Europe was changed for ever.

Grace and favour

One of the major splits between Left and Right had always been their attitude to the Church. Catholics were on the whole Royalist and Conservative. To be Republican was to be anticlerical. The division was aggravated in 1890, when Leo XIII advised the faithful of France to "accept and support the Republic". The Bishops, bound to obedience, regarded it as a temporary embarrassment that would disappear with the death of the current Pope, and the laity ignored it. As an attempt to establish a strong Catholic party within the Republican government, it was a signal failure.

The loyalty and strength of the Royalist adherence to Church and Throne runs like a golden thread through the tapestry of violence and change that had beset France since the start of the Revolution. It was more than a political belief, it was a religious faith. Only the divinely appointed King could cure the diseases of poverty, immorality and corruption that were the scourge of his people. When Saunière denounced the Republic from his pulpit as Anti-Christ, he was promulgating no more than the dogma of the faithful.

The death of the Comte de Chambord had been a shattering blow to the Legitimists, but in supporting the Comte de Paris in the 1885 elections, they were no longer assenting unwillingly to an uneasy alliance with the despised Orléanists, they were supporting the next heir to the throne, much as they disliked the idea. Only the really rigid die-hards continued to regard no king as preferable to an Orléanist, an attitude that relied on emotion rather than logic, since they had never forgiven Louis-Philippe's father for attempting to throw in his fortunes with the Revolutionaries and voting for his cousin, Louis XVI's execution.

The Orléans branch of the Bourbons were the direct descendants of Philippe, Duc d'Orléans, the second son of Louis XIII. The House of Bourbon had always practised the law of male primogeniture, and the senior branch, descended from Louis XIII's eldest son and Maria Theresa of Austria, ended with Chambord, who was childless.

The Comte de Paris was the son of Ferdinand-Philippe, Duc de Chartres, the eldest son of France's constitutional monarch, Louis-Philippe I. Louis Philippe, Prince of France, Comte de Paris, was born in 1838 in Paris, while his grandfather was still the King in residence. He married Isabelle, Infanta of Spain, in 1864, at Kingston-on-Thames when the family were living in exile in England, and they had four sons and four daughters. The hereditary Prince of France, Louis Philippe Duc d'Orléans, was their second child, born in 1869. He sadly had no children, and the title passed to his cousin Henri, grandson of Robert, Duc de Chartres, called Robert le Fort, Ferdinand-Philippe's second son. Henri married Isabelle d'Orléans Bragance, and they had a son Henri, who had a son François born in 1961, so that the line has continued.

There was, in fact, another possible claimant to the throne. Chambord had no son, but he did have a nephew, the son of his sister Louise, Princess of France, and Charles, Duke of Parma. Their son Robert was born in 1848, and he had twenty-four children, twelve by each of his two wives. Charles was himself a Bourbon, descended from Felipe, second son of Philip V of Spain, and he was named by Chambord as the Regent of the Traditional Monarchist Community. France had always adhered to the Salic law, under which a woman could not inherit, but it was a law that could easily be put aside, as Ferdinand VII of Spain had done in favour of his daughter Isabelle, who in consequence became Queen in her own right at the age of three. England had long abandoned the Salic law. Mary Tudor, Elizabeth I, and James II's daughter Anne had all inherited the English throne, and Victoria was still Queen of England at the time of Chambord's death in 1883.

Interestingly enough, under the ancient Celtic tradition, the hereditary ruler was not the son of the King, but the son of the King's sister. This was a way to ensure the purity of the royal blood, since all men knew their mothers, but not every man could swear to his father. In the medieval Arthurian legends, Mordred is cast as the villain who tries to usurp the throne, whereas in fact, according to the Celtic roots of the tradition, Mordred was the rightful heir, being the son of Arthur's sister Morgan.

Had the Legitimists agreed to recognise Louise's son Robert, and perhaps some of them did, he could have proved a strong leader for the royalist cause, and an important focus of their continued attempts to bring about the restoration of the monarchy. His descendants in fact still maintain that they are the true successors to the Comte de Chambord, and are the true kings of France.

Chambord's obsequies at Goritz in Slovenia were presided over by his brother-in-law, Jean III (Don Juan), who as the nearest male kinsman briefly became Head of the House of Bourbon, but he lived only four more years. The new Head of the House was Charles XI (Don Carlos) who married Margherita Marie Enrichitta, Louisa and Charles' daughter, at the Chambord castle of Frohsdorf on 4 February 1867, and their son, Don Jaime, was born in 1870 and brought up there. Jaime was very close to his uncle, who left him the archives of the House of France. Jaime also inherited Frohsdorf from his grandmother, the Comtesse. He had strong hopes of reviving the monarchy, and was involved in a number of loyal demonstrations while living in Paris. As a direct descendant of Louisa, the daughter of the Duc de Berri, heir apparent of King Charles X, he had a strong claim to the throne.

Don Jaime died in 1931, and his octogenarian uncle Alphonse briefly succeeded him as Head of the House. Alphonse's successor was Alphonse XIII of Spain, grandson of that Queen Isabelle who had inherited the throne due to the abolition of the Salic law. In theory, Alphonse XIII became King of France as Alphonse I, and he took the arms of France, raising a border of gules around the fleur de lys.

His son, Jacques Henri, who renounced the Spanish throne in 1931, claimed his rights as Henri VI, King of France, before the European Court. He spent a great deal of his time in France, and published a number of political manifestos, the most notable of which castigated the French Government for their failure to come to a settlement in French Algeria. In 1975 his son, Alphonse II, Duke of Anjou and Cadiz, succeeded him and continued his father's work. In particular, he was involved with the Capetian Millennium, the success of which owed much to his efforts.

He was accidentally killed at Beaver Creek (USA) on 30 January 1989, and his son, Prince Louis, then aged 14, became Head of the House of Bourbon and King of France as Louis XX. Louis Alphonse, Duke of Anjou and Cadiz, born on 25 April 1974, 760 years to the day after his illustrious ancestor Saint Louis, is a young man of his time, an accomplished sportsman and a brilliant horseman, like all the Bourbons. "History teaches us never to give up hope. Even the worst events offer us another chance to do better" he said at the celebration of the Festival of St. Louis at Aigues Mortes in 1992, "the throne of France is a task that has devolved upon me, and it is incumbent upon me to take up the burden...France may renounce the Bourbons, but the Bourbons will never renounce their responsibility. I did not choose to be born, but it is for me to keep alight the flame that since the baptism of Clovis has burned for a thousand years. It is a torch that has illuminated the world, and it can enlighten us today. In recalling the ancient dynasty of France, as in other countries, I am drawing attention to a regime that has contributed so much to mankind's happiness... With the help of Saint Louis, my ancestor and my patron saint, and with the support of my friends, I assume absolutely the duties bequeathed to me by my father".

Bethania – the secret enclave

Although royalist feelings ran high during the 1885 elections, the results made it plain that there was not going to be a sufficient majority of Right supporters in the National Assembly to ensure the defeat of the established Republican government. The Restoration was not going to be achieved by democratic vote, and the only way open was by a coup, such as had brought Louis Philippe I, and later Napoleon III to power. Such a coup was regarded as a possibility, but it required much organisation.

It is evident that there was a strong royalist party in the Carcassonne area. Saunière had come out into the open and declared his views, and the Bishop had covertly supported him by ensuring that he was given a job at Narbonne after the Left dominated local council had suspended him. Saunière's father had a prestigious position with the local landowner: his brother was tutor and chaplain to nobility. He himself was said to entertain wealthy and noble clients at Bethania, a conveniently quiet place for discreet secret meetings. He also had access to a house in rue des Maccabees in Lyon, where he apparently stayed on occasion, and used as an accommodation address for correspondence he did not wish sent to the Presbytery. Invoices sent to him there still exist, two of which refer to the hire of a horse-drawn vehicle for unrestricted use, on a number of occasions between May and September 1898, April and July 1899, and in May and June 1900. The inference inevitably is that the rue des Maccabees was perhaps a "safe house" for Royalist agents.

The Church was Royalist, and a number of the local priests, as well as Saunière himself, appear to have been involved in some extra-curricular activities. Most authors who have researched the Rennes-le-Château mystery, starting with Gérard de Sède, agree that Saunière could not have carried out the programme he did had he been acting alone, and that there was some kind of organisation behind him. This has been labelled as the Prieuré de Sion, which for convenience may be called Prieuré Two.

De Sède, and later Henry Lincoln, suggested that the Prieuré's job was to maintain and protect the latest descendant of the Merovingian Kings - in the 1980's designated as Pierre Plantard, in Saunière's time presumably his grandfather, Charles Plantard. This is a nonsense, because it has been demonstrated forcibly that the genealogy which is intended to support Plantard's claim is in fact a forgery, and in any case, even if the story were true, it is irrelevant. The Merovingian dynasty had been set aside hundreds of years before in favour of the Carolingians from whom the Bourbons claimed to be descended.

That Prieuré Two did have a political agenda cannot be dismissed. If they were using the local Catholic Church as a stalking horse to further the Royalist cause, they were doing no more than attempting to bring about what the Church desired and approved. If Saunière was dealing with party funds, it is understandable that he would not explain their origin, and if he was involved in a plot to overcome the Republic he did well to keep quiet. The government had no mercy on dissidents, as witness the massacre of the Paris Commune, and the totally dishonest cover-up over the Dreyfus affair. The rewards for Saunière were considerable, the re-establishment of the Catholic Church in France, and a Conservative, Right-Wing government that would protect its interests. In the short-term, he enjoyed a good life, with plenty of action and money to make it feasible, and the company of the type of people he liked and respected. Overall, it meant the Restoration of what the Royalists considered the true authority duly appointed by God - the Bourbon dynasty.

Chapter Five

'The actors, sir, will show whereuntil it doth amount'

Love's Labours Lost: V.2

Dramatis Personae
Chambord – The Miracle Child

The little Dauphin in the Temple, who became Louis XVII when his father went to the guillotine, died on 4 March 1795, and the exiled Duc de Provence succeeded him as Louis XVIII. There were certain cynics who said that Louis was not displeased at his nephew's death, and it was even suggested that he may have been a party to it, but there is no evidence that the child died of anything but natural causes, aggravated by imprisonment and misery. Some years, however, were to elapse before Louis XVIII benefited by anything more than the empty title of King of France. In fact he never was officially crowned, claiming that his health prevented him from undergoing the arduous ritual.

By the time of the Restoration of the Bourbon monarchy in 1814 he was already an elderly man, a widower and childless. He died in 1824, and his younger - but not much younger - brother, succeeded him as Charles X. On 25 May 1825 Charles, who in his rather giddy youth had delighted in the soubriquet of "Monsieur", was crowned at Rheims with full ceremonial. He was a kind and indolent man, but ultra Royalist, and unpopular with the general public.

Charles' eldest son, Duc d'Angoulême, was married to his cousin, Princess Marie Thérèse Charlotte, Louis XVI's daughter, who was Princesse Royale in her own right, and but for the fact that France adhered to the Salic Law, would have been Queen.

The d'Angoulèmes also were childless, and in addition the Duc, always unbalanced, had by this time become totally insane.

Charles Ferdinand, Duc de Berri, Charles X's second son, was therefore Dauphin in all but name. His wife, Marie Caroline, was the daughter of Francis I of the Two Sicilies, and she not only expected, but was determined to be Queen of France. She had a daughter Louise Marie Thérèse, an attractive and clever child, but female. Then, on 13 February 1820, it was confirmed that the Duchesse was pregnant again, and hopes of a legitimate heir ran high.

The Duc had chosen to attend a performance at the Opéra, where his favourite dancer - and supposedly mistress - Virginie was appearing. The Duchesse insisted on going with him, but half way through the evening she was unwell and decided to go home. The Duc accompanied her down the steps to her carriage, when a young man precipitated himself out of the surrounding shadows and stabbed him. The Duc fell, and his assailant was immediately apprehended by the guards. He had neither hope nor expectation of getting away with the murder.

The Duc was carried into the foyer of the Opéra and died the next morning. The evidence showed that the crime was not politically motivated, but a personal attack perhaps prompted by jealousy or revenge, and the Duc, who had inherited not only his father's sexual proclivities and also his amiable nature, left instructions that the young man was to be released and not punished. Nonetheless, after the Duc's death, as a matter of course the murderer went to the guillotine.

On 19 September, seven months later, Marie Caroline bore a son, Henri Charles Ferdinand Marie Dieudonné, Duc de Bordeaux, Comte de Chambord, l'Enfant de France. If she could not now be Queen, she was determined she would be Queen Mother, and her status among the Legitimists was almost akin to that of the Virgin Mary herself.

The young Duc was brought up in every way to regard himself as the next true King of France. Louise, "La petite Mademoiselle", was shocked when she was separated from her little brother. He had his own household, and his tutor, the Baron de Damas, dined apart from his charge who was allowed only one main dish and inferior well-watered wine, a diet the Baron would supplement from his own table. The Duc's regime was strict, but if his mother maintained her distance and state, his sister Louise adored him, and they in fact remained close friends all their lives.

In 1830 Charles X, worn down by ill-health and political pressure, abdicated naming his grandson, the young Comte de Chambord, as his heir. As a sop to the Left Wing element he appointed as Regent Prince Louis Philippe, son of Philippe Egalité, the Duc d'Orléans who had supported the Revolution.

On his accession Louis XVIII had reinstated the Orléanist branch of the family, and in all fairness Louis Philippe had had nothing to do with the infamies of his father, being with the Army in Morocco at the time. However, his politics did lean towards the Left, as he had been brought up by his father's Republican mistress. It was not long before the Regent began to have ambitions of his own, and he was already the virtual Head of State. In 1831 he was offered the crown as Constitutional Monarch, and accepted as Louis Philippe I, King of the French. The Legitimists could not believe such treachery, especially as relations between the "true" Royals and the Regent were ostensibly cordial. Louis Philippe visited at the Palais Royale, and he was especially fond of Louise, who from the age of ten was already taking an interest in public affairs, and who danced very prettily with him.

Marie Caroline and her children fled to her homeland of Italy, but she did not long remain quiet. In 1832 she landed at Marseille, and dressed in men's clothes made her way to Brittany, where the Legitimist faction was strongest. She thought she had only to appear and they would rise to support her son's restoration to the throne. "Vendéans, Bretons, all you inhabitants of the faithful provinces of the West, Henri V calls you..." she cried. Nothing happened.

On 16 May Henri V was proclaimed King at Nantes, but again there was very little response. Louis Philippe suddenly realised there was trouble brewing, and countered by sending troops against the little Legitimist army. Without money or arms, Marie Caroline was reduced to sleeping under hedgerows and begging for bread. Then came disaster.

In October, five months after her triumphant return to France, Marie Caroline was captured at a Breton farmhouse where she had hidden in a chimney, and imprisoned at the Chateau de la Duchesse Anne. Louis Philippe would willingly have deported her back to Italy, except that his wife Marie-Amélie, who was Marie Caroline's aunt and only too familiar with Italian court intrigue, would not permit it. Marie Caroline was an embarrassment to him. A gallant, pretty young woman won far more sympathy in prison than when she was rampaging around Brittany dressed as a man. Presents, food, flowers and sympathy poured in, and support for her cause looked like escalating, but Louis Philippe was fortunate. A policeman called Inspector Joly reported to the King that in his opinion the Duchesse was pregnant. A doctor was despatched secretly to investigate, and found the rumour to be true.

Harassed by endless questioning, in February 1833 Marie Caroline admitted her pregnancy, and on 10 May gave birth to a daughter. Count Hector Lucchesi-Palli of Palermo came forward, claimed paternity, and said that he and the Duchesse had been secretly married. It may or may not have been true, but as the wife or mistress of her father's Gentleman of the Bedchamber, Marie Caroline did not have the same romantic appeal as the Virgin Queen Mother of the last legitimate heir to the throne of France. Scandal was avoided, but she and her "miracle child" myth took a steep dive into obscurity. She returned to Italy and fades from the political scene.

In 1848 Louis Philippe in turn fled to exile in England. The Bourbon dynasty in France was finished.

Unlike his flamboyant mother, the Duc de Chambord was a quiet, slightly lame young man, of delicate health and a poetic turn of mind, but although he lacked Marie Caroline's driving ambition, he had a firm belief in the divine right of Kings. On 17 October 1843, when he was just twenty-three years old, he went to London and took a house in Belgrave Square. Here he sent out his manifesto, and on 30 November he was acclaimed by the remnants of the *ancien regime* in exile as King Henri V. Louis Philippe was not pleased, and sent a complaint to Queen Victoria, who accordingly ignored the sad little court in Belgrave Square. Discouraged, Chambord returned to the Continent.

It was apparent that he must marry, and he applied to the Duc de Modène for a bride. He was in love with one of the younger daughters, Marie Beatrice, but she was promised to Don Juan, the son of Don Carlos, Pretender to the throne of Spain. He was offered instead Marie Térèsa. She was plain, deaf, and ultra pious, much given to charitable works, but he married her anyway. She was by her own lights a good wife, but added to her inadequacies by proving to be childless.

There was still a strong Legitimist faction in France, who continued to anticipate, and work for the restoration of the Bourbon monarchy. They even trained a beautiful horse that would not be upset by music or cheering, which Chambord was to ride on his triumphant entry into Paris. They spent time, energy, money and blood, and asked for only one thing - that the Prince, their Icon, their Oriflamme, should come and lead them. He never came.

In 1850 the Chamber of Deputies numbered five hundred Royalists amongst its members, and agreed to support Chambord's claim to the throne on condition that he retained the tricolore flag and ruled as a Constitutional Monarch. Chambord refused. In 1871 and 1873 the offer was repeated, and again refused. He wrote saying "I will never accept it" (the Tricolore). The cynics shrugged their shoulders and said he was the only man ever to refuse a kingdom for the sake of a pocket handkerchief.

Marie Caroline's "miracle child", the fairytale prince of the Breton rising, the romantic exile of lost love and forlorn hopes, had declined into a middle-aged, overweight, rather pompous Bourbon Pretender. For Henri V, childless, trapped in a barren marriage to a good woman he had never wanted, all that was left of so much adulation, blood and passion spent, was the lily banner for which so many Frenchmen had fought and died over almost a thousand years. He could not for a matter of expediency deny his heritage. "What am I without honour but a fat man with a limp?" he said. All the bitterness of frustration and despair echo in that one banal sentence, and it is a final irony that the name of his home in exile, "Frohsdorf", translates as "joyous village".

It has been suggested that Chambord was perhaps uncertain about the legitimacy of his claim, and believed that there may, just possibly, be someone with a better right - that Louis XVII or his descendants were still alive. There had been many claimants, but none of them had proof. The Royal family had long accepted that the child in the Temple did not survive, Louis XVI's daughter would not even consider it, and Chambord's own upbringing is far more likely to have reinforced his belief in his own divine right to the throne.

For ten more years he ruled only his phantom kingdom at Frohsdorf, where on 25 August 1883 he died. Henri Lavedan of the Académie Française gives an eye-witness account of the obsequies, and his reaction to them:

"At that time I was thirteen years old. That summer of 1883 we lived near Blois...at about 6 o'clock of a quiet evening, I saw my father coming towards us. He was carrying, spread open, a newspaper with a wide black border...'The Comte de Chambord is dead' he said. ...

On August 28th as arranged, my brother-in-law and I arrived in Vienna, after twenty-four hours on the train...we found a hotel near the Church of St. Etienne...Another short journey next day, and at the station carriages were waiting, drawn by immaculate white horses. We got into one of these with two other people. After a quarter of an hour more, at a good regular pace, the carriage slowed down and turned into a main courtyard filled with people: there it was, Frohsdorf!

I expected to have to push through a crowd to get to the place where the Prince was lying, but no, before I had had time to prepare myself, I was surprised to find him in the first ground floor chamber where he had been brought from his bedroom: "Most High and Mighty Henri Charles Ferdinand Marie Dieudonné, Duc de Bordeaux, Comte de Chambord, Head of the Royal House of France". He was laid out in a black suit and polished shoes on a little, narrow bed, his head slightly raised...it was possible for me to see only his profile, but in this position he looked exactly like the effigy stamped on royal medals. People from the village were allowed to approach; women, children led by the hand or carried, who blew kisses to the deceased, father of his country; and the sick, the poor with huge rosaries, priests, monks, nuns with outmoded medieval head-dresses; entering by one of the open doors from the garden and going out of the other, they filed past, very slowly, in front of the funeral bier, where they were allowed to stop for a few seconds.

Although I was not tired, I rapidly retreated. In the flood of new arrivals, ever more numerous, I had become separated from my brother-in-law... I made my way to where I knew I would find him, alone in the open air, trying to master his emotion...

When I returned I could not hide from my father the revulsion I had felt in the mortuary chapel, and which the sight of the Prince had aroused in me... It was said he wanted to reign. Without a doubt, momentarily he wanted to reign, and then he desired it no more, at least not on the terms offered. But worst of all, when everything had been arranged, even the day when it was to happen, he had broken faith and destroyed it all. A great misfortune for him, and for France...we need say no more".

Louise died in 1864. Her daughter's husband, Don Carlos de Bourbon, Duke of Madrid, Carlist Pretender to the Spanish throne, was the Comtesse de Chambord's nephew, the son of her younger sister, Marie Beatrice, the girl whom Chambord had once wanted to marry. The union of the children of the two families must have been a joy for him, and their son Jaime became his heir.

For the Legitimists, the Comte de Chambord was more than just the true heir to the throne. He embodied the whole concept of kingship - authority, justice, loyalty, protection, mercy, righteousness. Their devotion had a mystical quality to it - the king ruled by divine right, he was, without blasphemy, God's appointed deputy on earth. The fact that Chambord was a posthumous child added an extra dimension of magic; like the ancient priest kings of myth he had no apparent father, but was the child only of a specially chosen mother. Even a congenital limp was regarded by mythographers as a legendary mark of royalty, arising from the Bible story when Jacob wrestled with the angel and was lamed.

In September 1820, at the time of his birth, Lamartine wrote:

He is born, the miracle child!
The inheritor of a martyr's blood,
He is born of a belated oracle,
He is born of a last breath.
France awakes and wonders
At the fruit by death engendered,
Ordained by the divine will.
Thus flowers upon the ruins
A lily that the storm has planted.

Reporting on the coronation of Charles X, when Chambord was five years old, Châteaubriand wrote:

But what is this child? The future of France!
God's promise that engenders hope!

His brow crowned only by his fair hair,
Ignoring the rank which is his birthright,
Freed from the ties of his high destiny
He smiles beneath the burden of his fate,
His blue eyes wide, reflecting the blue sky,
All ceremony forgotten.
Only the twig remains where once the tree had
flourished.
The smoke of incense mounts and streams,
The light of torches glinting on steel,
Plumes wave on the soldiers' crests,
And like Astanax in his mother's arms
He reaches out to clasp his father's sword.

How could any human live up to such expectations? The Legitimists were adamant that France should adhere to the Salic Law. This decreed that succession was a matter of heredity and not administration, that it was by primogeniture and must pass directly from male to male in order of seniority, and that women could not inherit since by doing so the Crown ran the risk of falling into the hands of a foreign dynasty. In the event of the first branch becoming extinct, succession passed to the eldest male of the next immediate branch of the family. The États-Généraux, convened at Blois in July 1588, added a rider to the effect that France must be ruled by a Catholic King. Thus, in 1589 when Henri of Navarre, a Protestant, ascended the throne of France, he could not be consecrated until he had converted to Catholicism. According to legend, Henri declared that "Paris was worth a Mass".

With Chambord's death the direct line from Henri IV ended. The Legitimist claim passed to Don Juan who was directly descended from Philippe, grandson of Louis XIV, the second son of Louis the Grand Dauphin. In 1700 Philippe became Philippe V, the first Bourbon King of Spain.

Archduke Johann - the Operetta Prince

Among the dramatis personae of the Rennes-le-Château epic there appear from time to time small-part characters who enter, say a few lines, and exit unsung. Such a one was Archduke Johann Salvator of Hapsburg, who is said to have opened a bank account on the same day as Saunière, transferred a large sum of money to him, and then bowed out of the action. Who was Johann, and what was he doing there?

In the 1885 elections, a large proportion of the public favoured a return to the old system of monarchy. The deaths of the Prince Imperial in 1879 and the Comte de Chambord in 1883 left only one candidate - the Comte de Paris, grandson of the Orléanist King Louis Philippe, which had resulted in an uneasy, but necessary Right-wing coalition. Saunière, royalist to the backbone, denounced the Republicans from his pulpit as followers of the anti-Christ. The local authorities promptly suspended him from office, leaving him without means of support.

The Bishop of Carcassonne, prompted no doubt by Saunière's friend and mentor, Abbé Henri Boudet of Rennes-les-Bains, in December 1885 appointed Saunière to a temporary position at the University of Narbonne. The Bishop was under an obligation to Boudet who had been instrumental in obtaining large donations for the diocesan funds. These may in fact have come from Archduke Johann, who knew Boudet and stayed with his family at Axat when visiting Languedoc.

It is possible that Saunière first became acquainted with Johann at Narbonne, as when he was reinstated at Rennes-le Château in July 1886 Saunière brought with him the promise of 3000 Frs. towards the church restoration fund. The money had been donated by the widowed Comtesse de Chambord via Archduke Johann, who appeared to be acting as her agent. Johann and the Comte de Chambord were first cousins; Johann's mother, Maria Antonia, and Chambord's mother, Marie Caroline, were half-sisters, both being daughters of Francis I, King of the Two Sicilies by his two wives.

Though the Comtesse died later that year, the system had been set up, and according to Saunière's accounts the money was paid in two instalments, 1000 Fr. immediately and 2000 Fr. two years later. It was apparently compensation for his overt Royalist support, and the Comtesse was a noted philanthropist - she had donated a million francs to the building of Sacré Coeur, a national bribe to God to treat France better in the future than he had in the past, when he had allowed the Prussians to win the Franco-Prussian war. It has been suggested that Johann was negotiating the purchase of Saunière's secret treasure on behalf of the Hapsburg Empire, but the more likely explanation was that the money was a down payment to the Royalists to further their plans for the Restoration of the Bourbon monarchy.

Johann was the youngest son of Grand Duke Leopold of Tuscany, and belonged to the cadet branch of the Hapsburgs descended from Empress Maria Theresa's second son. He was romantic, the archetypal Prince of operetta - energetic, intelligent, well-educated, and attractive to women; a good linguist and musician, an able gymnast, and an expert horseman and swordsman. With a wide brow, a firm mouth, large dark eyes, and a charming smile, he was striking rather than handsome; and what he lacked in height he made up for in personality. Above all, he possessed that most unfair advantage - star quality.

The Italian Hapsburgs had ruled Tuscany since the middle of the eighteenth century, and although in theory they were autonomous, they had to conform to the Emperor's policy; all important decisions had to be referred to him. They were easy-going, democratic, and their Court demanded no formality or ceremonial. Tuscany was a model state, and its standard of living was higher than that of any other European country. Franz Joseph disliked "Die Toskaner", regarding them as Latinised, fantastic foreigners.

After the Austrian's defeat at Solferino, "the good Prince Leopold" abdicated in favour of his eldest son Ferdinand, fled to Bohemia, and bought Schloss Schlackenwerth, where he lived comfortably in retirement until his death in 1879, taking no further interest in politics or his children. Ferdinand, known as "Nando", was a handsome, amiable man. He built himself a villa at Lindau on Lake Constance, negotiated with Italy, and handed over the family estates in favour of keeping his title. When Prince Hohenlohe, the Emperor's Chamberlain, deplored the loss of Tuscany to Johann, Johann replied "I do not agree with you at all...The Italians wanted unity, and the existence of the Grand Duchy was an obstacle to this; it was necessary for it to be abolished."

The second son Karl, like all Leopold's family, disliked Court life. He was an excellent craftsman, and earned a good living in Vienna as a locksmith and clockmaker. His favourite pastime was to ride on buses and trams, which the Emperor regarded as eccentric but harmless.

The third son Ludwig simply left, and spent his time voyaging round the Mediterranean with an exquisite curly-haired youth as his companion. When the boy died at the age of 23 Ludwig had a marble statue made of him almost wearing an artistically draped toga, in the tradition of the Emperor Hadrian who had raised nude statues all over the ancient world to his favourite, Antinous. Rumour had it that the ship's crew were young women dressed as sailors whose accommodation Ludwig shared, but in view of his sexual preferences, the reverse was probably the case. When not at sea, Ludwig lived in Majorca and wrote books about geology and the natural history of North Africa and the Balearic Islands. He dressed in sandals, old linen trousers, fastened his shirt-cuffs with string, and was believed to be a sun worshipper. The Empress Elizabeth rather liked him, but the rest of the Imperial family thought he was distinctly odd, and were grateful that his more scandalous exploits were carried on outside their territory.

Johann was his mother's favourite, and the hope of his house. He was born in 1852, and was seventeen years younger than Ferdinand. Maria Antonia was a devout Catholic and thoroughly disapproved of Ludwig. Her other two sons she discounted as boring. Johann - she called him Gianni, as she spoke only Italian - was a bright boy, and although in theory he joined the Army at the age of thirteen, Franz Joseph made himself responsible for Johann's education. He spent the next six years at the Viennese Court, where he was expected to take part in royal ceremonial occasions which he disliked intensely. When his father died the Emperor refused to allow him to return to Rome for the funeral, for which Johann never forgave him.

He chose a commission in the Artillery as offering the best opportunities for promotion, rather than serving in a line regiment. He was hard working and ambitious, and before he was twenty he had been promoted to Major. His interests were eclectic, and included architecture, painting, drawing, turnery, photography, sculpture and music. Early on, he acquired the old château of Orth, which he personally set about restoring. What he did not like was shooting parties and fashionable balls. He considered Court life was both dull and corrupt.

As a young cadet he had witnessed the terrible depredations of war. He greatly deplored what he considered to be the gross inefficiency of the Army, which he regarded as ill-equipped and worse commanded. A great deal of his service career was spent in planning and reorganising the Empire's total military commitment, but not only did he receive no thanks from the Emperor, official steps were taken to make sure that any moves he made in that direction were blocked. In any matters concerning political authority Johann was too brilliant for his own good. With no justification, the Emperor not only considered Johann presumptuous, but believed him untrustworthy.

A few weeks after his promotion was announced Johann left for a tour of the eastern Mediterranean, and it was then, on board ship, that he first fell in love. The object of his devotion was an

English girl, and he was willing to give up everything if she would agree to marry him. As a Hapsburg Prince, albeit a minor one, Johann required the Emperor's consent for his marriage. He wrote to her saying "My darlingest of angel girls...as you can never be an Archduchess, I should be only too happy to cease to be an Archduke..." He was even willing for them to emigrate to Australia, where he said he could easily earn a living - "managing a theatre, teaching French, German and Italian, as the curator of a zoo or botanical gardens, as a riding master or a stock rider". The lady obviously had other ideas, and nothing ever came of the romance.

In 1875 his mother was assiduously searching for a suitable bride, and suggested one of the Orléans princesses, but three years later Johann was still a bachelor, and quite definite in stating "For the present I have no intention of marrying". Before embarking on active service he made a will, setting up a trust fund of 40,000 gulden, the income from which was to go to Ludmilla Stubel.

Johann's life-long mistress, Ludmilla or Milli Stubel, was an opera-dancer. She came from a lower middle-class family and was the third of four sisters. The death of their father had meant that the girls had to earn a living, and Milli was fifteen when she went on the stage. Her mother was hopeful that it would bring Milli a rich lover. Johann was attracted to her, and contrary to expectations, the affair lasted.

Milli was uneducated and not very talented, but she was a pretty blonde, warm-hearted, good-tempered, and she shared Johann's love of music. She called him her "arch-duckling". With Milli he could relax. He found her company soothing, and an escape from the stress of his official life. True to operetta traditions, they met at the theatre. By bribing the Aunt who was supposed to be her chaperone, Johann and Milli would have supper together after the show, or meet during rehearsals. He would have married her, except that it would have meant dismissal from the Army. He took her with him as his housekeeper when he was posted abroad, causing considerable innuendo and unkind comment, which worried Johann not at all. "Everyone admires her..." he said, "she makes me forget all the troubles I have to endure in Vienna".

Pressure was still being brought on him to marry. In 1883 he decided to propose to the widowed Countess Attems, whom he decided might be bearable, and she accepted. She was not royal, but she was aristocratic and held a position at Court. A morganatic marriage was possible if the Emperor would agree. The Emperor refused. Johann asked his mother to intercede on his behalf, but again the petition was refused. Johann gave up, and went happily back to Milli for the rest of his life.

In 1878 Johann was appointed Colonel Proprietor of an artillery regiment, and a few months later found him on active service in Bosnia Herzegovina. It was customary for Princes to take servants and possessions with them to ensure their comfort in the field. Johann arrived with his charger and a mounted groom, his luggage in two packs slung across the horses. He expected his staff to behave in the same way, and met with strong objections which he ignored.

Conditions were appalling, and the wagon trains carrying food and ammunition lagged behind, taking two weeks to cover sixty miles. The Army met with unexpectedly fierce opposition, and guns had to be manhandled up mountains. By the time the Austrians arrived at Travnik Johann was very ill with typhoid, and had to go back to Brod in Croatia to recover. On his determined and premature rejoining his troops, he was appointed acting Divisional Commander, and when they left he remained behind as Military Commandant of the district. He wrote to his mother telling her of the problems. These included "...a host of things which take time to study, prudence to decide, and energy to carry out. You can imagine the difficulty of the language, of having to deal with anyone who speaks nothing but Turkish through two interpreters...However, I have succeeded in establishing the necessary order, public safety and in enforcing the law". In November he returned to Vienna, ill and disillusioned.

The same year Johann was involved in the election of a King for the Bulgarian throne, which had been created by the Treaty of Berlin on condition that the ruler was not a member of any of the existing European dynasties. There were forty contenders, and Johann himself was nominated but refused. He had seen too much of the Balkans during his active service. "Only an imbecile would accept such a throne", he said. He supported instead the candidature of Ferdinand, son of Princess Clementine of Belgium. Ferdinand could not have been more different from Johann. Pale, plump, fond of pretty clothes, furs and prolific jewellery, he painted his face, and was reputed to sleep in a pink frilly nightie. He was also said to practise black magic. Crown Prince Rudolph was offended as he had not been consulted about the nomination, and betrayed the scheme to the Emperor. Ferdinand was elected regardless, but Franz Joseph disliked him. Johann fell under the Emperor's displeasure and was forced to resign his Army commission.

Johann heartily disapproved of the Emperor's policies which he considered outdated and repressive, and had no hesitation in saying so, in public and in the press. His sympathies lay more with Crown Prince Rudolph who was active in encouraging the younger liberals.

Apart from political affiliations, Johann and Rudolph had little in common. Rudolph was six years younger than his cousin, but his dissolute life had undermined his health, and at thirty he was neurotic, syphilitic and drug-addicted. Trapped in a loveless and sterile marriage, thwarted in his ambitions by the father he hated and had once tried unsuccessfully to kill, in 1889 at Mayerling Rudolph shot himself and his young mistress, Mary Vetsera. Mary was a romantic girl obsessed with the dream of love and death, and she was infatuated with Rudolph. Later historians have suggested that it was a political assassination, or that Johann had quarrelled with Rudolph and killed him, but the evidence is against it. Rudolph left a suicide note, and every attempt was made to hush up the scandal. Although the truth leaked out, he was given a state burial in the family vault in Vienna. Mary's body was hustled away into an obscure grave.

According to Milli Stubel's sister, a locked casket was delivered to Milli on the day of Rudolph's funeral, with strict instructions to give it only to a messenger with a specific password. In due course the stranger arrived, only to Milli he was no stranger - it was, of course, Archduke Johann. Rennes-le-Château mythographers have suggested that the casket contained the secret of the fabulous treasure that Saunière found in his church and sold to the Hapsburgs, but history maintains that the contents were dangerous papers, either Mary and Rudolph's love-letters, or details of treasonable plots hatched between Rudolph and Johann to take over the Empire, which they intended to split - Rudolph to take over Austria, and Johann to have Hungary.

Although no longer an Army officer, Johann was still subject to Imperial discipline. Discouraged, and thoroughly disenchanted with the political situation, in 1889 he resigned his rank and position, and became simply citizen Jean Orth, exchanging his Army pension for a one-off down payment. Taking Milli with him, he fled to England.

He wanted to keep his Austrian citizenship, but in fury the Emperor branded him a traitor, stripped him of his Order of the Golden Fleece, and forbade him to re-enter the Austrian-Hungarian Monarchy. As a last spiteful gesture, he ordered Johann to take the necessary steps to adopt Swiss nationality.

When he was an Archduke Johann had not required any identity documents, and on becoming an ordinary citizen he had been given an Austrian passport for just six months. All his family were attracted to the sea, and Johann planned to buy a ship as a means of earning a living. Swiss nationality would mean that his Master Mariner's Certificate would become invalid. His only course was to acquire and register a vessel under the Austrian-Hungarian flag before his passport ran out.

He spent his entire capital on the "Saint Margaret", an iron three master of 1,368 tons, meaning to tramp around the world, trading as and where he could. He obtained a contract to transport a cargo to Valparaiso, and sailed on 26 March 1890, arriving off la Plata on May 30th. Before leaving England he had made a will leaving Schloss Orth to his mother, and his house in Vienna and 100,000 gulden to "my dear companion in life Ludmilla Stubel". Milli's relations later alleged that once he was clear of his Archducal prohibitions Johann had married her, but there was no documentary proof.

It was agreed that Milli should rejoin Johann in South America, and accompanied by a maid she crossed second-class by passenger ship to Buenos Aires. It was an uncomfortable voyage, and she was not very happy at the thought of another two months at sea. She wrote to her mother "God knows if I will survive it..."

The "Saint Margaret" left la Plata on 12 July for the voyage round Cape Horn with Johann in charge, and Milli on board. On 5 November Lloyds of London were notified that the "Saint Margaret" was overdue and presumed lost, but they decided to wait for further evidence. On 9 December they were told that the ship had been sighted on 31 July in a raging storm off Cape Horn. Franz Joseph ordered a search to be made, but nothing was found. The "Saint Margaret" was never heard of again, and it was assumed that she had been lost at sea with all hands.

But - did Johann drown? Or did Jean and Milli Orth live happily ever after on a paradisiacal tropical island? His mother refused to believe her beloved son was dead, and made him her sole heir. When she died, it was said a mysterious stranger came to pray beside her coffin, and then disappeared again.

Rumours that Johann was still alive continued to circulate. He had been seen in Japan, in the Argentine, in Cannes, and at the Paris Opéra. A lady named Percy Fergusson from South Carolina said she had met him disguised as a Russian sailor. In 1911 he was officially declared "presumed dead", and his nephew applied to wind up the estate. In the legal petition Johann was described as "An Archduke without external privileges...who called himself Jean Orth, but nevertheless an Archduke and a member of the

Imperial Family." The privileges were done away with, the Archduke remained.

Whatever his fate, Johann had achieved what he finally desired, escape from the stifling constrictions and empty ceremonial of the Hapsburg Empire before it disintegrated in the holocaust of the Great War. Johann's tomb, destined for the dusty vault under the Viennese Capuchin church which housed his ancestor Maria Theresa and - in spite of controversy - his tragic cousin Rudolph, would remain eternally and triumphantly absent.

Jean Cocteau - the chameleon poet

In the Dossier Secret Jean Cocteau is listed among the famous and talented as Grand Master of the Prieuré de Sion from 1918, presumably until his death in 1963. If Philippe de Chérisey, self-styled creator of the so-called Saunière parchments, also compiled the list of Grand Masters, then his choice of Jean Cocteau was an admirable, but also an obvious one. Like Cocteau, de Chérisey was both an actor and writer. Henry Lincoln regarded him as a very good novelist, and he and Plantard were involved with the original book on which de Sède based *Le Trésor Maudit*. Moving in theatrical and literary circles de Chérisey could not fail to be familiar with Cocteau's work, and may perhaps have known him in person. He also shared with Cocteau a perverted and sometimes malicious sense of humour, tempered by wit and generosity.

They both enjoyed practical jokes. As a teenager Cocteau, returning by train from a holiday in Switzerland, persuaded his mother to buy some cigars as a present for Auguste, one of their Paris servants, and to put them in the inside pocket of her petticoat. When at the frontier the Customs Officers came to their carriage Jean pointed to his mother and said "That lady is hiding a box under her skirt". It was intended as a charade, but the joke turned sour when Mme Cocteau was taken into the corridor and strip searched. De Chérisey, "The Trickster" who set up the scenario of the Rennes-le-Château mystery, was surely the prime practical joker, and could never have foreseen the results of his essay in literary deception.

All the Grand Masters are named or pseudonymed "Jean". The alleged list includes an impressive array of celebrated writers, philosophers and at least one great painter, and Cocteau was all these and more. The list also includes a number of magicians, and although Cocteau never admitted to being a member of an occult group, his work is widely based on mystical and magical symbolism. It is perhaps significant that he signed his work with a six-pointed star, commonly called the Seal of Solomon, and which is cabalistically a glyph of Macroposopus and Microposopus, the Greater and Lesser Countenances, symbols of creation.

The Prieuré was politically right wing, and its "house mag" *Vaincre*, published during the Second World War, is overtly pro-Nazi. Cocteau also was accused of being a collaborationist and like Pierre Plantard believed that if an artist wished to survive under the Occupation, then some lip service had to be paid to the enemy. Cocteau was a patriot rather than a politician, and Plantard would no doubt have made a similar claim. Although classified as unfit for Army duty - his health had never been good - Jean voluntarily served with the Red Cross at the front during the first world war. The horrors of trench warfare appalled him, and he tried, without success, to publicise in the Paris press the human tragedies he was witnessing.

Jean was born on 5 July 1889 in the Paris suburb of Maisons Laffitte, then a rural area mainly devoted to the raising of race horses. It was a profession that had no attraction for the Cocteau family, and they lived for most of the year in central Paris. Jean's mother had inherited money, and Georges Cocteau early abandoned a desultory career in law in favour of the bohemian life of an amateur artist. There were two older children - Marthe and Paul - and Jean seems to have had little affection for them, and even less for the father who committed suicide in 1898.

Jean's closest companion was his cousin, Marianne Lecomte, who shared his pleasures of dressing up and play-acting. Marianne tells how "Jean and I came home from a walk one day and were told that his father was dead. The news made little impression on us at the time - I remember that we were soon laughing and playing as usual".

Cocteau Père, aged 55, took to his bed and without explanation or apology blew out his brains. The matter was hushed up, and he was ceremoniously buried in his wife's family vault in Montmartre cemetery, but the indications are that he was homosexual and about to be involved in a scandal which at that time would have resulted in a heavy prison sentence. In the circumstances, and in view of the lack of feeling between them, the inevitable suspicion arises that Jean was not his son. There is a hint that Auguste, he of the smuggled cigar fiasco, who Jean seemed to regard as a friend, may have been Mme Cocteau's lover.

Jean himself made no secret of his own homosexuality, although he was always discreet in his affaires. His preference was for young men, whom he was inclined to regard with paternal affection. His great love was the dissolute young genius Raymond Radiguet. Radiguet was almost 16 when he and Jean met, probably in 1919 at the "matinee poétique" where Radiguet read a tribute to Apollinaire, and Cocteau performed his own poem *Coupe a ta muse les cheveux*. When Radiguet died of typhoid on 12 December 1923 Jean was distraught. He wrote "I suffer night and day, I shall never write again..." He refused to get up, or to go to the funeral. The coffin was white, the coffin of a child, because for all his precocity Radiguet was not yet twenty-one.

In May 1909 Diaghilev's Ballet Russes burst upon the Parisian theatrical scene. The dancers included Nijinsky, Fokine and Coralli; décor was by Benois, Bakst and Nicholas Roerich. Audiences were stunned. Cocteau attended a performance with his family, an occasion which changed his life for ever. At curtain fall he left the auditorium and never returned to it as a mere theatre-goer. He crashed backstage, met the artists and fell in love with Nijinsky, an unpopular move with Diaghilev, although later the maestro was to commission Cocteau to write several ballet libretti for the company. Jean said that all his life he suffered from "the red and gold disease". He had caught the bug in childhood, making his own toy theatre for which he wrote and designed the plays, and performed all the parts.

Jean's talents were so diverse that he has been denigrated by many critics as a mere dilettante. Actor, artist, playwright, film-maker, novelist, critic, theatre designer, creator of fabrics, jewellery, posters and ceramics, he accepted only one title - "poet". For Cocteau drama and dance were poetry in motion, painting was poetry made visible, literature was poetry in prose. He drew his material from myth and legend, the deep subconscious levels of racial memory. Imagination was just another way of illuminating poetic truth.

He rapidly won recognition among the avant-garde clientele of the Parisian salons where painters, composers and writers were seeking a new way of looking at art. His great friend and "master" was Picasso, of whom he said "Stravinsky was one of my great encounters, Picasso was THE great encounter".

Jean knew the value of exclusivity, and his youth, charm and good looks helped. Always thin, he deliberately starved himself down to a mere skeleton, and contrary to the fashion of the day for flowing locks, cut his unruly dark hair into the familiar wire-wool brush that became his trademark.

Although Cocteau is regarded as one of the most important pioneers of the modern theatre movement, his plays have never achieved the popularity of his films - *La Belle et la Bête* and *Orphée* in particular, both of which have become "cult" epics - and outside France his poetry, of all his work the most personal and treasured, is virtually unknown. "Cocteau" to most people means the lively little drawings that he scribbled on any- and every-thing, and which he regarded as mere doodles.

With the outbreak of the Second World War in September 1939 Jean Marais, Cocteau's current lover, was called up for service with the French Army, and Jean moved in with his friends, the stage-designer Christian Berard, and Boris Kochno who had been Diaghilev's secretary until Diaghilev's death in 1929. Their main concern was how to obtain the opium to which all three were addicted.

When the Germans invaded Holland and Belgium in May 1940 and the blitzkrieg swept on into France, Jean like many of his compatriots fled south. He stayed with friends in Perpignan until France collapsed and Marais was demobilized, when they returned together to Paris and the macabre existence under the Occupation. Every artistic activity required a German licence, and just to exercise one's own profession attracted the stigma of collaborator. Cocteau unhesitatingly sought German authorization for production of his plays and publication of his writings. His dictum was that a poet must express himself regardless of language, and he said he spoke German anyway as he had had a German nanny in his youth.

Meanwhile, faced with drug shortages, Marais weaned him away from opium, and Jean kept to this abstention throughout the war. With the cessation of hostilities he resumed the social round, wrote a celebratory poem *25 Aôut 1944* which was published in the first issue of *Les Nouvelles Litteraires* to be printed after the Liberation, and was officially exculpated from any accusation of fraternising with the enemy. The nervous strain however had brought on a debilitating skin disease, for the relief of which Jean returned to smoking opium.

Marais had a reasonably successful career in the theatre, but he wanted above all to be a film star, and it was his influence that led Cocteau to experiment with cinema. While Marais was in Italy in 1942, filming as Don José in a non-operatic version of *Carmen*, Jean undertook to write the dialogue for a B-Grade movie of a romantic "soap" called *Le Baron Fantôme*. His next project was *L'Éternel Retour*, for which Marais was recalled to play Tristan to Madeleine Sologne's Iseult, and for which Cocteau wrote both scenario and dialogue. It met with only moderate critical success, but audiences liked it, and it gave Marais the star status he craved. Women mobbed him in the streets, and camped out on his staircase. They even brought their own chairs and sat in rows in his garden like a theatre audience, eyes riveted to his windows as if to the stage. One evening when Marais was signing autographs outside the stage-door of a theatre where one of Cocteau's plays was being performed, a fan spotted him in the background and was heard to say "Look, there's the author, he's connected with the play too". Marais was angry and ashamed, but Cocteau merely smiled. He had his own priorities.

L'Éternel Retour launched both Marais and Cocteau on their joint screen triumph. Jean returned to the world of ballet with *Le Jeune Homme et la Mort*, created in 1946 for Jean Babilée and Nathalie Phillipart; and the same year also saw *The Eagle has Two Heads* in which Marais co-starred on stage and screen with Edwige Feuillere. A small part in the film was played by Edouard Dermit, actor and painter, who like many of his young men became one of Cocteau's adopted "sons", and was to become his heir. For the last fifteen years of his life Dermit was Jean's inseparable companion in Paris and at Milly-la-Fôret, where Cocteau decorated the little chapel that was designed to be his sepulchre.

Painting murals was his last innovation, and it was while working on the decoration of the Romanesque Chapelle de St Pierre at Villefranche in 1960 that he suffered two serious illnesses, a heart attack and a haemorrhage. Regardless of his somewhat erratic lifestyle, Jean had never deserted his Catholic upbringing, and he now turned again to the comforts of religion. In 1961 he wrote one of his finest poems, *Le Requiem*. A second heart attack in May 1963 found him with an image of the Virgin over his bed. He died at Milly on 11 October, and his funeral oration was delivered very conventionally by a member of the Académie Française, to which august body Cocteau had been elected on 20 October 1955.

It is the ultimate paradox that such an *enfant terrible*, artistic rebel against the Establishment, professed homosexual, confirmed drug addict and suspected collaborationist, should have been awarded this conservative accolade. Perhaps the justification was what Brother Pascal of Citeaux, a lifetime friend, wrote about him:

"A great poet is always an incalculable benefit to humanity...Cocteau had not only genius of language and images, he had also that of friendship...besides all those heaven-sent gifts that sparkled in him he had humble and beautiful qualities as a man, unsuspected by many of those who considered themselves his friends, and of which historians (and there will be many) will probably know nothing."

Allowing for the partiality of friendship, this is the other side of Cocteau, the opposite of the exhibitionist and cynical opportunist that Jean himself sought to portray, and was the armour with which he protected his vulnerability. It is impossible to disentangle the many strands of so complex a personality, or the reasons that led him to adopt a chameleon's colourful camouflage that so successfully hid the true poet. Like Oscar Wilde, Cocteau could honestly say "I put my talent into my works and my genius into my life".

Emma Calve: A singer for all Nations

Among the lesser luminaries circling around the story of Rennes-le-Château , the brightest is undoubtedly Emma Calvé. If one were setting out to draw up a late 19th century list of contemporary "beautiful people", Calvé has to be first choice. She was a Star in all senses of that word: talented, famous, glamorous, temperamental, exciting, wealthy - the "Maria Callas" of her day. She played many of the major operatic heroines, and was in demand at the great national opera houses - including San Carlo, l'Opéra Comique, Covent Garden, and the Metropolitan - touring continually and extensively in Europe, America and the Far East. Like Melba and Pavlova, a "sweet" was created for her: Coupe Calvé, consisting of strawberry sherbet and thin slices of poached apricot, topped with crème Chantilly.

She was born Rose Emma Calvet, not in 1862, the daughter of a Spanish nobleman - as the official biographers will have it - but in 1858 at Decazeville in Aveyron. Her father, Justin Calvet, is described as a contractor, which seems to have been something to do with public works and mines, and if not actually aristocratic he was wealthy enough to own land. In 1856 he married Leonie Adèle Astorg, a girl from his own neighbourhood, and they had three children. Rose Emma was the eldest. Next was a boy, Paul Justin, born at Montpellier in 1865, who died when he was ten years old. The third was Adolphe, familiarly called "Adol", born at Turin in December 1868. In due course he married Marguerite Puesch from Aurillac and they became the parents of Elie, Emma's beloved godson.

At the time of Adol's arrival Emma was living with her aunt Caylet at Labastide-Pradines, her father's home, where her parents had left her so as not to interrupt her education. She attended schools at Millau, Tournemire and St. Afrique, and although not brilliant, she was intelligent and regarded as an exemplary pupil. In 1878 she went to Paris to study singing with Jules Puget, who advised her to drop "Rose" and the final "t" of her surname. So Rose Emma Calvet became Emma Calvé.

Her big chance came when Calabresi, the director of the famous Monnaie Theatre in Brussels, offered her a two-year contract to sing leads. She had made a few tentative appearances in concerts, but this was real grand opera. She made her debut as Marguerite in *Faust*, a performance described by the American primadonna Claire Louise Kellogg as "a mixture of red peppers and vanilla blancmange". This was followed by Cherubino in *The Marriage of Figaro*, always one of her favourite operas, in which she later also sang the Countess and Susanna.

In her *Memoires* Emma writes about the first night of *Figaro*. She says "...I was very thin then, and my legs were spindly, like a grasshopper's, which really worried me. Then I had the bright idea of padding them out by wearing enormous cotton stockings underneath my silk ones..." In the interval she was accosted by the Director who ordered her "to remove those monstrous calves immediately. They do not match your figure, and make you look ridiculous." In fear and trembling Emma took off her cotton stockings, and played the second act with her legs reduced to their normal size. She says "I tried in vain to hide them under my page's cloak, which greatly amused the audience". Thinking it was all part of the show, they gave her a rousing reception. "I cannot ever remember hearing such a tumult of applause at the Monnaie as I did on that gloriously joyful evening" she adds.

She was enjoying life, and added several new leading roles to her repertoire. She was twenty-four and in the throes of her first real love affair. Henri Cain was a librettist, and owed much of his success to Calvé's performances in his operas. He was also a celebrated painter - his portraits included the Duke of Orléans, Leon Carvalho and his father Auguste Cain who was a famous sculptor - and his ambition was to become a horticulturist. He collected roses. Emma always kept at her bedside a Russian cross and chain that he had given her, and she wore it on stage as one of Marguerite's jewels in Faust. Their idyll had something of the character of a 19th century operetta, but the end came when a friend reported seeing Cain in Nice, with a "triumphant young lady on his arm". He had married Guirdaudon, a charming actress from l'Opéra Comique, and they set up house in Paris, where they became famous among friends for their good humour, the pleasant décor of their home, and their admirable lunches.

Jules Blois was quite a different type. He was intellectual, a "man of letters". The son of a merchant from Marseille and a Spanish mother, he had lived in Paris from the age of twenty, where he became interested in occultism, wrote books on metaphysics and philosophy, and became a disciple of the Swami Vivikanenda who was visiting Europe in 1900. It is probable that Emma met Blois at one of the occult groups of which they were both adepts, and they attended séances together at the Avenue

Victor-Hugo. He went on tour with her, and accompanied her to the Orient. On 6 January 1903 *The Times* in New York announced their engagement, but it was categorically denied in April. In 1915 Blois went to the States to live, and remained there until his death in 1943, although he never adjusted, and could neither speak or write easily in English. In old age he reverted to Catholicism.

The oddest of Emma's emotional excursions was her relationship with an American, who is identified only as "Higgins". In 1906 Emma gave up her smart apartment, decorated by Lalique, at the Course-la-Reine in Paris, saying she intended to spend more time at her château of Cabrière in the Cervennes, but in the meantime was leaving for a Mediterranean cruise on a superb yacht at the invitation of a "gallant American gentleman of culture and distinction". She added that she was considering matrimony. The "gallant American" was reputed to be a millionaire many time over, and offered to buy Emma a theatre of her own.

In March she was singing at l'Opéra Comique in *The Marriage of Figaro* and a new work, *Lara* by Nail d'Isadora, when *The Times* announced that the marriage would take place at the end of June. Reynaldo Hahn, in his *Journal of a Musician* says "...yesterday I had lunch at Durant's house where I met Calvé...she is, she tells me, engaged to a half-blind man who has sixty millions..." The press took up the story and embroidered it a little, saying the bridal couple would honeymoon on their yacht accompanied by an orchestra from one of the top Italian theatres. "In the clear evenings" it adds, "the divine voice of the one and only Carmen will enchant the fishermen..." In February 1907 Emma was in New York when the *Herald Tribune* published an announcement that the marriage was entirely a figment of the media's imagination. They said they were authorised to confirm that Mme Calvé did not know, and never had known, a "Mr Higgins".

Something - never revealed - had happened to make Calvé retract her original announcement. The mystery remains unsolved.

In *Le Trésor Maudit*, Gérard de Sède names Emma Calvé among the high society gatherings at Bérenger Saunière's Villa of Bethania at Rennes-le-Château , and inevitably the suggestion has arisen in later accounts that she was his mistress, although there is nothing to support such an allegation. It is very tempting to add a postscript to this mythical romance by naming Saunière as the father of Emma's mysterious daughter who, if she existed, was kept such a dark secret.

The suggestion is that Emma was introduced to Saunière in Paris by Debussy, who was a mutual friend of her own and Emile Hoffet, the young palaeographer whom Saunière perhaps consulted about the documents he was reputed to have found in the Rennes-le-Château church of St.Mary Magdalene. There is, in fact, no proof that Sauniere ever went to Paris, but he could have met Calvé locally, because she was a friend of Dr. Gérard Encausse (Papus of Tarot fame) who had connections with Jules Doinel's neo-Cathar church at Carcassonne, and Doinel was known to Saunière. Also she lived reasonably near at her château of Cabrière, where she taught young singers, and entertained a great deal when not engaged on her world tours.

The château was said to date from the thirteenth century, and Emma had spent a fortune on restoring it. There was a local legend connecting the château with the famous alchemist Nicholas Flamel, who was supposed to have made the first transmutation of gold, aided by a book known as the *Book of Abraham*, dictated to him by an angel. This book had been bought by an old man immediately afterwards, and had subsequently disappeared, but it was believed it may have been acquired by the then owner of the château of Cabrière, and was still hidden there. Emma knew the story when she bought the château, but never made any extravagant claims about it.

Emma had a curious and original mind, and with her thirst for knowledge it was inevitable she should be drawn to the occult sciences, particularly spiritualism and astrology. M. de St. Paterne, in his exhaustive survey, wrote that in 1891 Paris was the Ville-

Luminaire, the City of Light, where more than 20,000 of the inhabitants followed various esoteric cults, "all pretending to evoke the hidden forces of nature, and renewing the misdeeds of sorcery". There were among them such extremists as Cabalists, Theosophists, Spiritualists, Buddhists, Hermeticists, and Astrologers, experts in dream walking and "readers of the destiny of France and the World in tea-leaves", all of whom believed that there was an accord between mysticism, magic and "the great and noble aim of Peace". The common denominator was spiritual perfection, and the achievement of Utopia.

Emma was part of the Parisian occult scene that included not only Jules Blois and "Papus", but Josephin Péladan, the founder of the Order of the Rose Cross of the Temple and the Grail, and the famous seer Mme de Thebes. On 21 June 1904 the astronomers Camille and Gabrielle Flammarion invited Emma to witness the sunset from the top of the Eiffel Tower on the occasion of the Summer Solstice, in the company of all the most eminent French astronomers. Camille asked her to enchant them by providing an invocation to the sun, for "Dear and shining star…you love the sun, he is your brother, and as a star you are his sister…" and added, rather more prosaically "M. Eiffel sends you this day an invitation to dinner, for it appears to us right that the most glittering star in our sky should not miss the feast of the Solstice…"

In her *Memoires* Emma mentions an occasion in New York in 1899 when she and the tenor Salignac, whom she describes as intelligent and well versed in occult science, were discussing spiritualism with Grau, the company manager. Grau was a non-believer, and said to Emma "What nonsense. Come my friend, you who loved your little girl, do you believe that you will see her again? Why then, if one can regain everything, will I get back the money I have lost?" Emma writes "What can one reply to that? He is a blind soul… there is nothing to be done."

This is the only known occasion on which any mention is made of the hypothetical illegitimate child that Emma may, or may not, have borne some time towards the end of the 19th century.

Rumour reports that the little girl was severely handicapped, either mentally or physically or both, and died in adolescence. There is no mention of the supposed father, and it is surmised that the relationship was a "guilty" one. Whether or not the child ever existed, or whether it was just a rumour is not known, and those in a position to know have never spoken, but perhaps if Emma did have a child in these tragic circumstances, it may account for her great love for, and sympathy with children.

She did an enormous amount of work for children's charities, and she loved her godson, Elie, like her own child. He was an attractive boy with artistic leanings, and every year he composed a new poem for her birthday. He decided to enter the Academy of Drama in Paris, and at the end of his three year course in July 1929 entered for a special prize, which there was a good chance of his winning. The audition piece called for his taking part in a duologue on stage. When he failed to enter on cue he was called, but still did not appear. After repeated calls he was searched for, and found unconscious on the floor of a room under the stage. He was thought to have fainted, which was attributed to overwork or stage-fright. Dr François Poncet, who was in the audience, applied first aid, but all efforts failed. Elie was taken to the Hospital de la Pitié, but was found dead on arrival from a cerebral embolism. His favourite maxim had been "Do not weep for me...I die of joy". Emma was inconsolable.

Among her extensive operatic repertoirc, Emma is probably best known, even today, as the greatest exponent of *Carmen* of her time. She first sang the part on November 1892 at l'Opéra Comique in Paris, and had misgivings about following such great earlier Carmens as Galli-Marie, the creator of the part, Minnie Hauk and Pauline de Luca, all of whom had received rave reviews. One of the librettists, Henri Meilhac, sent Emma a first night present with a note saying "My dear, wonderful Star, I am sending you a little dagger with which to threaten Don José at your pleasure. I take this opportunity to send you my sincere and heartfelt compliments. Your grateful author, H. Meilhac." She need have had no fears of the outcome. She was acclaimed as the only Carmen since Galli-Marie. The great Coquelin himself was almost incoherent in his praise: "Carmen, you ARE Carmen, you are totally she whom Merimée painted in colours so vivid, so true...and you are not only Merimée's Carmen, but also Bizet's..." Calvé's great advantage was not only did she have a superb soprano voice, but she was also a very good actress.

There is a story that during one performance she became angry with the famous tenor, Jean de Reszke, who was co-starring with her, and in the final scene after her dramatic operatic death she got up and walked off stage. He rushed after her and dragged her back on, whereupon Emma resumed her position as the corpse, and proceeded to sing along with her distracted Don José for the whole of rest of the performance at the top of her not inconsiderable voice.

It was during a European tour of *Carmen* in 1910 that Emma first met Gaspari, and fell wildly in love with him. She was fifty with many love affairs behind her, he was thirty-five with many opportunities before him: Eugenio Galileo Gaspari, born at Santa-Maria in Fiore, Italy, on 26 April 1875. He was handsome, intelligent, charismatic - with a beautiful head, a tenor voice, and a roving eye. Emma was enchanted with him. She married him on 4 February 1911 in New Jersey, and adopted the name of Mme Calvé-Gaspari.

The marriage lasted for ten years, mainly due to Emma's sincere love, and her everlasting patience with his extravagances, greed for money, and many infidelities. He was mean in small ways. Emma had a long necklace which she always wore. After each success she would add to it another pearl of great price. Occasionally Gaspari would surreptitiously cut one or two off and sell them to settle his debts. Emma had for a long time been willing to shut her eyes to his misdemeanours, but on an April day in Paris he was discovered in adultery with one of her close friends, which aroused her to an unprecedented storm of fury... Gaspari regained his liberty, and Emma reverted to her single name of Calvé.

She was in the States when Queen Victoria sent for her to come and sing at the Jubilee celebrations. This was not Emma's first Command Performance. She had been invited to Windsor in 1892 when she was singing in *Cavalleria Rusticana* at Covent Garden, and the Queen had been so delighted with Emma's rendering of *Ave Maria* that she had three times got up to congratulate her, and presented her with a superb piece of jewellery. In 1894 the Queen asked her to come and sing extracts from *Carmen* at Windsor, and to return for another visit in 1900.

In 1916 she was back in the States, singing in charity concerts to raise money for the war effort - she had always been very patriotic. At one such concert in San Francisco there was a scandalous scene when two hundred Germans in the audience continually whistled throughout her performance. In June she was in New York, where she sang *La Marseillaise* draped in a French flag and wearing a Poilu's helmet.

In 1917 her cousin Lt. Marcel Marceau was killed in action. Only an hour earlier he had written to Emma to ask if she would embroider a pennon-flag for the ll Cie du l32e Regiment d'Infanterie. The letter was retrieved from his body and sent to her. She was living in Paris at that time, and she arranged for masses to be said there for the repose of his soul, and the souls of his hero companions.

After the war Emma resumed her gruelling schedule of tours and concerts. In 1921 her mother died and was greatly missed. Emma was always close to her family, even though she was so often separated from them.

In 1941 she became ill with liver problems. She went to Lamalou-les-Bains for thermal treatment and then on to Montpellier for a check-up. The prognosis was not good. In November she entered Dr Pares' clinic. December was a long agony of physical and mental pain, and she died on 5 January 1942. She was buried in the cemetery at Millau beside her parents, in a tomb designed by Denys Puesch which she had commissioned in 1899.

Thanks to the Gramophone and Typewriter Company, the ghost of Calvé's voice remains. She made her first recording in 1902. The studio was in a disreputable part of London, and when Emma's cab arrived she refused to get out, convinced that she was being kidnapped. The celebrated accompanist Landon Ronald, who was in charge of the event, solved the problem by rapidly despatching a messenger to the nearest Bank, and pouring a stream of golden sovereigns into Emma's lap. She gathered them quickly into her handbag, seized her mantilla, and shouting "Come, come, little Ronald" dashed into the Studio. She was ruinously generous, but she liked money.

The quality of the recordings, even allowing for the primitive equipment of the time, varies enormously, because Emma could never master the problem of singing while standing still. Even alone in the Studio she insisted on full costume, choreography and props. Thanks to modern technology many of her recordings have been enhanced and transferred to C.D., and the last, which she supposedly made at the age of 82 four days before her death, includes a recitation of *La Marseillaise*. Her motto could indeed have been "semper fidelis".

The Pretenders

The concept of the "lost king" is buried deep in the human psyche. History and legend are littered with examples: King Arthur, Simon-bar-Kochba, Barbarossa, Sebastian of Portugal, Drake, Che Guevara - the story is always the same. The hero is not dead, for there is no body, or the body is not the actual body, and somewhere - in Avalon, the Fortunate Isles, Glass Castle - he waits for the call that will summon him to return and lead his people to victory at the time of crisis. The little boy in the Temple was an obvious candidate.

After the fall of the Bastille in 1789 the Royal family were more or less confined to the Tuileries. In 1792 they were moved to the

Temple. This was not a prison, being in use as a Palace by the
Comte d'Artois, but it was an old Templar Commanderie, and
so partly fortified and more easily defended. Although under
restriction, they were not too uncomfortable until the Revolution
escalated into violence. In January 1793 Louis XVI was arrested,
tried and executed. The Queen was separated from her children,
and in October she too went to the guillotine. Louis' two brothers,
the Duc de Provence and the Comte d'Artois, had escaped to
England and both lived to become Kings of France.

By his father's death, the Dauphin Louis Charles, aged eight
years, became Louis XVII. He was moved to the Temple Tower,
and Antoine Simon, a cobbler, was appointed his guardian. Simon
was uncouth and foul-mouthed but not unkind, and his wife did
her best to alleviate the suffering of the little prince.

In January 1794 Simon was dismissed, and no replacement
was appointed. The window and door of the boy's room were
sealed, and his food was henceforth pushed through a hatch. Two
guards would peer through a small aperture night and morning to
check that the prisoner was still there. He had little light or air, no
change of clothing, and no contact with any other human being.

Six months later Barras, the new Dictator, visited the Temple
and was appalled at the condition of the prisoner. He was filthy,
verminous, and starving. Barras insisted that the place was cleaned
up, and the child bathed, clothed and fed. However, the boy
appeared to be in a state of shock, his mind gone, communication
impossible. He ignored anything said to him, and never spoke.
A young Creole, Christophe Laurent, was appointed to look after
him.

A few months later Laurent was replaced by Etienne Lasne, an
old soldier, who said that the prisoner, although very frail, had
spoken to him. The following March Lasne reported that the
boy was unwell, and on 8 June 1795 that he was dead, it was
assumed of natural causes. He was buried in an unmarked grave
in the cemetery of St. Marguerite.

Almost immediately the rumour began spreading that the child who died in the Temple was not the real Louis XVII, which inspired Regnault Warin, a second-rate author, to write a romance on the subject. It was published in 1798 under the title *Le Cimetière de la Madeleine*, and was the textbook used as a basis for the claims made by most of the Pretenders.

It was inevitable that the Legitimists, traumatised by Louis XVI's execution, should believe that his son did not die in the Temple, but at the right time would emerge to ascend the throne of his ancestors. The belief persisted, even after the Restoration of Louis XVIII in 1814. There was no lack of contenders.

The most believable of the claimants was Karl William Naundorff, who said he had letters of identity, but they were all lost or stolen. He had no passport, and his identity was never proved, though he was thought to be of Eastern European origin, and in fact spoke very poor French.

None of the other pretenders could aspire to written proof, and relied on hypothetical memories of childhood or verbal support from aged so-called witnesses. The legend grew that the child in the Temple had survived. "The Saviours of Louis XVII" began as a political movement, and ended as a quasi-mystical one. Naundorff was the front runner, and his claims were supported by Eugène Vintras, the renegade priest who claimed to have in his possession Hosts that bled for the infamy of France's sin in denying her true King and supporting a usurper.

One of the essentials a Pretender must have is documentary proof. Indisputable, legal, binding, unassailable proof. It is the one thing they never have, because if they had, they would not be Pretenders, but the real thing. Circumstantial evidence there is in plenty, but it is inevitably wrapped in a shroud of mist and mystery. Documents are said to exist, but are never seen, and their provenance varies from account to account, their ultimate destination remains obscure.

Plantard claimed to be the rightful King of France, descendant of the Merovingian King Dagobert II, but there was no evidence beyond the suspect genealogy in the Dossier Secret. The Rennes-le-Château authors were inspired when they tied the story of "le roi perdu" to hidden treasure, but Plantard himself never showed any interest in Saunière's mysterious wealth or the documents he supposedly found in his church that led him to the secret. Plantard's interest was centred on his royal lineage and the Prieuré de Sion who were his supporters. But hidden treasure, like the hidden king, provides both purpose and glamour to the story.

It is an interesting coincidence that there is also a lost treasure story connected with Naundorff. After his death, his wife and family settled in Holland under the name of "Bourbon". In 1866 they were approached by the son of Bremond, who had been Louis XVI's private secretary and who claimed that he had recognised Naundorff from childhood. When Bremond died, a document was found among his papers, and according to his will it was to be offered to the Naundorff family for the sum of 10,000 francs and a guarantee of 50,000 francs if the treasure it described was found. This 60,000 francs was equivalent to the amount Bremond had loaned to the Naundorffs from his own pocket.

Bremond said he had been given the document by his great friend, de Monciel, one of Louis XVI's Ministers. In 1792 de Monciel told Louis XVI that he knew the existence of a source of enormous wealth. The King had replied that he and the King of Spain were both aware of this treasure, but the time was not yet right. It was to be used only for the restoration of the Bourbon monarchy.

In 1872 a Dutch newspaper *The Panama Star* reported that the Bourbon family (that is, the Naundorffs) had offered to sell to the Colombian Government a description of the site of some fabulous platinum mines, the knowledge of which had been bequeathed to them by the Queen of Spain. The proposal was being considered by the President of Columbia.

The news created great excitement, but it was discovered that in 1735 the mines were said to have been filled in by order of the Spanish Government, so that over-production of platinum should not depreciate its value. The secret location of the mines was contained in Bremond's document.

Negotiations started in 1870, but came to nothing, and two years later Gruau, the Naundorff's lawyer, concluded an agreement with two Dutchmen for exploitation of the mines. Almost immediately a Colombian citizen, Saravia-Ferro, arrived in Europe and explained that as he lived near the site of the mines he was the person to undertake the survey most easily and cheaply. Accordingly, a new contract was drawn up to which he was made a party.

The Colombian Government then sent ex-Minister Pradilla to the Naundorffs to say that Colombia was now ready to negotiate. The "Bourbon consortium" initially declined, but the task proved to be beyond their capabilities. They made a new offer to Colombia who was by that time no longer interested, and the project went into abeyance. When Gruau died in 1883 he left instructions that the document was to go to Amélie, Naundorff's eldest daughter, who had married a Frenchman, Abel Laprade, and so was the only member of the Naundorff family to obtain legitimate French citizenship. Everyone concerned firmly believed in the existence of the platinum mines, but nothing ever came of it. The Naundorff treasure, like Saunière's, was most probably fictitious.

Lacking proof, the identity of any Pretender is, of necessity, left open. The most interesting part of their histories is the evidence created from assumptions, half-truths and plausible lies. De Chérisey and Plantard are both dead, and apparently profited little by being the creators of the Rennes-le-Château mystery. Naundorff died in exile, a disappointed man. None of the other Pretenders gained anything. Saunière's will showed that he owned nothing, and Marie Denarnaud died in poverty.

So who gains? The writers of the books perhaps, and the readers for whom the stories provide conjecture and entertainment.

A Plethora Of Princes – Jean Marie Hervagault, Bruneau, Baron de Richemont

The first of the many contenders for the crown was Jean Marie Hervagault, born in 1781, and supposedly the son of a tailor of Saint-Lo. He was handsome, aristocratic in appearance and bearing, and attractive to both men and women. He may have been the illegitimate son of the Duke of Valentinois, whose mistress his mother had been before her marriage.

As a young teenager he ran away from home on a number of occasions and wandered the countryside where his pleasing looks and charming manners easily earned him board and lodging. Dressed as a girl, a disguise that his long hair suited well, in 1797 he was arrested for fraud and imprisoned at Chalons, where he proceeded to hold court. A lady from the town provided him daily with fresh bed linen, another gave him her best furniture for his cell, a tailor made him new clothes, and an apothecary supplied him with expensive bottles of toilet water. The Governor of the prison allowed him to run up a debt of 2000 francs and himself paid it off.

On occasion Hervagault said that he was the son of the Duke d'Ursel, on others that he was the son of the Duke of Monaco. Finally he asserted that he was the son of the Marquis de Longueville and that his Christian names were Louis Antoine Joseph Frederic. The Longueville family were natives of Normandy, and because his name was Louis, Hervagault's supporters rashly came to the conclusion that he must be the Duke of Normandy, that is, the son of Louis XVI. Hervagault enthusiastically encouraged the idea, and declared that he had been rescued from the Temple in a washing basket.

On release from prison he was welcomed into society, but in the midst of a party, when he was about to display a tattoo of the Fleur-de-Lys on an intimate part of his person, he was again arrested for misrepresentation and sentenced to a further four years in gaol. In 1806 he joined a colonial regiment and spent two years at Belle-Isle-en-Mer, where he became the close friend of his commanding officer, who gave him a house and servant to himself and allowed him to wear civilian clothes.

In 1809 he deserted and returned to France, and was once more arrested and imprisoned at Bicetre, where he died on 8 May, 1812.

Hervagault did not set out to claim to be Louis XVII, the role was more or less thrust upon him. Because he was always somewhat ambivalent about his age and origin, the usual stories arose that the young man who died in Bicetre was not Hervagault, but that he had escaped and resurfaced as the next Pretender, Mathurin Bruneau.

Bruneau was born in 1784 at Vezins in the department of Maine et Loire, the son of a cobbler. When he was only seven he was left an orphan and adopted by one of his married elder sisters. He was a good-looking and intelligent boy, but lacked Hervagault's aristocratic heritage, and by the age of eleven his sister found him unmanageable and turned him out of the house.

He supported himself by begging and theft, and in the winter of 1795 arrived at a farm-house about nine miles from Condé. When the farmer asked where he was from he said "Vezins" which was the truth, but the farmer misunderstood and thought he meant he was from the noble family of Vezins in la Vendée, who had lost everything in the war. He therefore took the boy into his home and looked after him.

The news came to the ears of the Viscountess de Turpin, who lived at the Château d'Angry nearby, and she agreed to take charge of Mathurin. He quickly adapted to his new circumstances, and convinced the Viscountess that he was indeed a son of Baron de Vezins, but when shortly afterwards the Chevalier de Vezins returned from England and learned that one of his nephews was living at the Château d'Angry, he denounced the impostor because "none of his nephews remained in France". The Viscountess, disillusioned, sent Mathurin back to Vezins.

His sister, Mme Delaunay, had no wish to have him back, and returned him to the Viscountess, saying she could not afford to keep him. The Viscountess, being a philanthropist albeit a sensible one, took the boy in but relegated him to the servants' quarters.

It is not known how long he stayed there. He was next heard of in 1803 when he was imprisoned at St Denis as a vagrant and considered to be insane. He was presumably still attempting to pass himself off as a nobleman or prince. On his release he enlisted in the Marine Artillery, and sailed on the frigate *Cybele* for the New World, but deserted in 1806 to live in America for the next nine years.

In September 1815 he arrived back at St Malo with an American passport in the name of Charles de Navarre, and proceeded to convince a widow, Mme Phelippeaux, that he was her son whom she had believed killed in Spain. As a result he received a considerable amount of money from her.

Shortly afterwards he proclaimed himself to be Louis XVII, and succeeded in recruiting a reasonable amount of local support. He said that he did not wish to dethrone his uncle, and would be willing to serve him on condition that on the king's death Bruneau himself should succeed him. This was embarrassing to Louis XVIII, newly restored to the throne, and committed to the Comte D'Artois and his son, the Duke of Angoulème, as the next heirs.

Bruneau was arrested and imprisoned at Rouen. Although he was officially forbidden to see anyone, his adherents quickly bribed their way in, and Bruneau held court in his cell, drinking and smoking, and allowed his visitors to kiss his hand. His letters, written by a "secretary", were sealed with "Charles de Bourbon, King of France and Navarre, by the grace of God". His life story was written by a man named Griselle, based on the novel *La Cimetière de la Madeleine* by Regnault Warin, which described how a boy was smuggled into the Temple in a cardboard toy horse, and substituted for the Prince who was smuggled out again by the same device.

The deception was finally exposed when M. de la Paumelière, an old Vendéan officer, saw Bruneau in prison and thought he recognised the boy befriended by the Viscountess de Turpin twenty years earlier. Reporting his suspicions to the Viscountess, she in turn went to Rouen to confront Bruneau who admitted he was indeed the same person. He did not think there was any harm in this, as the time he first arrived at the Château D'Angry coincided with the date of Louis XVII's supposed rescue from the Temple. The Viscountess felt she had been hoaxed and was furious.

In 1817 Bruneau issued an appeal to the French people, and was moved to the Conciergerie, where an enquiry was made into his case, but no evidence was forthcoming to support his claims. He was eventually put on trial, identified by his sister and other relatives, and sentenced to a long term of imprisonment. He is reported to have died in 1822 before the term was completed.

The third pretender, Baron de Richemont, is something of an enigma. His origin is unknown, but it is believed his real name was either Herbert or Perrin. The first that is known of him is that he was imprisoned in Milan at the same time as Silvio Pellico, the Carbonari poet and author, who recognised "the easy and refined tone of a man of the world who had received a good education". Richemont told Pellico that he was the Duke of Normandy, Louis XVII, which Pellico did not believe, although he said that Richemont bore a striking physical likeness to the Bourbons.

In 1825 Richemont went to Paris and started to press his claims. In 1828 and 1829 he addressed petitions to the Chamber in which he claimed to be Duke of Normandy and heir to the throne. He wrote to the Duchesse d'Angoulême, his reputed sister, and to the Press, and was involved in various political intrigues. He was clever enough not to press for restoration to the throne, but he coveted a share of the Duchesse d'Angoulême's inheritance, which although officially entailed to the male heirs, had been granted to her as the only surviving child of Louis XVI and Marie Antoinette.

In his published *Memoires*, Richemont follows the version of the rescue favoured by Regnault Warin, using a substitute child concealed in a toy horse. Richemont, however, adds his own fantasy to the story, stating that he was kept in hiding until nightfall, when he was put inside a life-size model horse which was then harnessed to a cart with two leaders in front and a wheeler behind it, making it difficult to distinguish between the real horses and the model. This was truly a mechanical marvel, having legs with flexible joints which enabled it to move in a life-like way, and was covered with a real horse's skin. The inside of the body was padded to make the journey comfortable for the passenger, and air holes pierced in ears, nostrils and under the tail to allow him to breathe. In this wondrous contraption Richemont says he was conveyed out of Paris.

He was taken to Charette in La Vendée and then to Germany to join the Prince de Condé who, fearing that Richemont's uncle - the Count de Provence - might harm him, placed the boy in the guardianship of Kléber, under whom he later fought in Egypt. When his health broke down he returned to Paris and sought the protection of Fouche, who advised him to take refuge in America, which he did. Here he lived with the Mamelucks (South American Indians) in Brazil until 1815, when he returned to Europe. After unsuccessfully endeavouring to obtain recognition from Louis XVIII and the Duchess d'Angoulème, Richemont wandered through Europe, Asia and Africa, and so at length arrived at Mantua where he was arrested and transferred to Milan - which is where his official history begins.

In 1833 Richemont was introduced to the Countess d'Apchier de Varbre through a mutual friend, Viscount d'Orcet, and she became his devoted supporter, accepting all his claims without question. In her youth she had been a Lady of Honour to the Princess Royal and had known both her and her brother as children. The Countess was a widow, and after the Restoration did not feel inclined to resume life at Court, preferring to live retired at Vaurenard. In the summer of 1833 Richemont visited her there and she entertained him like a king. She was well over fifty, but fell madly in love with him, and placed her home and fortune entirely at his disposal. She even forgave his philandering with her maidservants, believing it was the *droit de seigneur*.

1834 Richemont was arrested for misrepresentation and sentenced to twelve years hard labour, which he elected to serve on the roads of Paris. He escaped soon afterwards and fled to the protection of the Countess at Vaurenard. He discovered that Viscount d'Orcet had come to the rather strange conclusion that he (Richemont) was the same person as Hervagault and Mathurin Bruneau, and had confided his beliefs to the Countess. Feeling that the surest way to keep her faith in him from suffering, Richemont himself told her that much of the information contained in his *Memoires* was fiction, and that he had not been in Brazil, but was imprisoned at various times under the names of Hervagault and Mathurin Bruneau. Incredibly, the Countess believed him and continued to regard him as the true King Louis XVII. He had become her whole life, and to accept that he was an impostor would have broken her heart.

In 28 October 1834 Karl William Naundorff sent a letter to the President of the Court before which Richemont was on trial, pointing out that Richemont could not be Louis XVII because he (Naundorff) himself was the true King. In the letter he says "...The man who secretly employs the charlatan Richemont knows that the real son of Louis XVII is armed with all the proofs necessary to establish his origin...he knows equally well that every time the royal orphan attempted to obtain recognition by his family a new Louis XVII appeared who was just as much an impostor as the man whom you are called upon to judge today..." Naundorff believed that Hervagault, Bruneau and Richemont were all government agents employed to ridicule and discredit the claims of the true Louis XVII - himself. Inevitably Louis XVIII and Charles X were the wicked uncles who persecuted him, although he never blamed the Duchess d'Angoulème for her treatment of him, believing that she was ill-advised and misled by his enemies.

Richemont continued until the end in his attempts to get the Duchess d'Angoulème to acknowledge him as her brother, but the Duchess never moved from her resolve not to be involved in the matter of Louis XVII's alleged survival. The fact that the government left him unmolested after his escape from prison until his death seems to indicate that they did not take his claims seriously. He never achieved a crown, but he lived in comfort for the rest of his life, and died in 1853 at the Countess' château at Gleize on the Rhone. If, on his own admission, much of the account of his early life was a lie, who in fact was he?

Augustus Meves – Le Roi malgré lui

The most interesting among the Pretenders was an Englishman, Augustus Meves, the only one who made no effort to assert his claim. For twenty-three years life had held no surprises for him; it was typically that of an English middle-class family. Then in 1818 his reputed father, William Meves, died of cholera, leaving "to my natural son Augustus" one half of his estate. Augustus' mother took great exception to this, since it implied that Augustus was illegitimate, and she revealed to him that he was not, in fact, the son of William Meves, nor of herself, but the legitimate child of Louis XVI and his Queen Marie Antoinette. She said he had been rescued from the Temple, brought to England in 1793, and placed in her care.

The news shattered Augustus who became ill and totally distracted, and he does not appear to have done anything about establishing his new identity until the death of his mother in 1823. He then began laboriously to recreate the supposed life of Louis XVII compiled from scraps of childhood memory, accounts from surviving friends and members of the Meves family, and such documentary evidence as could be found. He wrote a somewhat hypothetical biography and it was published in 1868, with a commentary by his son who called himself Augustus de Bourbon the younger, by William Ridgway of 169 Piccadilly, London, under the title of *The Authentic Historical Memoirs of Louis Charles,*

Prince-Royal, Dauphin of France, who subsequently to October 1793 personated through supposititious means August Meves. These Memoirs were dedicated to the French Nation. There were obvious omissions and errors in his account, specifically regarding dates, which his son not always satisfactorily explains away, but there remains a grain of truth.

The following is the story told, AS IF it were true.

Mary Anne Crowley - she liked to write it "Marianne" - was born at Bath in April 1754, the younger daughter of Cornelius and Mary Crowley, and educated at the Convent of St. Omer in France. Marianne had pretensions to being an opera singer, and at the age of twenty-three went to London to study music with Signor Sacchini, the celebrated Italian composer. When the death of her mother cut short this ambition, Sacchini obtained an appointment for Marianne at the French court as lady-in-waiting to Marie Antoinette, with whom she was soon on terms of intimacy.

In 1781 her father became ill, and although she hastened to Bath she was too late, he was dead when she arrived. He left very little, and Marianne went to London where at the house of the Reverend Charles Wesley she met the Dowager Duchess Caroline, Countess of Harrington, who invited the girl to stay with her. It was during this time that she became acquainted with William Meves, a portrait painter and miniaturist, and in 1784 was said to have married him secretly at an unspecified Roman Catholic church.

She went to France, travelling under the name of Madame Schroeder, which was William's mother's name, and resumed her position at Court. In February 1785 Marianne gave birth to a son, and paid a flying visit to London to register him and have him baptised at St James's, Piccadilly, under the name of Augustus Antoine Cornelius Meves, which gave him the right to inherit under English law. She then went to live at Boulogne-sur-Mer supported by a Court pension and an allowance of £200 a year from her sister, who had been married and widowed twice, both husbands being men of substance.

In 1788 Marianne returned to London, and in February 1789 a daughter, Cecilia Marianne, was born. Her sister considered Marianne something of a light-skirt, and reduced the allowance to £40 a year, but finding this left her in dire penury, the allowance was restored. Marianne was said at this time to have married William Meves by Protestant rites as a sop to her sister's moral principles, dropped the name of Schroeder, and became "Mrs Meves". No record exists of either marriage, religious or civil, and William and Marianne never lived under the same roof. After the birth of Cecilia they parted, Marianne supporting her daughter by giving music lessons, and William accepting responsibility for Augustus.

In August 1793, at about the time that Marie Antoinette was removed to the Conciergerie, Mrs Carpenter, a friend of Marianne's, received a letter from Tom Paine, author of *The Rights of Man* and a member of the French National Convention, asking her to find a child answering to a certain description and bring him to Paris "for purposes required by him". By a questionable coincidence, Augustus Meves answered this description well, except that he was fairer than stipulated. William took him to Paris and handed him over, plus a good sum of gold, to Antoine Simon with the intention of exchanging him for Louis Charles, to whom Augustus bore a very strong resemblance. The exchange was accomplished in October 1793, and William returned to London with Louis Charles, whom he placed in a boarding school while he learned English. Augustus remained in Simon's care in the Temple Tower.

In January 1794 Mrs Meves left England for Paris with a deaf and dumb child. A second exchange was made, and the deaf mute replaced Augustus Meves, whose subsequent fate is left ambivalent. According to this scenario, it was the deaf and dumb child who was shut up in solitary confinement and suffered so shockingly, and it was for this reason that when Barras tried to talk to him six months later he could not get any response to his questions. The boy could not hear them, nor speak the answers.

As it was politically undesirable that Louis Charles should be seen to be murdered, it was obviously hoped that by subjecting the prisoner to such atrocious treatment he would die, but children afflicted with physical handicaps are often very strong and the boy survived. At some point therefore a further exchange was achieved, whereby the deaf mute was replaced with a child terminally ill with rickets. This must have been accomplished before the appointment of Lasne, who had never previously seen the prince so would not have known the difference, and accounts for his saying that the prisoner spoke to him.

The question arises - why was William willing to sacrifice his reputed son? There was the inference in his Will that Augustus was illegitimate, but no right thinking man would count that as sufficient reason. Was he, in fact, not William's son at all? Marianne was back at the French Court between June 1784 and February 1785 when her son was born, and she made her home in France until he was four years old. There was his convenient - and considerable - resemblance to the Bourbons. Inevitably the implication arises that he was, in fact, the bastard son of one of the Royal princes.

In his search for his true identity, Augustus - or Louis Charles - met Karl Wilhelm Naundorff, who also bore a great likeness to his reputed father Louis XVI, and who claimed to be Louis XVII. Naundorff, like Augustus, had fleeting memories of the Temple, his escape, and subsequent adventures in Europe. Augustus, accepting that he was himself Louis Charles, believed that Naundorff was the real Augustus Meves, bastard son of Marianne and perhaps a Bourbon prince, who had in the first instance replaced himself, and was later rescued from the Temple by the second substitution of the deaf and dumb child.

Why did Augustus never attempt to claim his supposed royal birthright? The answer was, he did not wish to be King. He wrote on two occasions to his supposed sister the Duchesse d'Angoulème, but was not distressed to receive no reply. He had a wife and children, a comfortable life in England, some prestige, and an assured income. Apart from his inheritance from William, his puritanical Aunt left him property and £12,000. He loved music, was a sufficiently good performer to give public piano recitals, and was recognised as a distinguished composer. His "fine touch and exquisite execution" gained him somewhat spurious comparison with Mozart. He just wanted to know who he really was.

On 14 May 1859, at the age of seventy seven years, Augustus died of a heart attack in a cab on the way to University College hospital. At the request of his sons, post-mortem examination confirmed the existence of certain moles, birthmarks and scars upon the body which were said to correspond exactly with those of Louis XVI's son. There was the question of colouring - the Augustus in London before 1793 was fair haired and blue eyed, while the Dauphin had chestnut brown hair and hazel eyes. After 1793 the reverse appeared to be the case. Young children's colouring can darken with age - but science declares it cannot get lighter.

This evidence, however, relies on eye-witness accounts, and people are subjectively inaccurate when describing colour. Moreover, contemporary portraits show Louis XVI's first son, Louis Joseph who died of a bone disease in 1789, was blonde. If Augustus was not Louis XVII, then he was subject to delusions, fostered perhaps by his likeness to the French royal house. He had a history of mental illness.

He certainly did not wish to use his supposed identity for profit. He had a true love for France, and wrote an anthem for her, with the refrain -

> *Dieu et mon droit, Dieu et mon droit,*
> *Vive La Liberté Française.*
> *God and my right, God and my right,*
> *Vive La Liberté Française.*

Le Roi perdu - le Roi retrouvé - le Roi malgré lui. Perhaps. ...

August de Bourbon (Meves)
*The Lost Dauphin Louis XVII,
King of France,* 1976

Emma Calvé as "Ophelia"

Emma Calvé's Château at Millau

Karl William Naundorff
The Shadow King, 1928

Eleazer Williams
*The Lost Dauphin Louis XVII
or Onwarenhiiaki*, 1878

Grave of Gérard Encausse (Papus)
Père Lachaise cemetery, Paris

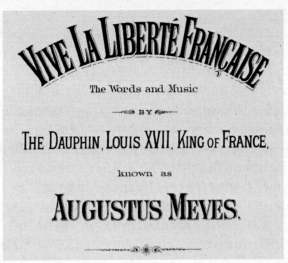

VIVE LA LIBERTÉ FRANÇAISE

The Words and Music

— BY —

THE DAUPHIN, LOUIS XVII, KING OF FRANCE,

known as

AUGUSTUS MEVES.

Title page of *Vive La Liberté Française* by Augustus Meves, 1876

Karl William Naundorff – The Shadow King

Among the numerous claimants to be Louis XVII probably the most plausible, and certainly the most persistent, was Naundorff. His passport, admittedly false, listed him as Karl William Naundorff, watch-maker, born in Weimar, but the civil authorities of Weimar said no family of that name had ever lived there.   He has been variously described as a Prussian adventurer, a Polish Jew, a Prince of the Holy Roman Empire, a great-grandson of an Albanian king, the agent of a secret society, an émigré nobleman, a valet of Louis XVI and a page to Marie Antoinette.

Naundorff himself claimed that he was the legitimate king, Louis XVII, and there are those today who still believe that he was. The one verifiable fact is that he was indeed a watchmaker, and earned his living as such from time to time. He was adept at mechanical invention, and when he died in Holland he was working on a gun which had the approval of the Netherlands Government. Eric Rede Buckley, author of Monsieur Charles (published in London in 1927) stated that at that time it had recently been discovered that Naundorff's real name was Karl Benjamin Werg, and that he was born at Halle-on-Saale in May 1777.

Naundorff's best evidence was his likeness to the Bourbon family. There is a theory that he was the illegitimate son of the Comte d'Artois (afterwards Charles X) and Mme Simon, who with her husband Antoine were the guardians of the little Prince in the temple. This would have accounted for Naundorff's Bourbon characteristics and familiarity with the layout of the Temple prison. Simon was dismissed in January 1794 and went to the guillotine for some unspecified crime. Mme Simon was put into a home for incurables (for which read insane asylum) in May 1796 and remained there until her death in 1819. Those who saw her there said she was perfectly lucid and talked a lot about "her children" by which it was assumed she meant the two little "royals" in the Temple, for there is no evidence that she had children of her own.

Naundorff's book entitled *The Misfortunes of the Dauphin, son of Louis XVI*, published in France in November 1836, and in an English translation in London in 1838, contains a one hundred and twelve page long semi-fictional memoire, signed *Charles Louis, Duc de Normandie*. It details his life up until his arrival in Paris and includes a description of his escape from the Temple and his subsequent wanderings around Europe. A large part of it is devoted to tirades against the enemies whom he says have persecuted him and denied him his identity, his inheritance, and his civil rights. The alleged villains of course are Louis XVIII and Charles X, the usurpers of the French throne. The remaining five hundred and seventy-seven pages of the book list more than 400 letters, articles and statements swearing that Naundorff is the surviving legitimate heir to the throne, but as these are all written by himself, his legal advisers, friends and supporters, they contain not one shred of real evidence.

Naundorff could never produce a birth certificate nor the proof required to obtain residence in Prussia and Germany, and although he repeatedly stated that he held identity papers, including letters written under the royal seal by Louis XVI and Marie Antoinette which had been smuggled out of the Temple sewn into his coat collar, he never showed them. When pressed, he said all his papers had been taken by the secret police, stolen or confiscated, or alternatively that he would only show them at the right time.

His account of the rescue from the Temple follows the usual story of substitution. He states that a dummy in his likeness was smuggled into the Temple in a washing basket, and placed in his bed. He was then drugged, placed in the same basket, and taken up to a disused attic in the Temple, where he lived in concealment among the discarded furniture for some months. When his gaolers found their prisoner gone, they brought in a deaf and dumb child to take his place, and gave him poison. In order to have a death-bed witness they called in a certain Dr. Desault, but Desault had seen the Prince before, and stated roundly that this was not him. He administered an antidote and the boy recovered. Desault and his apothecary were said to have died mysteriously a few days later. A second substitution then took place, and a terminally ill child was brought in who conveniently died on 8 June 1795. The body was removed, and Naundorff - or as he says the Prince - was again drugged and placed in the coffin, from which he was released on the way to the cemetery. He claims he remembers nothing about this until he woke up and found he was free.

He was then taken to La Vendée and put in charge of a Swiss woman who taught him German, so that he could pass as her son. They were caught and imprisoned, but rescued through the good offices of the widow Josephine Beauharnais, who later married Napoleon I, and had royalist sympathies. The story then becomes very vague. Naundorff says he spent most of the time in prison for vagrancy since he could not obtain a residence permit, and falsely accused of fraud, theft, attempted murder, misrepresentation and arson, all of which charges he strongly refuted. He finally arrived in Berlin where he tried to join the Army, but was refused as a foreigner. Lecoque, the Chief of Police, said it was too dangerous for Naundorff to remain there, and in 1812 he moved to Spandau where on Lecoque's recommendation he was allowed to stay.

He was at this time living with a widow, Mme Sonnenfeld, and when she died in 1818 he married Johanna Einert, the beautiful fifteen year old daughter of a manufacturer of Havelberg. She was devoted to him, gave him nine children, and had a comfortable retirement in Holland universally venerated as "The Old Countess".

The Bourbons returned to France in 1814, and from 1816 onwards Naundorff continually wrote to them demanding recognition and a share of his reputed sister, the Duchesse d'Angoulème's inheritance. This included Marie Antoinette's diamonds, 1,300,000 livres and her dowry of 200,000 gold thalers. His representations received no acknowledgement, although Naundorff claimed he had in his possession an autograph letter from the Duc de Berri promising his help. If it existed, the letter was never found. It seems an unlikely claim since the Duc de Berri was the heir apparent, his brother the Duc d'Angoulème (the Dauphin) being childless. The Duc de Berri was assassinated on 13 February 1820, which Naundorff attributed to this alleged support.

The July revolution in 1830 deposed the legitimate Bourbons, and drove Charles X and his family, which included the Duc and Duchesse d'Angoulème, into exile. This did not stop Naundorff from continuing his campaign. He said as he was married to a commoner he was willing to recognise the Comte de Chambord, the Duc de Berri's posthumous son, as his heir. He repeatedly requested the Duchesse d'Angoulème to grant him a personal interview, even sending a legal representative, Morel de Saint Didier, to Prague in 1834 to try to see her. The Duchesse maintained that she was certain her brother was dead and "...the man is nothing but an impostor, though he may be a very clever one". She affirmed throughout that she saw no reason to change this opinion.

Naundorff arrived in Paris in 1833 and set about finding any witnesses still alive who could be induced to recognise him. These included M. Joly, Louis XVI's last Minister of Justice, Mme de Rambaud who had been the Dauphin's governess from birth until

1792, and M. and Mme Marco de St. Hilaire, respectively Louis XVI's chamberlain and lady-in-waiting to the King's Aunt Adelaide. All three declared their belief that Naundorff was indeed Charles Louis, son of Louis XVI. Mme Rambaud said she recognised the marks on his body, a mole on his thigh, prominent front teeth, and the scar on his upper lip where he was bitten by a rabbit. None of these people would have seen him for getting on for forty years, and were all over seventy, so that it was easy to doubt their evidence.

One can only sympathise with Naundorff's frustration. His letters to the French royal family and various crowned Heads of State in Europe went unanswered, or were returned unopened. He was not treated with the malice he averred but rather with contempt, his every effort to gain a hearing ignored. Finally on 13 June 1836 he lodged a civil action against Charles X, ex-King of France, and the Duc and Duchesse d'Angoulême, to appear before a civil court in the Department of the Seine to answer his claims. Two days later he was arrested and imprisoned without trial, and twenty three days later escorted by armed Police to Calais and deported from France. Four Barristers at Law - MM. Gruau, Bourbon-Leblanc, Xavier Laprade and Briquet - wrote to Louis Philippe (now King of the French) objecting to this illegal action, which was strictly against French civil rights. There was no reply.

Naundorff went to London and took up residence in Clarence Place. His application to King William IV of England for sanctuary and a request for an interview were politely refused by Lord Palmerston, the Prime Minister, but no further action was taken. In the meantime, the case against him for fraud and misrepresentation continued to be prosecuted in France.

While in London, Naundorff met the English pretender, Augustus Meves, who truly thought that he himself was the genuine son of Louis XVI and Marie Antoinette. Meves believed he had been rescued from the Temple and that the "real" Augustus had taken his place, and that the reason the child in the Temple did not answer his gaoler's questions was not because he was deaf and dumb, but because he could not understand French. Meves was convinced that the "real Augustus" was in turn rescued and taken to Eastern Europe, and that Naundorff was this child grown up, under an alias.

In August 1838 Naundorff's wife and children, who had been living in Switzerland, joined him. They moved to Minerva House at Camberwell Green, where later that year an attempt was made on Naundorff's life. On a foggy November night he had just emerged from the lavatory, which after the custom of the time was situated in the garden, when a man shot him at point-blank range. Two bullets lodged in his arm and narrowly missed killing him. Next day a Frenchman named Desiré Roussel, who had previously contacted Naundorff on the pretext of asking for help as a political refugee, was arrested. His footprints were found in the garden, but Naundorff said he was unable to identify him, and he went free.

This was not the first time Naundorff had been attacked. When in Paris he had been stabbed and seriously wounded by two unknown men who may have been assassins, but could have been ordinary muggers; and on two occasions his workshop at Camberwell had been blown up and caught fire. This could have been arson, or carelessness on his own part as he was experimenting with explosives.

In July 1839 the French Minister for Foreign Affairs issued a statement saying that the Prussian Government had published an official communication stating that Naundorff "belonged to a Jewish family which is settled in Prussian Poland". Naundorff countered by writing to the King of Prussia for verification. In reply he received a letter from the Prussian Minister of the Interior, dated Berlin 27 August 1848, stating that he could not make such a declaration as he had no knowledge of any circumstances by which such an origin could have been established.

Naundorff considered this vindicated him, and as a French newspaper, *Le Capitole*, had published an offensive account of the allegation, Naundorff promptly sued them for libel. The case was quashed on the grounds that Naundorff had entered his plea under a false name, and by this time the newspaper had folded. Naundorff's advocate, Jules Favre, wrote to him saying that he had succeeded in getting an official ruling that it was no presumption to call oneself the son of Louis XVI, which rendered void the suit against Naundorff for misrepresentation, but added ."..the King of France and other sovereigns of Europe are deliberately deaf...neither the King nor his Ministers will allow you to return to France".

In 1841 Naundorff's affairs took a turn for the worse. He was arrested for debt and imprisoned at Horsemonger Lane. He owed some £5000. At last he was beaten. He wrote to his daughter Amélie "...your father never meant any harm, but his hard fate sometimes drove him crazy..." He had lost a great deal of support among his faithful followers, most of whom as Royalists were also Catholic. Naundorff never had any formal religious education, and in 1839 he wrote a book entitled *Partie Préliminaire de la Doctrine Celeste* and had it privately printed in Geneva. It was a foolish, ill-considered and untimely action. The book was regarded as heretical by orthodox Catholics, placed on the Index by the Holy See, and Naundorff condemned as a blasphemer. The Church offered aid if he would recant, but he refused.

In 1841 he was again in prison for debt, and his household goods were sold by auction. These included some magnificent portraits of the House of Bourbon, Amélie's harp, a piano, 1500 tools, a state bed in Spanish mahogany, and a bomb. The house at Camberwell was let, and the family moved to Holland, where Naundorff continued his pyrotechnic experiments, but his health had broken down, and he died on 10 August 1845. He was buried at Delft as Louis XVII, Charles Louis Duc de Normandie, King of France and Navarre, and the Dutch authorities refused to change the inscription on his tombstone in spite of all Louis Philippe's protests.

His eldest son Charles Edouard, continued with the ballistic experiments and received 20,000 gulden in payment. He died in 1886, and Naundorff's second son Louis Charles - daughters being ignored under the Salic law - was styled Charles XI. Both were childless. The third son was Edmond, whose eldest son, Auguste Jean, was born in 1872, and was accepted by some Legitimists as Jean III, but he had no interest in claiming the throne. He was married to a French woman and lived quietly in Paris, and he and his two brothers petitioned the French government to be reinstated as French citizens. Naundorff's youngest surviving son, Adalbert, had taken Dutch citizenship, and his son Henri was a high ranking officer in the Dutch army. Henri promptly issued a proclamation disassociating the Bourbon family from Auguste Jean's action, since he considered the French Government to be the successors of the regime that murdered their ancestor, Louis XVI. *Le Matin* rejoiced in the quarrel and published scurrilous accounts of "Bourbon v. Bourbon", scoffing at the dispute and saying it was all nonsense as they were only Pretenders anyway.

The last shot in the identity battle was fired in 1913 when Louis de Bourbon, Henri's son, won an action for libel against Henri Rochefort, a newspaper tycoon, who in one of his publications disputed the Naundorff family's right to use the name of Bourbon. The Naundorffs had received official sanction in Holland to use the name of Bourbon, and the Court upheld that the Dutch ruling was valid in France. The defendant was fined 500 Fr. Francs. Since then no-one has disputed the right of Naundorff's descendants to use the name.

Eleazer Williams - The Missionary Monarch

Among the Pretenders to be Louis XVII perhaps the most fantastic is Eleazer Williams, also known as Onwarenhiiaki, the Indian Iroquois Chief.

The story starts, as all Pretenders' claims do, with the account of how the little son of Louis XVI and Marie Antoinette was imprisoned in the Temple Tower, and was reported as having died there in May 1795. Even at that time rumour was rife that the body that was buried in an unmarked grave in St. Marguerite cemetery was not that of the Prince, but a substitution - a deaf mute boy, or a child terminally ill with rickets. It is perhaps circumstantial that Louis XVI's first son died of a congenital bone disease.

In this particular case no details are given of the escape. It is merely said that the boy - automatically created Louis XVII on the execution of his father - was abducted and taken to America. The Comte de Provence, Louis XVI's brother, had declared himself Regent on behalf of the boy king, and was said to have had aspirations to the throne before that, in anticipation that the unpopular King Louis XVI would abdicate. The Comte de Provence, and the third brother, the Comte D'Artois (later Charles X) had emigrated at the first signs of trouble in France, and continued to regard themselves as the senior representatives of the monarchy in exile.

It was surmised that the Comte de Provence and the right-wing elements of the Revolutionary Government had conspired together to get rid of a mutual encumbrance, which on the face of it seems an unlikely alliance. Whether or not the Comte de Provence was implicated in the removal of the child from the Temple, it was certainly to his advantage that the boy should disappear, without obviously being murdered.

Eleazer Williams in later life received a letter from a Mr Kemball of Barton Rouge, in which it was stated that a French gentleman named Bellanger who had died in New Orléans said "he was the person who aided the escape of the Dauphin from the Temple in 1795, his transportation to North America, and his adoption by the Indians, so that he could be hidden from his enemies". Like the other claimants, Eleazer was said to have birthmarks, scars and a distinctive vaccination mark that corresponded with those borne by the Dauphin, though it is significant that in most cases the marks displayed by the various claimants, each supposedly identical to the Dauphin's, did not correspond to each other's.

In 1795 a family arrived in New York from France. They gave their name as de Jardin. Mme de Jardin was aristocratic and claimed to have been a lady-in-waiting to Marie Antoinette. The man was older and rougher, and the two children - a boy named Louis and a girl named Louise - were obviously not their own children. The boy suffered from ill-health and appeared to be simple minded, and both children were kept out of sight. The family had in their possession a number of valuable articles including a golden bowl stamped with the French royal crest which they sold to support themselves. They then left New York, and dropped out of sight, except possibly the boy.

Later the same year two Frenchmen, one having the appearance of a Roman priest, arrived at Lake George (Ticonderoga) bringing with them a sickly, apparently mentally deficient child about ten years of age, who was adopted by Thomas Williams and named Lazu or Eleazer. Thomas was pro-British, would disappear for long periods without any explanation, and probably acted as an undercover agent for the British government. It was during one of these journeys that the child was handed over to his care. He apparently received money from France, supposedly to support the boy, but perhaps for other more secret services.

Thomas' great-grandfather, the Reverend John Williams, was living in Deerfield when in 1704 it was sacked by Indians. His wife and two of his children were killed, but he and the other two were taken prisoner and removed to Montreal. Eunice, his daughter, married an Indian named Turoges, learned their language and adopted their customs. They had three children, one of whom, Mary, married an English physician named Williams - no relation - and they became the parents of Thomas who adopted the little French imbecile. Thomas, or Tehorakwaneken, had close Indian ties, and married an Indian girl named Mary Ann Konwatewenteta in January 1799. They had eight children, all baptised as Catholics, and all with distinct Indian colouring and features.

Little Eleazer improved in health, but his mind remained clouded, until one day when out hunting with his foster-father he fell from a rock and severely cut his head. After that, he regained all his mental faculties except his memory. He could remember nothing before that time. At the age of fifteen he was sent to the Reverend Nathaniel Ely to be educated. Ely knew Eleazer was French, and had in his possession two boxes that had been left with him at the time of the adoption - perhaps he was the "Roman seeming priest" who had been instrumental in arranging it. It was said that one of the boxes contained three medals, of gold, silver and bronze, struck at the time of Louis XVI's coronation. The bronze one remained in the possession of the Catholic Bishop of Montreal, the gold and silver medals disappeared.

In 1812 Eleazer was acting as Agent of the American Board of Missions at Sault St Louis, where he was made a Chief of the Iroquois Tribe under the name of Onwarenhiiaki or Tree Cutter. He decided to devote his life to the Indians as a missionary, and in the 1811-1813 war he was recruited by the US Government as a liaison officer, for which he was paid £2000, money he spent on building schools and supporting the Indian Mission.

In 1815 he approached Bishop Dr Hobart of New York about ordination, and was appointed as a lay reader, catechist and schoolmaster to the Indians, finally being made Deacon in 1826. In 1818 he acted as mediator when the New York Indians were forcibly moved to Green Bay, Wisconsin. Eleazer went with them, and in 1823 he married Madeleine Jordan, a beautiful Creole girl with a half-Indian mother, who possessed considerable land holdings in the area.

It was in 1818, when Mr Richards of the Montreal Catholic Seminary told Eleazer that he was a foreigner of noble birth, that he first had doubts about his identity. In spite of looking quite different from the other members of the family, Eleazer presumably had up to that time had no doubts about his being the true child of Thomas Williams. On checking the parish register at Sault St Louis, he found there was no record of his birth, although all

Thomas Williams's other children were listed. Whatever his origin, Eleazer obviously was an adopted child.

Apparently, however, he took no further steps until 1841, when the Prince de Joinville, son of Louis Philippe the constitutional King of the French, allegedly arrived in America and sought out Reverend Williams and informed him that Eleazer was the legitimate King of France. He brought with him a declaration of abdication, and asked "Charles Louis, son of Louis XVI" to resign the crown in favour of Louis Philippe who would "pledge himself to secure the restoration or an equivalent of all the private property of the royal family rightly belonging to him" and offered him "a princely establishment to be secured to him either in America or France".

In fact, Louis Philippe was not in a position to give away the private property of the royal family. Louis XVI's daughter, Marie Thérèse Charlotte, had been granted the right to inherit her parents' private property on her release from the Temple in 1795 as part of an exchange of prisoners with Austria. She went straight to Vienna where she was royally treated, and a marriage arranged for her with Archduke Charles. The Comte de Provence, however, had other ideas. She was the Princesse Royale, the legitimate Dauphine, and although she could not herself inherit the crown, her husband would have had a good claim in the event of a Bourbon restoration. The Regent had no wish to open such an opportunity to Austria. He arranged instead for his niece to marry the Duc d'Angoulème, the eldest son of the Comte d'Artois, the heir apparent. Marie Thérèse refused all her life to recognise any of the Pretenders' claims to be her brother, since to do so would have been both politically and personally inexpedient.

Eleazer thought about it, and then refused to sign. He said he had considered the matter fully, but could not barter away the rights pertaining to him by birth. He wished only to retain his name, considering that his upbringing, religious convictions and training were unequal to the demands of being King.

It was an empty victory. The Prince de Joinville returned to France, Louis Philippe continued to reign as King of the French until his abdication in 1850, and Eleazer dropped back into obscurity. He himself came to believe in his royal birth, but he never sought greatness for himself. He wanted money only to further the work of his Indian Mission. He loved his Indian flock and desired their advancement, although he was constantly repudiated and persecuted by those he was trying to help.

There was no proof that he was Louis XVII although he looked very like the Bourbons, and there was some circumstantial evidence. He never remembered anything about his childhood, though when he recovered his mental abilities he could speak some French. Many aristocrats who fled the Revolution found refuge abroad, some in America, and Eleazer could have been the son of a French noble family, if not the royal one. Many of the valuables of the aristocracy were looted and sold, and the bronze medal could easily have found its way to the States - there is no evidence that the gold and silver medals existed. In later life Eleazer was haunted by strange dreams, which may have been a symptom of mental instability.

In his book *The Lost Dauphin* published by George Allen in London in 1887, which was not very long after the events may - or may not - have taken place, the author A. de Grasse Stevens cites a number of statements and letters from contemporaries of Eleazer's who believed in the validity of his claims. The case must, inevitably, rest there.

Chapter Six

"To what end are all these words?"

The Taming of the Shrew:1.2

CONCLUSION
How it was - the evidence

Once it has been admitted that Prieuré Two was a political organisation, and that Saunière and his gaggle of priests were political activists, much that was hitherto unexplained becomes clear.

The domaine was built for a reason. Saunière said Bethania was intended as a home for aged priests, but no aged priest ever set foot across the threshold. It was a comfortable, moderate sized villa, suitable for providing accommodation for visiting VIP's, and sufficiently remote for them to visit unobtrusively. The whole domaine was cut off from the village, and no unauthorised foot could profane its precincts. The Tour Magdala was a strong room which Saunière said was to house his papers and his library - if they were confidential political documents he needed that sort of security. The ramparts ensured that strangers could be monitored since they could enter the village only by the main street, and travellers could be seen miles away from the walkways.

The local tradesmen's bills show that Bethania was supplied with quantities of good food and drink for the guests to enjoy. Among the aristocratic and prestigious visitors were Emma Calvé, the famous diva who had connections with the Royalist occult societies of Paris, and was passionately patriotic; and Dr Gérard Encausse, Papus, who had been appointed Bishop of Jules Doinel's neo-Cathar church at Mirepoix.

Encausse was life Grand Master of the Martinists, whose avowed policy was the establishment of a new state based on theocracy, and whose political influence stretched across Europe to Russia where he was an acknowledged friend of the Tsar and Tsarina. It is possible that Saunière was himself an initiated Martinist, and he is listed as attending a meeting at the Lyon Lodge on ll May 1900.

Calvé had connections with the Martinists. On 11 November 1892 her signature is included among the guests at Le Chat Noir Cabaret, Paris, over the words "St. Superieur Inconnu, third degree Martinist". Stanislas de Guaita, Magus of the Cabalistic Order of the Rosy Cross, and the eminent astronomer Camille Flammarion, are also listed among those present. On another occasion, after dining at the Flammarion house, Emma noted in her diary: "Conversation very interesting about astronomy, hypnotism, spiritualism and telepathy..." She also organised her own séances at her house on the Course-la-Reine, where as well as the Flammarions and Mme de Thebes, the company included the famous spy Mata Hari, who performed the dance of the seven veils.

The quasi-Rosicrucian societies of the French occult revival were inevitably Catholic and Royalist. It is not inconceivable, therefore, that a Royalist cell had been set up centred on Rennes-le-Château: perhaps part of the larger National lobby for the Restoration, perhaps working alone in Southern France, which had always been a place of refuge and rebellion.

In spite of the disappointing results in the 1885 elections, which the Right did not win, the fact remains that they had doubled their number of seats, and the shocked Republicans were forced into a coalition with minority parties in order to maintain their majority rule. There was still hope for the Royalists.

Money came in from loyal supporters and was administered by Henri Boudet, who paid it out to the local activists. He gave Marie the money for the domaine, and the land was registered in her name, although she always said it was not her property. Marie also covered for Saunière when he was away, dealing with his letters and sending out replies which would conceal his absence.

Much of his correspondence came from abroad, and that fits in with the theory that the conspirators, exiles perhaps themselves, or secret agents working at foreign courts, reported by post. Saunière's unexplained movements around the country - on local excursions which he said were to gather rocks suitable for his landscape gardening, or on unauthorised visits to places like Lyon or Toulouse - can be attributed to meetings with members of Prieuré Two. It is probable that he visited Paris, and Marie Denarnaud confirmed that he did, perhaps to contact Royalist supporters for whom the occult societies provided secure cover.

Fr Boudet's account books show specifically that the money Saunière used to refurbish St Mary Magdalene was provided by him and paid through Marie. Boudet apparently had no money of his own, his family origins were humble, but he had access to a gold-seam the origin of which remains obscure. Perhaps the original contact was through Fr Cayron, who had been responsible for young Boudet's education, and acted as his sponsor as priest in charge of the parish of Rennes-les-Bain. Fr Cayron had access to money, and had spent a great deal on refurbishing his church; and then, like Saunière, he refused to move.

Boudet gave large donations to the Diocese of Carcassonne, and had himself paid the very considerable costs of publishing his book *La Vraie Langue Celtique*. In his Preface to a reprint, Pierre Plantard says that Henri Boudet was the main protagonist in the mysterious activities that were centred around Rennes-le-Château. His grandfather Charles Plantard had been invited to visit Boudet at the Rennes-les-Bain presbytery, and remarked on the fact that Boudet lived very quietly, but could afford to buy expensive photographic equipment, and although his meals were austere they were eaten with good silver tableware from porcelain dishes.

Boudet also spent a great deal of money on decorating his church, though in a somewhat more restrained fashion than the style that appealed to Saunière. Like Saunière, and perhaps other priests in the diocese of Carcassonne, which had such a sympathetic bishop in Mgr Billard, Fr Boudet apparently received recompense for his part in organising the Prieuré Two activities. He was the brains, while Saunière was the hands and legs of the local activists.

Marie appears to have been the "cut out" between Boudet and Saunière, and indeed the whole Denarnaud family, who moved into the Presbytery and remained there throughout Saunière's lifetime, acted as "smoke". Saunière told the Court of Enquiry that was investigating his finances that the money earned by the Denarnaud family went into the communal purse, but the amounts credited in his accounts as being earned by Denarnaud père and fils are nearly 29,000 Fr. more than they could possibly have earned at the Espéraza hat factory where they were employed. Saunière also put in fictitious amounts of salaries paid to Mme Denarnaud and Marie. This was obvious laundering of money which he had no intention of explaining.

According to the accounts that Saunière did provide, there were large donations from local nobility, and considerable sums were paid through Alfred, Saunière's brother, who worked for one wealthy aristocrat and was reputedly the lover of another. The first donation of 3000 Fr. came from the Comtesse de Chambord, and who had a greater interest than her in the Restoration of the Bourbons? Her agent was her nephew, Archduke Johann Salvator, who had been politically active in the Balkans, and had been forced by the Austrian Emperor to resign his Army commission, give up his title and revenues, and go into exile. He would have been very happy to become involved in any plans that might embarrass Franz Joseph, who disliked the "Latinised Hapsburgs", and had always treated Archduke Johann abominably.

Calvé, who was certainly a friend of Saunière's and perhaps something warmer, was also a possible source of funds - she earned thousands and was notoriously generous. Wherever it came from, Saunière used the money he received to build and supply the domaine for some purpose other than his own enjoyment, and what better reason than for the convenience of Prieuré Two who required availability, comfort and discretion, and were prepared to pay for privacy and service.

With Boudet's death in 1915 the money ceased, and Saunière's accounts show that there were bills outstanding which he could not meet, or had to settle by instalments. Perhaps owing to the war Boudet's paymasters had not been able to reorganise the gold-seam, or it may have been that Saunière himself, with his health breaking down, and desperately involved in litigation, had become a political embarrassment and was quietly being dropped. The war would in any case have effectively put an end to any internal political intrigues. France was fighting for her life, and had no time to consider minor problems like the rights of outdated dynasties. Empires crashed throughout Europe, and the question of the Bourbon restoration was buried in the debris. Prieuré Two would have been one of the first casualties.

The question inevitably arises as to why Saunière should have involved himself in dangerous political activity. Certainly he was Royalist by upbringing and conviction. He presumably enjoyed intrigue. There were fringe benefits. But there had to be a stronger incentive. He was playing a dangerous game, and the stakes were high. The horrific murder of Fr Gélis at Coustassa is explicable if the intruder was searching for politically sensitive documents. The old man perhaps had been indiscreet, and it was expedient that he should be silenced, although unwillingly - hence his being so solemnly composed in death, and the fact that nothing obvious was missing from the Presbytery although there was evidence of search. Alternatively, the very nature of the bizarre murder may have been a warning to others to keep their mouths shut. The murderer was never brought to justice, understandable if it was a political execution.

The reason for Saunière's involvement is simple: he was ambitious. Henri Boudet's village of Rennes-les-Bain was thriving, doing a good trade in visitors and patients coming to drink or bathe in the medicinal waters. Saunière had a vision that linked

Rennes-le-Château as a place of spiritual refreshment to Rennes-les-Bain's health-giving popularity. He envied Puivert, with its miraculous virgin and renewed pilgrimages; he adored Lourdes and made several visits there. At considerable personal expense and effort he had created an outdoor sanctuary dedicated to Our Lady of Lourdes, with her statue perched on the pseudo-Visigothic pillar that played such a large part in the de Sède/Lincoln story. He spent a great deal of money on refurbishing St Mary Magdalene, lavishly painting and decorating it, providing it with statues of all the main saints and many of the minor ones. The cemetery was cleared, and a chapel created over the ossuary. The Presbytery was restored and made comfortable for his adopted family. The cost was high, although the local craftsmen were induced to donate some of the decorations.

The church restoration fund was presumably separate from the money that was later given to him for the domaine and its upkeep. The inference is that it was a bribe given to Saunière in advance for services to be provided, and it was an offer he could not refuse. He did not want it for himself, he wanted it to make his church beautiful and attractive to visitors. He wanted a mission and pilgrimage centre, with himself as the presiding genius. He lacked only one thing - a miracle. No visiting saint or apparition of the Virgin came to oblige him. If he had found an object of religious significance such as the Holy Grail, as suggested by the early Rennes-le-Château writers, he would not have hidden or sold it however suspect its provenance. He would have shouted it from the housetops. It would have provided just the extra inducement he needed to make Rennes-le-Château famous.

He never gave up, and plans for the future included a baptismal pool and a ziggurat from which he could conduct outdoor services and preach. Fortunately the money was never available to implement these extravagant plans, the war interrupted them, and he died before they came to term. The church remained, as it still does, a bright and somewhat garish example of 19th century French bourgeois taste for Catholic "bondieuserie", and nothing else.

It is perhaps ironic that Saunière's own story and the mysterious origin of his wealth has created a huge tourist industry, far in excess of his anticipated pilgrimages. Books, films and the media have created world-wide interest in his village and his church, so that in a way he is now the source of a different kind of miracle, which has made him and his village more famous than he could ever have envisaged or hoped.

ʜᴏᴡ ɪᴛ ᴡᴀꜱ – ᴛʜᴇ ᴍyᴛʜ

It is obvious that Saunière's wealth had no legendary origin, but was provided by misguided enthusiasts who were supporting what was doomed to be a lost cause.

The story of the coded documents that Saunière supposedly found in his church has been discredited by subsequent revelations. Plantard admitted that the copies of the documents which he gave to Lincoln were written by Philippe de Chérisey, although he said they were based on genuine originals. No originals have ever been seen. Pierre Jarnac, an indefatigable researcher into the Rennes-le-Château mystery, said that the documents were definitely the work of de Chérisey; and Jean-Luc Chaumeil, an original member of the Plantard cabal until they fell out over money, said that he had copies of the documents and the "key" to the code, written in de Chérisey's own hand and signed as authentic.

Some authors, notably Schellenberger and Andrews, who use the coded documents as a basis for sacred geometry, are convinced that if the documents are modern, then they were written by initiates who know the real secret of Rennes-le-Château, but this is whistling in the dark. No proof has ever been found of the various solutions which sacred geometry has reputedly revealed.

If the documents are forgeries, then it follows that the tombstones are similarly modern inventions, and were created by de Chérisey specifically to provide the key to the code. There is no evidence of their existence apart from the sketches in the Dossier Secret lodged by Plantard and de Chérisey in the Bibliothèque Nationale in Paris. The copy of the "Et in Arcadia" stone which is said to have been published in a rare booklet entitled *Engraved Stones of Languedoc*, is signed by Eugene Stublein but the signature is different from that verified as Stublein's own; and the *Bulletin de la Société des Études Scientifiques de l'Aude*, which supposedly contains a copy of the epitaph stone, is unobtainable.

The Coume Sourde stone, first mentioned by de Sède, exists only as a sketch in the Dossier Secret. It is not involved in any way with the code, its provenance is vague, and the Latin inscription is illiterate and untranslatable. There appears to be no reason for its invention other than to provide artistic misinformation.

If Saunière found valuables buried in his church, then it was by chance during the building work, and not as a result of secret information. It would have been a relatively small treasure. There may have been family documents, perhaps belonging to the Hautpouls who were the patrons of St Mary Magdalene, and it could have been these that Saunière left to his niece, Mme James of Montazels, and which she was said to have sold to the International League of Antiquarian Booksellers in 1965, although there is no evidence the she ever did so. There may have been some money, Saunière sold gold coins of not very ancient date at Perpignan; and he is said to have given pieces of jewellery to some of his parishioners. He could well have discovered the church plate which disappeared at the time of the Revolution, witness the gold chalice he gave in 1886 to Fr Graussaud, the priest at Amélia-les-Bain.

Saunière dealt in antiques given to him by grateful patrons, and also sold stamps to collectors. He photographed views and sold them as postcards to visitors, who may have been generous with donations in the church alms-boxes. He also wrote articles for local publications for which he received small payments. Catholic parishioners were expected to contribute to the upkeep of their church, but when it is remembered that the priest's stipend was 75 Fr. F. a month, and that on the whole the village consisted of poorly paid and generally illiterate agricultural workers, it is understandable that Saunière had to raise money to keep both himself and the parish solvent. These contributions, to which he admitted in his accounts, would in no way have covered the costs of the building and upkeep of the domaine, apart from the refurbishment and decoration of St Mary Magdalene.

The very large amounts which he received, and which he refused to account for, were obviously over and above the money which he laboriously earned for himself and his church. After the Boudet gold-seam failed, Saunière owed money on unpaid bills, and the good living ceased. When he died he apparently owned nothing at all. The domaine was in the name of Marie Denarnaud, although she did not regard it as her own property.

It was the First World War that ended the dream. France was now incontrovertibly a Republic. There was no hope of a Restoration. Empires throughout Europe had fallen, swept away in the bloody massacres of Flanders and Picardy. After the war, with the revaluation of the franc, Marie burned the old notes that were useless, but the origin of which she would still not reveal. She was poor, a little strange, living alone on the sadly disintegrating domaine. In old age she sold Bethania, now falling to pieces, to the Corbu family on condition that she could continue to live there until her death.

Rennes-le-Château appears then to have sunk back into obscurity, until Plantard and de Chérisey resurrected the story of Saunière and his hypothetical treasure. They wrote a book about it but failed to find a publisher, so took it to Gérard de Sède who had published other semi-fictional historical works. When Henry Lincoln in turn discovered the story through de Sède, the "mystery of Rennes-le-Château" was launched. Nobody at that time could have foreseen its extraordinary success.

De Sède's book, *Le Trésor Maudit*, is concerned mainly with the Saunière story, and only hints at the secret organisation behind the mystery, which he suggests had Rosicrucian origins. De Sède referred Lincoln to the Dossier Secret, a collection of papers deposited at the Bibliothèque Nationale in Paris, which included a document entitled *Le Cércle d'Ulysse*, giving an outline of the plot, including the finding of the coded documents, Marie de Négri's tombstones, and brief references to the Prieuré de Sion and Plantard's ancestry. Henry Lincoln and his co-authors added their own research to a revised version of the story, and the Prieuré de Sion really came into being with Lincoln's three BBC TV Chronicle programmes, and his subsequent block-buster *The Holy Blood and the Holy Grail*, which brought it to public attention.

Plantard told Lincoln that he was a descendant of the ancient Merovingian Kings of France, "le roi perdu", and that the Prieuré de Sion was intricately associated with this claim. De Sède later stated categorically that the genealogy in the Dossier Secret, supposedly supporting Plantard's royal ancestry, was a fake. It had been falsified from a table published in a school history book, and Plantard came from humble peasant origins.

If Plantard was the figure-head, there is no doubt that de Chérisey was the brains of the plot. It was he who originally created the documents in 1956 for a television programme, invented the code, and wrote the pamphlets disseminating the required disinformation about the modern Prieuré de Sion. In *The Messianic Legacy*, Lincoln pays tribute to de Chérisey as "...the most convivial, the most imaginatively resourceful, the most original and perhaps the most brilliant individual we encountered in the course of our research...deserving more recognition than he received."

The Marquis Philippe de Chérisey died suddenly on 17 July 1985. One of his friends, recalling their long friendship dating from the time when de Chérisey was working as a successful actor in Belgium, says "his dramatic death appears to have followed the dictates of his life and career". His obituary in *Études Merovingiennes*, the house-magazine of Le Cércle Saint Dagobert II, refers to his presence at one of their recent meetings "which he enlivened with his wit and scholarship".

The funeral mass was held at the church of La Trinité, near where de Chérisey lived in the rue St Lazare, and the celebrant in his oration made reference to de Chérisey's good taste, versatility, and the sense of humour which did not spare himself. Above all, he spoke of de Chérisey's great kindness and compassionate understanding. The obituary ends "Those who disagreed with him render him their homage: those who loved him will keep him always in their hearts". The Cércle's sheaf of white flowers accompanied the coffin to the family tomb at Roeux (Pas-de-Calais).

It has been suggested that the Cércle, a contemporary organisation operating in France, is the front for the modern Prieuré de Sion, which disappeared from public view with Plantard's resignation as Grand Master on 10 July 1984. Its declared manifesto is to promote interest in the Merovingian dynasty, and to restore and maintain ancient Merovingian sites in France.

What had started as a public relations exercise had become a burden. By publicly disassociating himself from the Prieuré, Plantard could no longer be hassled by the media or public demanding information about its activities or beliefs. He could just say he was no longer privy to their councils, and that was the end of the matter. There were no further leaks of information or disinformation. Plantard went underground, and de Chérisey refused to answer letters or the telephone. Perhaps the Prieuré ceased to exist, although there is a rumour that Plantard's son and daughter are still active.

The question inevitably arises - did the Prieuré de Sion as such ever exist? It is obvious that it did not, in the sense that it was promulgated by the early Rennes-le-Château authors.

Occult societies commonly claim origins dating from antiquity. Ancient records are notoriously inaccurate, but history indicates that in 1099 there was an Order of Augustinian canons at the Abbey of Sion in Jerusalem who moved to France in 1152. There is no record of their ever being known as the Prieuré de Sion, or of being officially affiliated with the Templars, although seven ex-members were said to have joined the Templars after the Order left the Holy Land. The romantic story of the "cutting of the

elm" at Gisor as an explanation of the separation of the Prieuré
of Sion from the Templars is apocryphal. The last existing mention
of the Order was in 1244 when it donated land to the Teutonic
Knights, and there is no evidence that it survived beyond the 13th
century.

The Rennes-le-Château legend tells how the Prieuré went
underground, gathering a distinguished list of Grand Masters,
including famous occultists, painters, politicians and writers. It
supposedly had connections with important organisations
throughout Europe, and became a kind of *eminence gris* exerting
secret powers behind governments and thrones. The declared
policy of most occult societies is to improve mankind's spiritual
and temporal condition, and establish a better world for all to
live in. Their method of operation inevitably involves attempts to
gain political power.

Had the list of Grand Masters been in fact genuine, then
undoubtedly the organisation they ruled would have been a force
with which to reckon, but evidence indicates that the list was no
more than wishful thinking, part of Plantard and de Chérisey's
fiction. It could not be challenged, as all the people concerned
were dead. Even Jean Cocteau, the last alleged Grand Master,
had died in 1963 before the list was published in *The Holy Blood
and the Holy Grail* in 1982. No Grand Master is named between
1963 and 17 January 1981, the date on which Plantard claimed he
was - most conveniently - elected.

Whether or not the 20th century Prieuré de Sion actually existed
remains in doubt, but true or false it was a brilliant piece of romantic
propaganda. The myth of "the hidden king" has universal appeal.
An occult society, guardians of an ancient secret, dedicated to
protecting the survival of the last descendant of the magical
Merovingian priest-kings, and in possession of a fabulous treasure,
could not fail to capture the imagination. Like the original
Rosicrucians, it was veiled in mystery, unavailable to investigation,
but carefully leaked pieces of information kept interest alive.

Now that Plantard and de Chérisey, the prime creators of the story, are both dead, it is unlikely that the truth will ever be known. Undoubtedly Plantard had esoteric connections - he had been involved with Alpha Galates, an occult society in the 1930's, and copies of its magazine *Vaincre* exist to prove it. *Vaincre* was right wing and anti-Semitic. Like many other occult societies, Alpha Galates was a supporter of synarchic policy, which advocated an elitist government dedicated to the preservation of traditional values. Guy Patton, author of *The Web of Gold*, suggests that the role of Plantard's Prieuré was to act as a centre for other similarly politically oriented secret organisations, and that the common agenda was "most probably to bring about a Synarchic government for Europe in the style of the Old Holy Roman Empire" (*R.O.*30, March 2001). In one of the *Vaincre* articles, Plantard does advocate a "united federal state of Europe similar to the U.S.A.".

Plantard was obviously ambitious, but so far as is known, he moved only on the outer fringes of power, if at all. His claims to have been involved with the French Resistance during the Occupation, and his later involvement in helping to bring Charles de Gaulle into power, are questionable.

There is no doubt that Plantard was extremely knowledgeable about what the public wanted, just as de Chérisey was clever enough to bring his ideas to fruition. Both of them remained discreetly in the background, leaving journalists like Jean Pierre Deloux, Jacques Brétigny, and Jean-Luc Chaumeil to spread the word in the right places. Unfortunately, Plantard seems to have had a habit of falling out with his colleagues, and de Sède, de Chérisey and Chaumeil later reneged on what they had formerly rigorously supported. Plantard, in fact, behaved as if he really were royalty, and perhaps he genuinely believed he was. He would not be the first to have delusions of grandeur. The difficulty was that it was not true, and even if it were, who would care today?

It was a stroke of genius to tie the idea of the Prieuré de Sion to the mystery of Bérenger Saunière's mysterious wealth. It provided a good plot by offering a reason for Saunière's obstinate silence about the origin of the money, and by hinting at the discovery of a fabulous treasure, or a dangerous secret, and the existence of an ancient secret society as its guardian. Plantard's obsession with his royal blood fitted neatly into the pattern, and the authors of *The Holy Blood and the Holy Grail* introduced the idea of descent from Jesus, the true King of Israel, as an added controversial, even shocking element. It couldn't fail.

On evidence, both the ancient Abbey of Sion, and the Prieuré de Sion of the 1980's, have nothing to do with what actually was happening at the end of the nineteenth century in Languedoc. That there was a great deal of clandestine activity going on around Rennes-le-Château is obvious. That Saunière received, and spent, vast sums of money is fact. That he refused to say where it came from is also fact. The records exist in the annals of the diocese of Carcassonne, and are supported by copies of real invoices.

Taking into account the political affiliations of the local nobility, the indissoluble ties between the Catholic church and the throne, the instability of the government with its small and insecure majority, and the dedication of the Right to the idea of the Restoration as an antidote to socialism and anarchy, it is reasonable to assume that what was going on was an active movement to return the Bourbons to the throne of France.

In his *Voyage to Rennes-les-Bains* the eminent writer Labouisse-Rochefort sums up the reasons for the Royalists' unswerving devotion. "I am royalist, devoted to the legitimate heirs by duty and conviction" he says, "...because I think that a Nation like ours cannot find peace, content, confidence, happiness, and security except under the legitimate and paternal monarchy. Destroy the monarchy and all the ties are broken, all minds overthrown, order disappears and ills are multiplied...one is not free because one is said to be free. The foundation stone of the column of liberty is virtue...but where to find this wisdom and wholesome liberty if not under the paternal and legitimate monarchy?"

The Legitimists had suffered a cruel blow with the death of the Comte de Chambord, but for the 1885 elections they had agreed to join with the Orléanists to promote the candidature of the Comte de Paris. The death of Napoleon III's only son, prompted the Bonapartists to join them. The political climate was reasonably encouraging, with the Right in the ascendant. There was money available, a widespread system of communication already existed through the clergy, and there was support from many Royalist-oriented occult societies.

Rennes-le-Château was suitably situated in a secure area, and it had an energetic priest in charge who was not only Royalist by upbringing and conviction, but had his own ambitions and plans which required financing. His parents and brother were involved with the local aristocracy. In the neighbouring village of Rennes-les-Bain was Fr Boudet, who had royalist, and wealthy, connections. The local Bishop was friendly, and not above a little quiet bribery. There was a Martinist lodge at Lyon, and Papus, the Grand Master, was associated with the neo-Cathar church of Carcassonne. Emma Calvé, famous, rich and Royalist, had a grand château at nearby Millau in the Ardenne available for discreet gatherings, and she was involved with the Royalist neo-Rosicrucian societies in Paris. The network almost created itself. It started with a gift of 3000 Fr .F from the Comtesse de Chambord towards the St Mary Magdalene Restoration Fund, and finished with a vast concourse of idealists pursuing an impossible dream amidst the luxury of a charming estate.

The assassin's shot that killed the Austrian Archduke Francis Ferdinand on 28 June 1914, and instigated the First World War, brought the Royalists' dream crashing to the ground. Gone too were Saunière's plans for St Mary Magdalene as a centre of pilgrimage comparable with Puivert or even Lourdes. Boudet was ill with cancer, and had retired to his brother's house at Axat, where he died on 30 March 1915. The gold-seam was closed.

There was no more money, and Saunière was being hounded by the new Bishop, suspended from office and threatened with excommunication. He was still only sixty-two, but his health was ruined, and the debts piled up. True to his principles and his profession, he continued to say his masses at the private altar in the garden of Villa Bethania, and the local congregation still came to him, in preference to Abbé Marty who had replaced him in 1909, whom they did not know, did not like, and did not want.

Jacques Rivière in *The Fabulous Treasure of Rennes-le-Château* does his best to give Saunière every possible benefit of the doubt. He says that he was a good priest, industrious and intelligent, whose one desire was to serve his parish and his church. He was painstaking in teaching the children, assiduous in organising processions around the village, charitable to the poor, and always had a gold piece for the young sons of the neighbourhood leaving for military service. But first and foremost he was a dreamer, the type of man who would immediately rush into action, and stop at nothing to achieve his aims.

Rivière does not believe in the treasure story, or indeed in any other untoward behaviour or mysterious activities on Saunière's part. According to his conclusions Saunière was a good man overcome by ambition, who after raising the money to restore St Mary Magdalene, got carried away and stole from the church funds to satisfy his own aggrandisement. He does not, however, suggest where the funds came from for Saunière to steal, preferring to accept the priest's assertion that they were the proceeds from his business ventures and the alms boxes, an explanation which is demonstrably untenable. Nor does it account for Saunière's obstinate refusal to discuss the origin of the money.

"If the Bishop had not questioned his accounts", Rivière says, "no-one would ever have heard of Saunière and his domaine...everything collapsed at a single blow and suddenly he realised he had gone too far." In his final valediction, Rivière adds "Being a priest, Saunière was no less a man, with a man's strength and weaknesses. One can criticise him or blame him for the way he behaved, reproach him for favouring Mlle Denarnaud at the expense of the Church, and for other things too, but one cannot be indifferent to the personality of such a man who, the priest of a remote village in Corbière, wanted above all to raise his parish from anonymity".

This Saunière achieved by default. For more than twenty years, since Henry Lincoln and his co-authors brought it before the public, the remote little village of Rennes-le-Château has held a central role in literature and the media. As each separate solution is put forward, another arises to discredit it. Where is truth? Somewhere under the rags of allusion, illusion and delusion, the bare facts exist.

François Bérenger Saunière, born at Montazels on 11 April 1852 died at Rennes-le-Château on 22 January 1917. His obituary denied him the courtesy-title of "priest", but throughout his turbulent life, Saunière never abandoned his vocation.

What was he? Treasure-hunter, political agitator, trickster, secret agent, opportunist, thief? A passionate loyalist of unshakeable conviction, or just a misguided, overly ambitious dreamer?

'He was a man, take him for all in all, I shall not look upon his like again'

Hamlet:II.1 - William Shakespeare

Perhaps the last word should rest with Saunière himself...

J'ai traversé la vie comble de tant de dons,
Rachete toute erreur, obtenu mon pardon.
Discouvrante le Royaume, françissant la barrière,
Mon Esprit a, de dieu, penêtre la lumière.
A chacun je declaré, ressentant la vraie joie:
Dieu emplit l'Universe, et il reside en Moi.
Mais libre ton Esprit et perçois le bonheur
En cherchant tout trésor au fin fond de ton coeur.
Ici et maintenant, goute, parmi les humains,
La joie de vivre, d'aimer, en suivant ton chemin,

Par les biens c'ici-bas, puisses-tu avoir compris
Que ta vie permettre l'envoi de ton Esprit.
Esprit indestructible, sortant de ton tunnel,
Tu sais qu'un divin souffle t'a rendu immortel.
Car en mourtant chenille, devenant papillon,
Seul, tu t'introduiras dans la résurrectcion.
B.S.

Moi - Bérenger Saunière Vol.1
Emile Saunière 1989

I have lived my life, received the gift of pardon.
Transgressions all repented, blessing given,
My spirit breaks the barrier, and flies
To God, enfolded in pure light.
This is the joyful news that I impart.
God fills the Universe and dwells in me.
Send out your spirit to seek happiness,
Seek the treasure that will fill your heart.
Here and now you can know earth's delights,
Good fortune, life and love along the way.
But free your spirit and find heavenly joy
Greater than anything mankind can know.
Immutable spirit, ascending from the dark,
One divine breath will render you immortal.
As dying, the grub becomes a butterfly,
Alone, you will embody Resurrection.
B.S.

Bibliography

Richard Andrews & Paul Schellenberger
The Tomb Of God
Little, Brown & Co. 1996

Theo Aranson
Prince Eddy And The Homosexual Underworld
John Murray 1994

Richard Bordes
Les Mérovingiens A Rennes-Le-Château
Philippe Schrauben 1984

Henri Boudet
La Vrai Langue Céltique Et Le Cromleck De Rennes-Les-Bains
Pierre Belford Paris 1886/1978
Belisane 1984

August De Bourbon
The Dauphin - Louis XVII, King Of France
Richard Bentley & Son, New Burlington Street 1876

J.P.T. Bury
France 1814-1940
Methuen & Co. 1949

Antoine Captier
Rennes-Le-Château Le Secret (Comic Book)
Belisane 1985

Lavender Cassels
Clash Of Generations
John Murray 1973

Monsieur Charles
The Tragedy Of The True Dauphin (Louis XVII Of France)
H.F. & G.C. Witherby, 3-6 High Holborn, London, WC 1927

Alfred Cobban
A History Of Modern France, Vol.1 - 3
Penguin Books 1957

Chris Cook & John Stevenson
Modern European History 1763 - 1991
Longman Group UK Ltd. 1987

Claire Corbu & Antoine Cartier
L'héritage De L'abbé Saunière
Belisane 1985

Gérard De Sède
Le Trésor Maudit
J'ai Lu Paris 1967

Gérard De Sède
Rennes-Le-Château Dossier, Les Imposteurs, Les Hypothèses
Robert Laffont Paris 1988

Marie De St Gely
Berenger Saunière, Prêtre 1887-1917
Belisane Nice 1989

Jean Pierre Deloux & Jacques Bretigny
Rennes-Le-Château, Capitale Secrète De L'histoire De France
Editions Atlas 1982

René Descadeillas
Mythologie Du Trésor De Rennes
Editions Collot 1991

René Descadeillas
Rennes Et Ses Dernier Seigneurs 1730-1820
Edouard Privat Toulouse 1964

Dossier Secret (Photocopy Extracts)
Bibliothèque Nationale Paris

André Douzet (Translated Gay Roberts And Philip Coppens)
Saunière's Model And The Secret Of Rennes-Le-Château
Frontier Publishing/Société Perillos 2001

H.Elie
Finis Gloriae Mundi
Belisane 1986

John Elliot
Fall Of Eagles
BBC London 1974

Lionel & Patricia Fanthorpe
The Holy Grail Revealed
Newcastle Publishing Co. Inc. 1982

Lionel & Patricia Fanthorpe
Rennes-Le-Château Mysteries & Secrets
Bellevue Books, 1991

Sylvia Francke & Thomas Cawthorne
The Tree Of Life And The Holy Grail
Temple Lodge Publishing 1996

Michael Gabriel
The Holy Valley And The Holy Mountain
Hurst Village Publishing 1994

Gérard Giraud
Emma Calvé, La Cantratrice Sous Tous Les Ciels
La Société Des Imprimeries Maury, 21 Rue Du Pont De Fer, 12101 Millau 1968

Marilyn Hopkins, Graham Simmans & Tim Wallace-Murphy
Rex Deus, The True Mystery Of Rennes-Le-Château And The Dynasty Of Jesus
Element Books Ltd 2000

Stanley James
Treasure Maps Of Rennes-Le-Château
Seven Lights Publishing (Bow) & Acorn (France) 1984

Pierre Jarnac
Les Archives De L'abbé Saunière
Collection "Couleur Ocre" Ass. D. L.I. 1984

Stephen Knight
Jack The Ripper, The Final Solution
Harper Collins 1977

Les Cahiers De Rennes-Le-Château Volumes I And XI
Belisane 1984, 1996

Henry Lincoln
The Holy Place
Jonathan Cape 1991

Henry Lincoln
Key To The Sacred Pattern
Windrush Press 1997

Henry Lincoln Michael Baigent & Richard Leigh
The Holy Blood And The Holy Grail
Jonathan Cape 1982

Henry Lincoln, Michael Baigent & Richard Leigh
The Messianic Legacy
Jonathan Cape 1986

Christopher Mackintosh
Eliphas Lévi And The French Occult Revival
Rider & Co. 1972

Hans Roger Madol
The Shadow King, The Life Of Louis XVII Of France
And The Fortunes Of The Naundorff-Bourbon Family
George Allen & Unwin London 1930 (Original German Leipzig 1928)

Franck Marie
La Résurrection Du Grand Cocu, Rennes-Le-Château
S.R.E.S. - Vérités Anciennes 1981

Augustus Meves
The Authentic Historical Memoirs Of Louis Charles Prince Royal,
Dauphin Of France, Who Subsequently In October 1793
Personated Through Suppostitious Means August Meves
William Ridgeway, 189 Piccadilly, London 1868

Jean Pierre Monteils
Le Dossier Secret De Rennes-Le-Château
Belford 1981

Karl William Naundorff
The Misfortunes of the Dauphin, Son Of Louis XVI
Translated From The French By The Hon.& Rev. C.G.Perceval,
Rector Of Calverton, Bucks
James Fraser 215 Regent Street London 1838

Neil Hudson Newman
Les Sentiers Des Dieux, Pathways Of The Gods Volume 1
Garth Books Reading 2000

Peter Partner
The Murdered Magicians, The Templars And Their Myth
Oxford University Press 1981

Guy Patton & Robin Mackness
Web Of Gold, The Secret Power Of A Sacred Treasure
Sidgwick & Jackson 2000

Lynn Picknett & Clive Prince
The Templar Revelation
Transworld Publishers Ltd. 1997

Keith Randall
France, The Third Republic 1877-1914
Hodder & Stoughton 1986

Jacques Rivière
Le Fabuleux Trésor De Rennes-Le-Château, Le Secret De L'abbé Saunière
Belisane Nice 1983

Gay Roberts (English Translation)
Dossier Of Rennes-Le-Château, New Insights Vol.1
Cep D'or Pyla
Rennes Observer, Rennes-Ie-Château Research Society 1997

Gay Roberts & Ron Boyd (Joint Editors)
Rennes Group Newsletters Nos 1 -10 1992
Rennes-Ie-Château Research Society 2000

Jean Robin
Rennes-Le-Château, La Colline Envoutée
Guy Tredaniel, Editions De La Maisnie 1982

John M. Saul & Janice A. Glaholm
Rennes-Le-Château, A Bibliography
The Mercurius Press 1985

Emile Saunière
Moi Berenger Saunière, Vol.1 And 2
Emile Saunière 1989

Simon Singh
The Code Book
Fourth Estate Ltd 1996

A. De Grasse Stevens
The Lost Dauphin Louis VII, Or Onwarenhiiaki The Indian Iroquois Chief
George Allen, Sunnyside, Orpington Kent 1887

Agnes De Stoecki
King Of The French
Butler & Tanner 1957

The Holy Bible Old And New Testaments, King James Translation
OUP 1902

Elizabeth Van Buren
Refuge Of The Apocalypse
The C.W.Daniel Co.Ltd. 1986

David Wood
Genesis, The First Book Of Revelations
The Baton Press 1985

David Wood & Ian Campbell
Geneset, Target Earth
Bellevue Books 1994

Frances Yates
The Rosicrucian Enlightenment
Routledge & Kegan Paul 1972

Index

Other Titles from Thoth Publications:

THE GRAIL SEEKER'S COMPANION
By John Matthews & Marian Green

There have been many books about the Grail, written from many differing standpoints. Some have been practical, some purely historical, others literary, but this is the first Grail book which sets out to help the esoterically inclined seeker through the maze of symbolism, character and myth which surrounds the central point of the Grail.

In today's frantic world when many people have their material needs met some still seek spiritual fulfilment. They are drawn to explore the old philosophies and traditions, particularly that of our Western Celtic Heritage. It is here they encounter the quest for the Holy Grail, that mysterious object which will bring hope and healing to all. Some have come to recognise that they dwell in a spiritual wasteland and now search that symbol of the grail which may be the only remedy. Here is the guide book for the modern seeker, explaining the history and pointing clearly towards the Aquarian grail of the future.

John Matthews and Marian Green have each been involved in the study of the mysteries of Britain and the Grail myth for over thirty-five years. In THE GRAIL SEEKER'S COMPANION they have provided a guidebook not just to places, but to people, stories and theories surrounding the Grail. A reference book of Grail-ology, including history, ritual, meditation, advice and instruction. In short, everything you are likely to need before you set out on the most important adventure of your life.

This is the only book that points the way to the Holy Grail Quest in the 21st. century.
ISBN 1-870450-49-3

DION FORTUNE AND THE INNER LIGHT
By Gareth Knight

At last – a comprehensive biography of Dion Fortune based upon the archives of the Society of the Inner Light. As a result much comes to light that has never before been revealed. This includes: Her early experiments in trance mediumship with her Golden Dawn teacher Maiya Curtis-Webb and in Glastonbury with Frederick Bligh Bond, famous for his psychic investigations of Glastonbury Abbey.

The circumstances of her first contact with the Masters and reception of "The Cosmic Doctrine". The ambitious plans of the Master of Medicine and the projected esoteric clinic with her husband in the role of Dr. Taverner.

The inside story of the confrontation between the Christian Mystic Lodge of the Theosophical Society of which she was president, and Bishop Piggot of the Liberal Catholic church, over the Star in the East movement and Krishnamurti. Also her group's experience of the magical conflict with Moina MacGregor Mathers.

How she and her husband befriended the young Israel Regardie, were present at his initiation into the Hermes Temple of the Stella Matutina, and suffered a second ejection from the Golden Dawn on his subsequent falling out with it.

Her renewed and highly secret contact with her old Golden Dawn teacher Maiya Tranchell-Hayes and their development of the esoteric side of the Arthurian legends.

Her peculiar and hitherto unknown work in policing the occult jurisdiction of the Master for whom she worked which brought her into unlikely contact with occultists such as Aleister Crowley.

Nor does the remarkable story end with her physical death for, through the mediumship of Margaret Lumley Brown and others, continued contacts with Dion Fortune have been reported over subsequent years.

ISBN 1-870450-50-7

THE WESTERN MYSTERY TRADITION
By Christine Hartley

A reissue of a classic work, by a pupil of Dion Fortune, on the mythical and historical roots of Western occultism.

Christine Hartley's aim was to demonstrate that we in the West, far from being dependent upon Eastern esoteric teachings, possess a rich and potent mystery tradition of our own, evoked and defined in myth, legend, folklore and song, and embodied in the legacy of Druidic culture.

More importantly, she provides practical guidelines for modern students of the ancient mysteries, 'The Western Mystery Tradition,' in Christine Hartley's view, 'is the basis of the Western religious feeling, the foundation of our spiritual life, the matrix of our religious formulae, whither we are aware of it or not. To it we owe the life and force of our spiritual life.'

ISBN 1-870450-24-8

*   *   *   *   *

PRINCIPLES OF HERMETIC PHILOSOPHY
By Dion Fortune and Gareth Knight

Principles of Hermetic Philosophy together with *The Esoteric Philosophy of Astrology* are the last known works written by Dion Fortune. They appeared in her Monthly letters to members and associates of the Society of the Inner Light between November 1942 and March 1944.

Her intention in these works is summed up in her own words: "The observations in these pages are an attempt to gather together the fragments of a forgotten wisdom and explain and expand them in the light of personal observation."

She was uniquely equipped to make highly significant personal observations in these matters as one of the leading practical occultists of her time. What is more, in these later works she feels less constrained by traditions of occult secrecy and takes an altogether more practical approach than in her earlier, well known textbooks.

Gareth Knight takes the opportunity to amplify her explanations and practical exercises with a series of full page illustrations, and provides a commentary on her work

ISBN 1-870450-34-5